Union Retreat and the Regions

Regional Policy and Development Series

Series Editor: Ron Martin, Department of Geography, University of Cambridge

Throughout the industrialised world, widespread economic restructuring, rapid technological change, the reconfiguration of State intervention, and increasing globalisation are giving greater prominence to the nature and performance of individual regional and local economies within nations. The old patterns and processes of regional development that characterised the post-war period are being fundamentally redrawn, creating new problems of uneven development and new theoretical and policy challenges. Whatever interpretation of this contemporary transformation is adopted, regions and localities are back on the academic and political agenda. *Regional Policy and Development* is an international series which aims to provide authoritative analyses of this new regional political economy. It seeks to combine fresh theoretical insights with detailed empirical enquiry and constructive policy debate to produce a comprehensive set of conceptual, practical and topical studies in this field. The series is not intended as a collection of synthetic reviews, but rather as original contributions to understanding the processes, problems and policies of regional and local economic development in today's changing world.

Union Retreat and the Regions

The Shrinking Landscape of Organized Labour

Ron Martin, Peter Sunley and Jane Wills

Regional Policy and Development Series 8

Jessica Kingsley Publishers
London and Bristol, Pennsylvannia

Regional Studies Association
London

The right of Ron Martin, Peter Sunley and Jane Wills to be identified as authors of this work has been asserted by them in accordance with the Copyright, Designs and Patents Act 1988.

First published in the United Kingdom in 1996 by
Jessica Kingsley Publishers Ltd
116 Pentonville Road
London N1 9JB, England
and
1900 Frost Road, Suite 101
Bristol, PA 19007, U S A

with Regional Studies Association (Registered Charity 252269)

Copyright © 1996 Ron Martin, Peter Sunley and Jane Wills

Library of Congress Cataloging in Publication Data
A CIP catalogue record for this book is available from the Library of Congress

British Library Cataloguing in Publication Data
A CIP catalogue record for this book is available from the British Library

ISBN 1-85302-255-1

Printed and Bound in Great Britain by
Biddles Ltd, Guildford and King's Lynn

Contents

Tables

Figures

Abbreviations

AEEU	Amalgamated Electrical and Engineering Union
AEU	Amalgamated Engineering Union
BIFU	Banking, Insurance and Finance Union
CBI	Confederation of British Industry
COHSE	Confederation of Health Service Employees
CSEU	Confederation of Shipbuilding and Engineering Unions
EEF	Engineering Employer's Federation
EETPU	Electrical, Electronic, Telecommunications and Plumbing Union
FBU	Fire Brigades Union
GCHQ	Government Communications Headquarters
GMB	General, Municipal and Boilermakers' Union
HRM	Human Resource Management
ILO	International Labour Office
IPM	Institute of Personnel Managers
ISTC	Iron and Steel Trades Confederation
LFS	Labour Force Survey
MSC	Manpower Services Commission
MSF	Manufacturing, Science, Finance Union
NALGO	National and Local Government Officers' Union
NAPL	National Association for the Protection of Labour
NEDC	National Economic Development Council
NES	New Earnings Survey
NIR	New Industrial Relations
NOMIS	National Online Manpower Information System
NSA	New Style Agreement
NUM	National Union of Mineworkers
NUPE	National Union of Public Employees
NUTGW	National Union of Tailors and Garment Workers
OECD	Organisation for Economic Cooperation and Development
TGWU	Transport and General Workers' Union
TUC	Trades Union Congress
UCATT	Union of Construction, Allied Trades and Technicians
USDAW	Union of Shop, Distributive and Allied Workers
WIRS	Workplace Industrial Relations Survey

Preface

The economic and social landscape of Britain has undergone enormous upheaval and reconfiguration since the beginning of the 1980s. Nowhere has this process of restructuring been more pronounced than in the realm of work and employment. Yet while geographers have directed considerable attention to the spatial impact and consequences of the contemporary transformation of industry, production and employment, by comparison they have tended to neglect the equally significant changes that are occurring in the institutional and regulatory structures of the labour market, especially the trade unions and the industrial relations system. This book is intended as a contribution towards rectifying this neglect.

Since 1979 the British trade union movement has been in freefall decline, and the traditional system of industrial relations has been subjected to a barrage of structural and legislative change. Trade unionism and industrial relations are at a critical historical crossroad. Although economists, labour economists and industrial relations analysts have made important contributions to our understanding of the ongoing shifts in labour organization and employment relations, we know relatively little about the impact and implications of these shifts in different areas of the country. This is an important omission. For not only has the historical evolution of trade unionism and industrial relations practices been inherently uneven geographically, with different labourist traditions and workplace cultures having developed in different areas of the country, the retreat of the unions since 1979 has likewise been regionally uneven, and this in turn has potentially significant implications for the labour markets in the regions and for the future trajectory of the trade union movement itself. It is the role of geography in shaping the contemporary retreat and restructuring of British trade unionism that forms the motivation for this book.

The book is based on a large research project funded by the Economic and Social Research Council (ESRC) (Contract No. R000 23 2943), whose financial support we gratefully acknowledge. In addition, the research for this book would have been impossible without the help and assistance of several individuals. In particular we would like to thank Dr Paul Callow, of the Computer Laboratory, University of Cambridge, who provided extensive assistance in deciphering and analysing the data contained in the three Workplace Industrial Relations Surveys; Michael Blakemore at the National Online Manpower Information System (NO-MIS), for responding so enthusiastically to our requests for detailed local employment statistics; and Suzy Reimer, now at the Department of Geography, University of Hull, who helped to carry out the union interview work. Neil Millward, of the Policy Studies Institute, and the leading researcher behind the Workplace Industrial Relations Surveys, gave us valuable advice. The various union officials and research officers consulted in the specific unions we studied are too numerous to mention individually, but Bill Callaghan and David Coats of the Trade Union Congress (TUC), and John Gibbons of the Amalgamated Electrical and Engineering Union (AEEU), deserve special acknowledgment. Similarly, our thanks are due to all those managers and personnel officers we interviewed and questioned. Finally, we would like to record our appreciation to Jenny Wyatt and Ian Agnew, of the Department of Geography at Cambridge University, for drawing the maps and diagrams.

Researching and writing this book has itself been an interesting geographical experience, 'embedded' (to use the current buzzword) as we are in three well-separated local contexts (Cambridge, Edinburgh and Southampton). The propinquity provided by copious use of the fax overcame our lack of spatial proximity. Although each of us was primarily reponsible for drafting particular chapters, extensive cross-critique and rewriting have, we hope, achieved a coherence of style and orientation. Some of our earlier joint publications from this research project have already generated a lively debate within the geographical literature in the pages of the *Transactions of the Institute of British Geographers, NS, 19*, No. 1, 1994. Our hope is that this book will also generate interest, not only from geographers and other regional specialists, but also from labour economists, industrial relations analysts, and the unions themselves.

Ron Martin, Cambridge
Peter Sunley, Edinburgh
Jane Wills, Southampton
December 1995

CHAPTER ONE

The Disorganization of Organized Labour

INTRODUCTION: A NEW ERA IN UNION HISTORY

In contrast to the long post-war boom years from the end of the Second World War up to the early 1970s, the past two decades have been a period of dramatic change and upheaval in the labour markets of the countries belonging to the Organization for Economic Cooperation and Development (OECD). Most, if not all, of the certainties and verities of the post-war boom – such as full employment, job security, a well-defined and stable occupational structure, and a convergent income distribution – have been undermined and even reversed. Almost all of the OECD economies have experienced a massive shift in their labour market structures away from manufacturing industry towards services, from male to female employment, from full-time to part-time jobs, and from manual to non-manual occupations. Only the United States, Japan and the Scandinavian countries have managed to create sufficient new jobs to keep employment levels buoyant and relatively stable. Elsewhere, there has been a marked secular rise in unemployment (see OECD 1994a). Economic globalization, rapid technological change and increasingly intense and volatile competition are recasting the quantity and nature of work at the same time that governments have been busy de-regulating and re-regulating labour markets in an effort to increase the 'flexibility' of their operation.[1] No aspect of the labour market seems to be immune from these 'restructuring' processes, which are reaching right down to the basic institutions of the workplace, namely unions and the system of industrial relations (see for example, Jacobi *et al.* 1984; Gilbert *et al.* 1992; Regini 1992a; Jacoby 1995).

---

1   The contemporary upheaval of labour markets in advanced industrial economies is the subject of considerable debate within the economics literature. Although some emphasize the impact of two deep recessions (in the early 1980s and early 1990s), and the lack of economic growth, others stress the increasing importance of structural change. There are three versions of the structural view. The first sees the shift from manufacturing to services as having profound effects on the labour market (see Nickell and Bell 1995). The second focuses on the impact of technological change on the demand for skilled relative to unskilled workers (Berman *et al.* 1994; Machin 1994). The third emphasizes the challenge to Western unskilled and semi-skilled labour posed by the trade competition from low wage Third World countries (see Wood 1994).

The collective organization of workers into trade unions and the spread of workplace industrial relations systems have been two of the key institutional developments of the labour market in capitalist economies during the twentieth century. The growth in trade unionism was particularly rapid from the 1930s through to the early 1950s, and by the 1960s several (mostly American liberal-pluralist) industrial relations theorists were arguing that the world was rapidly entering an age of total industrialism characterized by widespread unionization and formally codified employer/employee relations (Kerr *et al.* 1962). They claimed that social conflict and labour protest were symptoms of a transitional period and would decline with the progress of industrialization and unionization. It was further argued that the imperatives inherent in the 'logic of industrialism' (such as technological advance, competition, and trade) were essentially unifying and homogenizing forces which would eliminate national differences in labour organization and management-labour systems, differences that were considered in any case to be residual and archaic features of earlier phases of development. These two assumptions, of increasing unionization and progressive convergence in industrial relations systems, became typical of many pluralist studies of industrial relations of the 1960s and indeed the 1970s.

This scenario was also shared by more radical, Marxist studies of workplace industrial relations. While Marxist writers challenged the liberal-pluralist emphasis on 'job regulation' as the achievement of social order, they tended to substitute the 'logic of capitalism' for the pluralists' logic of industrialism, and likewise emphasized the fundamental evolutionary similarity of different capitalist countries. In Hyman's words, 'The grievances and deprivations inevitably created by work relations in capitalist societies cause a perpetual tendency for workers to organize in trade unions' (Hyman 1975, p.62). The general Marxist view has been that capitalism's competitive and exploitative pressures necessarily lead to an erosion of workers' rights and expectations so that, as a consequence, collective labour organization and trade union membership display a long-term upward trend. The assumption has been that deep-seated structural forces associated with the development of the labour process would promote a steady convergence in unionization and mass industrial relations across the industrialized countries.

However, over the past two decades this prognosis of a progressive extension of trade unionism and convergence and homogenization of industrial relations practices has been seriously undermined. For one thing, despite the remarkable similarity in the economic and structural trajectories of the advanced (OECD) economies after the Second World War, for example the rise of mass production, the growth of public sector employment, and increasing intervention by the state, all factors alleged to have played key roles in promoting the expansion of union membership, national patterns of trade unionism did not behave as predicted. Far from converging towards a norm of uniformly high density, significant and systematic differences in national unionization rates and industrial relations systems persisted (Visser 1991, 1992; Poole 1986). In fact, as Lange and others have noted, while changes have indeed occurred in the outlook, scale and behaviour of unions as industrial development has proceeded, 'Such change seems to [have led] as much towards divergence between different national movements as towards convergence' (Lange *et al.* 1982, p.5). Similarly, Blanchflower and Freeman (1990) have argued that despite the increased openness of national economies, trade unionism developed in remarkably different ways amongst Western countries during the 1970s and 1980s. What is now recognized is that social, political and cultural differences between countries – differences in the formative contexts of institutionalized practices and norms – have exerted a powerful influence in shaping national systems of trade unionism, to the extent that broadly similar economic developments and trends have had different outcomes for organized labour and industrial relations in different countries (see Davis 1986; Ferner and Hyman 1992; Crouch 1993).

Not only have national patterns of trade unionism failed to converge, but the assumption that the collective organization of the workforce was a progressive, ineluctable process has also proved erroneous. Unlike the buoyant decades of the 1950s, 1960s and 1970s, when in many countries unions attracted expanding memberships, enjoyed increasing industrial power and extracted progressively higher real wages, since the late 1970s trade unions in almost all the OECD nations have come under increasing strain, and have experienced declining memberships and sharp falls in economic, political and workplace influence. The 'golden age' of trade unionism, it seems, has come to an end, and a widespread process of de-unionization has set in:

> Trade unions today are in a state of transition. The economic and institutional crisis of the past decade, combined with some longer-run, underlying trends intensified by the crisis, has confronted the labour movements of many Western countries with the most serious challenges they have faced in a generation or more...The many challenges and problems encountered by...unions in the last few years raise difficult questions about their futures. Are unions passing from the scene, merely a temporary phenomenon in the history of industrial capitalism? What will be the role of unions in the highly internationalized and competitive economy of the future? (Edwards 1986, pp.1–2)

Yet, despite the common experience of trade union decline, there has been considerable national variation in the process of retreat.

DIMENSIONS OF DISORGANIZATION

The fall in trade union membership density began first in the United States, France, Austria, Japan and Australia, and can be traced back to the 1960s. It was not until the 1970s and early 1980s that decline spread to other countries like the United Kingdom, Italy, Canada, Belgium, and New Zealand, and only in the late 1980s that it appeared in others such as Sweden, Norway, and Germany (see Figure 1.1). If the timing of the onset of decline has varied across countries, so too has the rate of decline, with the contraction of unionism being much more rapid in the United Kingdom, Italy, Netherlands and the United States than in the Scandinavian countries, Germany or Canada. As a result of these variations in the incidence and speed of decline, by the beginning of the 1990s, differences in union density across the OECD economies had widened considerably, varying from a high of more than 80 per cent in Sweden to less than 20 per cent in the United States and to barely 10 per cent in France (Figure 1.2 and Table 1.1). Significantly, differences

Table 1.1: Union density in OECD countries, 1970–1990

	1970	1980	1990
Sweden	76.7	79.7	82.5
Iceland	–	68.1^1	78.2^2
Finland	51.4	68.8	72.0
Denmark	60.0	76.0	71.4
Norway	51.4^3	56.9	56.0
Belgium	45.5	55.9	51.2
Ireland	53.1	57.0	49.7
Luxembourg	46.8	52.2^4	49.7^5
Austria	62.2	56.2	46.2
New Zealand	–	56.0^6	44.8^7
Australia	50.2^8	48.0^9	40.4
United Kingdom	**44.8**	**50.4**	**39.1**
Italy	36.3	49.3	38.3
Canada	31.0	36.1	35.8
Greece	–	36.7^{10}	34.1
Germany	33.0	35.6	32.9
Portugal	60.8^{11}	60.7^{12}	31.8
Switzerland	30.1^{13}	30.7	26.6
Netherlands	38.0	35.3	25.5
Japan	35.1	31.1	25.4
Turkey	18.1^{14}	29.2	21.5^2
United States	24.8	22.3	15.6
Spain	–	25.0	11.0
France	22.3	17.5	9.8

Source: OECD Employment Outlook, 1994, Chapter 5.

Notes: 1. Trade Union members as percentage of all wage and salary earners (except 1970 figure for the United States, which is for non-agricultural union members and wage and salary earners).

2. Key to dates: (1) 1979; (2) 1989; (3) 1972; (4) 1981; (5) 1987; (6) 1985; (7) 1991; (8) 1976; (9) 1982; (10) 1986; (11) 1978; (12) 1984 (13) 1971; (14) 1975.

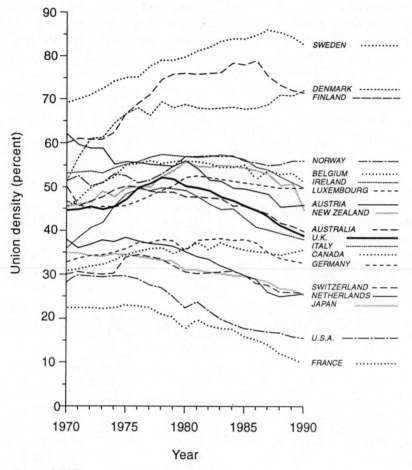

Source: OECD

Figure 1.1: Union density trends in selected countries, 1970–1990

in the rate of union decline across countries have varied inversely with national differences in the pre-existing degree of unionization. As Visser (1991, p.100) observes,

> In general, it seems that unions in weakly unionized countries weakened further, whereas unions in initially highly unionized countries stood better against the tide.

Union density has thus shown diverging trends in countries with otherwise broadly similar systems of industrial relations, and even modest differences in the institutions and regulatory frameworks that govern labour relations would seem to have exerted a substantial influence on the recent pattern of union decline (Wallerstein 1989; Freeman 1990; Visser 1992; OECD 1994a).

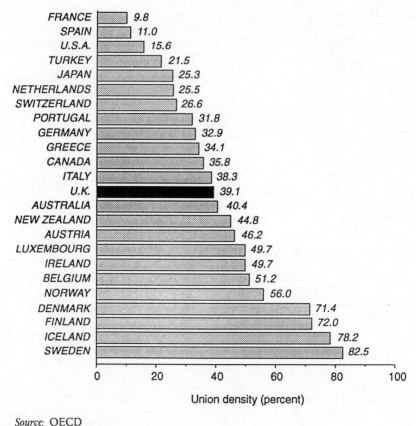

Source: OECD

Figure 1.2: Trade union density in selected countries, 1990

Another manifestation of the erosion of union power is the dramatic drop in strike activity that has occurred in Western capitalist economies since the beginning of the 1980s. Although there have long been significant international differences and marked historical swings in the incidence and intensity of strike activity (see Korpi and Shalev 1980), virtually all industrial countries experienced an intense phase of worker militancy from the late 1960s through to the late 1970s (Shalev 1983; Walsh 1983). The increase in strike action (in terms of the number of workers involved in industrial stoppages and the number of working days lost) was highest in those countries with extensive labour organization and high union densities, and several commentators saw this general wave of militancy as marking a 'resurgence of class conflict' (see Crouch and Pizzorno 1978).

Since 1979, however, there has been a pronounced fall in industrial militancy to levels comparable to, and in many cases (for example, in the United Kingdom) substantially below, those that characterized the years of relative industrial peace in the 1950s and 1960s (Table 1.2). Several factors have contributed to this

Table 1.2: Strike activity rates in selected countries, 1973–1992

	Number of working days lost through strikes per 1000 employed	
	1973–82	*1983–92*
Austria	6.5	2.6
Germany[1][2]	26.6	28.8
Netherlands	28.4	12.3
Japan	59.8	3.7
Sweden	136.7	73.8
France	143.8	34.8
Denmark[1]	241.3	116.9
United States	355.3	71.2
United Kingdom[1]	**405.9**	**200.9**
Finland	444.9	288.3
Australia	570.4	175.5
Italy	859.9	146.6
Canada[3]	907.4	210.4

Source: ILO *Year Book of Labour Statistics,* various.
Notes: 1. Strikes of less than 100 working days excluded.
            2. Refers to West Germany before 3rd October 1990
            3. Second period is 1985-1992.

'resurgence of labour quiescence' (Shalev 1992), not least the growth and persist-ence of high unemployment since the late 1970s and the shift in some countries (especially the United Kingdom) towards a much more restrictive legislative framework controlling the scope and form of industrial action. But it is also clear that the slide in strike activity has been closely correlated with the decline in unionism, and has been greatest in those occupations, industrial sectors, and countries which have witnessed the largest falls in union density (Shalev 1992). While the current travails of trade unionism as an encompassing social movement do not necessarily preclude the possibility of future strike waves, and although the general trend towards the erosion of overt labour militancy since the end of the 1970s, like the fall in union membership, has displayed considerable international diversity, there can be little doubt that with the retreat of trade unionism the organizational basis for mass collective action has been seriously weakened.

Inextricably bound up with this retreat in membership and militancy, the unions in many advanced industrialized countries appear to be experiencing a break-up of their traditional structures of organization and workplace negotiation. Indeed, one of the increasingly recurring themes in the industrial relations literature on the contemporary decline and reorganization of trade unionism in the West is that, like other aspects of the economy and society, the institutions of industrial relations are undergoing what is now widely referred to as 'decentralization'. As one industrial relations commentator puts it:

Much of the debate and controversy over emerging organizational forms and potential institutional futures has been driven by a concern to identify and extrapolate the underlying motor and direction of change, which is usually thought to necessitate a sustained move towards more decentralized, flexible and collaborative structures so that class and occupationally-based control systems fragment and eventually dissolve away. (Reed 1992, p.17)

According to many observers, the decentralization of industrial relations is now one of the dominant trends in contemporary European labourism. Protagonists of this thesis argue that employers' workforce strategies are changing in ways that require them to be dealt with on an individual workplace and individual worker basis rather than through collective institutions. Simultaneously, rising living standards and the expansion of the service sector are supposed to have fostered individual self-interest at the expense of collective regulation. And reinforcing these processes, the thrust of both economic change and government economic policies seems to be towards the fracturing of the structural and institutional bases of post-war 'mass' society, including the unions.

Several developments are held to be indicative of this trend away from national or sectoral structures of union negotiation and organization to more localized forms of representation and regulation, including the decline of collective wage bargaining, the increasing importance of individual employment contracts, the spread of employee profit- and performance-related pay schemes, and the emergence of alternative workplace-based structures of employee representation, such as works' councils. These are all features that run counter to the traditional role of and need for unions. Measuring the extent of this shift towards decentralization

Table 1.3: Collective bargaining coverage in selected countries, 1980–1990

	Proportion of employees covered by some form of Collective Wage Agreement		
	1980[1]	1985[2]	1990[3]
Germany	91	91	90
Australia	88	85	80
France	85	92	–
Netherlands	76	76	71
Great Britain	70	64	47
Canada	–	37	38
Japan	28	–	23
United States	26	20	18

Source: OECD Employment Outlook, 1994, Chapter 5.
Notes: 1. Except for Australia, 1974; France, 1981; Great Britain, 1978.
         2. Except for Canada, 1986.
         3. Except for Japan, 1989; Germany, 1992.

and decollectivization, even in the key realm of collective bargaining, is more difficult than assessing the trends in union membership and industrial militancy.[2] But what evidence exists suggests that, as in the case of union decline and strike activity, the 'localization', 'individualization' and 'flexibilization' of pay determination appear to be proceeding markedly unevenly from country to country. Thus while the degree of collective bargaining coverage has declined in certain countries, it has done so at quite different rates, while in others there has been little if any change (Table 1.3). Again, these differences appear to be the result, in part at least, of differences in national legislative and institutional environments, and of differences in the form and extent of state regulation.

Not surprisingly, there has been intense debate about the causes and future course of the contemporary 'disorganization' of organized labour. At one end of the interpretative spectrum are those accounts that see union decline as as an irreversible feature associated with the march of fundamental systemic structural tendencies in the socio-economy as a whole. In these accounts organized labour is caught up in a more general historical transition of industrial society, although views differ as to the precise nature and direction of this transition. The most influential, but also most debated, model is that which sees the current upheaval of industrial relations as inextricably bound up with the decline of the post-war 'Fordist' phase of economic accumulation and social regulation and emergence of a new phase of 'post-Fordist' or 'flexible' accumulation and regulation (see Boyer 1993).[3] A somewhat different perspective sees the retreat of trade unionism as part of a shift from organized to 'disorganized' capitalism (Offe 1985; Crouch 1993), in which 'industrialism' is being superseded by a service-based 'post-industrialism', and the collectivistic institutions associated with the former, from mass welfare to mass social classes, are being replaced by the more heterogeneous and pluralistic forms of the latter (see Lash and Urry 1987, 1994).[4] Still others regard de-union-

---

2   There are significant difficulties in classifying and comparing different national industrial relations systems. Given that most countries have complex multi-level bargaining systems, indices of the degree of collective agreements coverage and centralization of wage bargaining may not be strictly comparable from country to country (see Soskice 1990).

3   The literature on the supposed transition from Fordism to post-Fordism, both celebratory and critical in orientation, is now vast. Useful accounts can be found in Harvey 1989; Murray 1989; Sayer 1989; Hirst and Zeitlin 1991; Gilbert et al. 1992; Jessop 1992; and the collection edited by Amin 1994. Much of the discussion of post-Fordism has been associated with the so-called 'regulationist' school of political economy (see, for example, Boyer 1990). The focus of this work has been on questions of production, industrial organization and state intervention, and only recently have the post-Fordism debate and regulationist theory begun explicitly to address institutional issues such as industrial relations.

4   In some respects Lash and Urry's thesis of the 'end of organized capitalism' was pre-empted by Offe's (1985) book on 'disorganized capitalism'. While Lash and Urry's discussion looks at economic, political and social change, Offe focuses explicitly on the contemporary transformaton of work and labour market institutions in the advanced industrialized countries. Both contributions, however, stress the significance of the rise of services.

ization as the inevitable outcome of the rise of a new, increasingly globalized, market-driven and competitive world economy, as firms and governments have no option but to reduce the scope and power of organized labour in order to maximize the freedom of capital and the flexibility of the labour market in the struggle to maintain competitiveness, growth and profitability (Jacoby 1995). In contrast, at the other end of the spectrum are those who, more optimistically, see the decline of the unions as an essentially temporary or cyclical phenomenon, the product of a contingent conjunction of adverse economic and political events, namely the deep economic recessions of the early 1980s and early 1990s, and the rise to power of anti-union right-wing governments obsessed with reducing the power of organized labour. These observers tend to stress the underlying resilience of the union movement, and are more inclined to believe the decline is potentially reversible (Kelly 1990; Taylor 1994). However, even this group acknowledges that fundamental changes are taking place in the form and organization of work, in the structure of employment, and in social and cultural values, such that even if unionism were eventually to recover, the *nature* of trade unionism and the *role* of unions in industrial relations are likely to have been irrevocably transformed.

UNION DECLINE IN BRITAIN

These debates have attracted considerable attention in the United Kingdom, where the reversal in the fortunes of unionized labour has been particularly dramatic. Britain was the first nation to develop unions, reflecting the country's earlier industrial start, and during the course of the twentieth century the unions came to occupy a position of considerable power and influence, not only in the workplace but also in the regulation of the economy and in national political life more generally. In the post-1945 period, particularly, the unions enjoyed considerable success as far as their members were concerned. They helped to push up their members' wages, they tenaciously protected their members' jobs and skills, and they were able to influence or even defeat government policies. By 1979 trade union membership in the UK had reached 13.29 million, or in density terms 57.6 per cent of the employed labour force.

In stark contrast to much of the post-war era, the period since 1979 has been nothing less than traumatic for British trade unionism. By 1994 union membership in the UK had fallen to 8.28 million, a drop of more than a third, and density had declined to 38.3 per cent (Table 1.4). Thus by the early 1990s, the extent of unionization had fallen back to the levels recorded immediately after the Second World War, thereby removing all of the growth in membership made during the 1950s, 1960s and 1970s. The 1980s also witnessed the virtual rupture of union/government relations and the reversal of many of the gains in political recognition and influence that had been won over previous decades. Successive changes in employment legislation by the Conservative governments since 1979 have increasingly restricted the powers and freedom of action of unionized labour,

Table 1.4: Trade union membership and density in the United Kingdom, 1977–1994

	Union membership (000s, end of year)	Cumulative fall in membership since 1979 (000s)	Union density (membership as % of mid-year employees in employment)
1977	12,846		56.7
1978	13,118		57.5
1979	13,289		57.6
1980	12,947	342	56.5
1981	12,106	1183	55.1
1982	11,593	1696	53.8
1983	11,236	2053	52.2
1984	10,994	2295	50.6
1985	10,821	2468	48.9
1986	10,539	2750	47.4
1987	10,475	2814	46.3
1988	10,376	2913	45.7
1989	10,158	3131	44.8
1990	9947	3342	43.4
1991	9585	3704	43.0
1992	9048	4241	41.2
1993	8700	4589	40.3
1994	8278	5011	38.3

Source: Department of Employment (Union membership figures derived from the Certification Officer).

Note: Potential membership excludes self employed and unemployed.

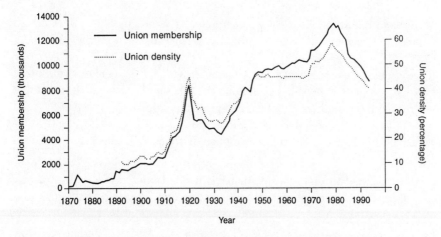

Figure 1.3: Trade union membership and density in the United Kingdom, 1870–1993

and effectively abolished the largely unregulated and basically voluntaristic system of workplace industrial relations that had developed over the post-war period (McIlroy 1988). Some industrial relations analysts have argued that the hostile legal framework for trade unions introduced since 1979 has been the decisive factor explaining the vast bulk of the decline in membership and density (for example, Freeman and Pelletier 1990). While such a monocausal explanation is obviously far too simplistic, it is clear that the legislative attack mounted by the Conservative governments (especially those under Mrs Thatcher) have seriously undermined the power, actions and appeal of the unions, and resulted in an environment of labour exclusion and union avoidance (Crouch 1986; Longstreth 1988). Aided by this legislative assault, and a labour market disciplined by persistent high unemployment and widespread restructuring, the balance of power has swung back to employers. Notwithstanding some large and drawn-out disputes in certain public sector industries (notably coal and the railways), aggregate strike activity has all but withered away. Whereas in 1979, some 29.5 million days were lost through strikes in Britain, by 1993 the annual number of working days lost through industrial action had fallen to 0.6 million. Moreover, not only has the incidence of strike action declined, but the unions' ability to win industrial conflicts (particularly in some of the large stoppages that have continued to hit public sector industries) has also weakened.

The British union movement has thus had good cause to feel besieged. As the Secretary General of the Trades Union Congress has stated,

> The key question [the unions] have to face is whether the decline of trade union membership, organisation and collective bargaining is long-term and irreversible or is a cyclical phenomenon linked to short-term political and economic factors, or somewhere between the two. (Monks 1993, p.228)

For many commentators, the answer to this question is clear: in their view the scale of de-unionization in Britain is symbolic of a profound and permanent transformation in the country's industrial culture. The falls in union membership, strike activity and industrial militancy are interpreted as signifying 'a major watershed in industrial relations' (Cadbury 1985), a 'decline in organization' (Beaumont 1987), 'a battle against oblivion' (Leadbeater and Lloyd 1987), and even the 'dissolution of the union movement' (Phelps-Brown 1990). There is a widespread view that 'union membership has become an irrelevance' (Bassett 1986), and that we are seeing the 'rediscovery of the mangement prerogative' (Purcell 1991), and 'the end of institutional industrial relations' (Purcell 1993). Certainly the Government is in no doubt about the transformation which is taking place in British industrial relations:

> Unions remain important participants in the labour market...[But] all the signs, however, point to their long-term decline. The main reason for this is their inability to adapt to rapidly changing conditions in the labour market

and the economy more generally where competitive pressures have become more intense. (HM Government 1994, p.6)

Others, however, deny that the decline of the unions in the UK since the end of the 1970s has been quite as significant or as climacteric as these jeremiads suggest, or that it has been as beneficial as the Government would like to think (Metcalf 1994). Kelly (1990) and Metcalf (1991), for example, prefer to view the decline more as a temporary downturn than the necessary onset of irreversible atrophy. Kelly draws a parallel with the dramatic collapse of trade union membership that occurred in Britain during the 1920s, which although viewed as catastrophic at the time, subsequently proved to be a short-term set-back. The challenge facing the unions then was to organize the new growth industries that were emerging. It was the success with which they responded to that challenge that underpinned the recovery and expansion of trade unionism from the 1930s onwards. In a similar way, Kelly and Metcalf see the present problem as one of penetrating the new growth sectors of the 1990s, such as private services and high technology industry. Both authors acknowledge that recovery will undoubtedly require a change of strategy on the part of the unions, but argue there is no reason in principle why the unions should not be able to regain at least some of the membership lost over the past decade and a half. A similarly 'up-beat' position is argued by Taylor (1994):

> The future of Britain's trade unions looks more promising in an age of rapid economic and industrial change than many people realize. The conventional view is that they are locked into a spiral of irreversible decline...Despite the formidable problems they must grapple with over the coming years, it is not inevitable that the trade unions face further contraction in their power and influence. They still have the opportunity to renew themselves. (p.217)

In one sense, this view is indisputable. Of course the unions have the power to shape their future; but the conditions under which they will have to do so will almost certainly not be of their own choosing. For most of their history the unions have had to face adverse circumstances. They rose to prominence in response to a polarized and deregulated labour market very much like that which returned to Britain in the 1980s and 1990s. However, whether they remain adaptable and pragmatic enough to shape the current agenda and grow once more into the next century, is an open issue.

And so the debate continues, with still no conclusive end in sight. Our concern here is not to add yet one more position to this discussion, still less to advance a particular manifesto for the renewal of the unions. Rather, we wish to focus on a somewhat different aspect of the contemporary upheaval, one that has received remarkably little attention yet which we believe to be of considerable interest and importance. The predominant way of analysing and explaining the decline and restructuring of British trade unionism has been to offer a national or aggregate account. Hence although much has been written on the broad features and

dimensions of the de-unionization of Britain, by comparison relatively little is
known about its *geography*, about how far and in what ways the spatial contours
of British trade unionism and industrial relations are being reconfigured, and what
the implications of this spatial reconfiguration might be, both for the unions
themselves and for different regional and local labour markets across the country.
Our view is that the industrial relations system is an integral component of the
process of uneven regional development, that each has significant implications for
the other, and that, as a consequence, a geographical perspective has much to
contribute to an understanding of the contemporary retreat and restructuring of
the labour movement.

GEOGRAPHY AND UNIONS

Traditionally, industrial relations analysts have not been particularly sensitive to
the significance of geography. They have conventionally viewed industrial relations systems as comprised of only two levels: the macro-level of national
institutions and their centralized practices and policies; and the micro-level of the
individual workplace, the site where specific day-to-day relations and practices are
implemented. The industrial relations system is typically seen as a *vertical* system
of concertation and articulation (Crouch 1993) in which the move upwards
through the capital/labour relationship is from company to economic branch to
nation state (and perhaps to supra-national bodies). In general, little or no
significance has been given to the role of 'horizontal' relationships shaping trade
unionism, to the role of the regional and local spheres in the capital/labour
relationship. Recently, however, there have been signs of a belated interest in
'regionalism' within the industrial relations literature. Teague (1993) for example,
suggests that the new dynamics of regional restructuring and industrial development have highlighted the fact that different regions have their own governance
and regulatory structures that generate norms and conventions which connect firms
with each another and with other institutions. He argues that as part of the
contemporary restructuring of the space economy 'virtually spontaneously a
regional dimension is emerging in industrial relations across the European Community' (p.172). According to Perulli (1993) this 'regionalization of industrial
relations' has exposed the long-overdue need for industrial relations theorists to
give greater attention to local and regional contexts and externalities in their
analyses of trade unionism and industrial politics. In the British case, one or two
industrial relations analysts have also argued for the importance of 'spatial
subsystems' of trade unionism and industrial relations (Beaumont and Harris
1988a, 1988b).

    We endorse this call for a spatial perspective in industrial relations research.
However, we would argue that the significance of geography in industrial relations
systems is in fact neither new nor simply 'spontaneous'. In Britain, as in most other
countries, geography has long been a key feature shaping the evolution of

organized labour. Certainly in some nations such historical patterns of regional unionism may well have become obscure or even obsolete with the march of economic development, but in these cases much of what is now being referred to as the 'new' regionalization of industrial relations is, we suspect, the rediscovery, reassertion or reconfiguration of those earlier union geographies. But if industrial relations analysts have neglected geography, so industrial and economic geographers have accorded very little attention to the role of industrial relations in their studies of the location of production, of spatial divisions of labour, or of uneven development. Economic geographers have conventionally viewed labour as a 'location factor', as one element influencing the distribution of industry. Over recent years this narrow view of labour has been heavily criticized and attempts have been made to construct a new conception in which the role of labour in production is seen as a social and political process as well as an economic one. Yet, although this revised perspective on the role and significance of labour has stimulated interest in the social organization of work across space (for example, Massey 1984; Sayer and Walker 1992), the social, political and institutional geographies of industrial relations and organized labour have remained largely neglected, and it is only in the last few years that geographical work on trade unions has begun to emerge. A good example is Clark's (1989) study of American unionism, in which he argues that the demise of organized labour in the United States is inherently geographical and not simply a national phenomenon. In his view, the local community context is an essential determinant of the way in which the effects of economic restructuring interact with the regulation of labour/management relations. As yet there there are no comparable geographical studies of trade unionism in the European countries, although recently the industrial relations bases of successful growth regions and districts in France, Germany and Italy have begun to attract the attention of industrial geographers (Storper 1995). Likewise in Britain, it is only in the last few years that geographical interest in industrial relations and trade unionism has begun to develop (Massey and Miles 1984; Southall 1988; Massey and Painter 1989; Martin, Sunley and Wills 1993, 1994a).

There are several reasons why the study of industrial relations should take geography seriously, and why economic geographers should give greater prominence to industrial relations in their studies of the spatial development process. The first, and most obvious, is that the principal institutions of industrial relations, not only the organizational forms such as trade unions, employers' associations and the state, but also the institutionalized practices of industrial relations, are themselves *geographically structured*. The institutions and processes of industrial relations operate at a variety of spatial scales, not only at the national and the individual workplace, but also at the regional and sub-regional. Most trade unions and employers' associations are organized into different geographical levels, for example into regional, district and local branch divisions, so that this itself imparts a material spatial structure into the industrial relations system. Furthermore, varying degrees of autonomy of orientation and operation, of custom and convention, may exist at these different levels, and such autonomy may serve to 'institutionalize' local and regional variations in trade unionism and industrial relations practices. At the same time, such regional and local variations in union organization and workplace relations intersect with national regulatory structures and forces. The concept of *institutional spaces* allows us to visualize this nested, multi-layered and multi-scaled system.

Second, industrial relations and industrial politics are *spatially embedded*, in the sense that they develop and are reproduced within locally-varying economic, social and cultural settings or contexts. Geography complicates the relationship between capital and labour because of the way places differ, not only in their economic structures and functions but also in their inherited cultural, political and social value systems. In most advanced countries, successive phases of economic development have led to specific regional patterns of industrial and labour process specialization, labour market regulation, and workplace norms and practices, which have significant implications for local social relations and cultural-political consciousness (see, for example, Massey 1984; Hanson and Pratt 1992; Peck 1992, 1994; Jonas 1996). In this way different union and workplace traditions have been established in different geographical areas in different historical periods. Yet once established, those locally-based traditions can exhibit a high degree of socio-institutional persistence over time, and, at the very least, influence the nature of subsequent changes and developments. Together, local embeddedness and the path dependence which it tends to foster, are major factors shaping the geographical patterns of industrial relations and union strength. This is not to imply that local trade unionism and capital/labour relations can be simply 'read off' deterministically from the uneven development of the economy and society, nor that the 'local repertoires' of collective organization and employer/employee relations are fixed or mechanistically reproduced over time. Specific outcomes are always in some sense contingent and uncertain, even sometimes counterintuitive (see Martin, Sunley and Wills 1994b). The basic point, however, is that local context matters, and that this context has a geography. In the same way that some industrial relations analysts now recognize that even small differences in socio-institutional arrangements can play a significant role in explaining national differences in trade unionism and systems of workplace regulation, so spatial variations in socio-institutional structures and practices within a country may exert an important influence on that country's trade union geography.

Third, such local contexts help shape the *strategic spaces* for action by employers and workers, the sets of institutional, economic, social and cultural *resources* on which unions, employers and even the state can draw selectively in developing their respective strategies. Local institutional resources are both enablers and constrainers of social action (see Giddens 1984). The ways in which such resources vary over space and time may help explain why particular strategies are more successful in certain places and times than in others. Employers, unions and the state all make strategic use of the 'power of place' and 'local context'. For example multi-plant firms and the state itself may attempt to 'play off' workers at different locations in order to push through particular policies with regard to investment, disinvestment, changes in employment conditions or industrial relations. Likewise, unions may use space strategically, sometimes in a cooperative or collaborative way by forging 'coalitions of solidarity' across groups of workers in different localities, and at other times in a more competitive manner by pursuing a fragmented 'defence of place'. The scope, nature and relative success of such employer, state and union strategies are shaped, in part at least, by the local circumstances under which they are pursued, which in turn depend upon the ways in which institutional spaces and the resources they provide vary from area to area. Those spaces and conditions are not, of course, immutable but themselves change over time. In particular, economic restructuring and legislative change may transform the institutional resources available to workers and employers in different local areas in quite dramatic ways. Understanding the geography of industrial relations, therefore, implies a need to explicate the role of economic, social and political resources in reproducing and potentially transforming the local institutional contexts that help to regulate those relations.

In sum, these considerations lead us to expect an uneven geography of industrial relations and trade unionization. This unevenness serves to determine the local impact of wider national developments and policies so that the latter have different specific outcomes and consequences in different areas. In turn, the development of the 'national' industrial relations system is itself an inherently geographically uneven process, the complex product of local developments and structures. Shifts and changes in unionization, in working practices, collective bargaining, and industrial relations do not, therefore, necessarily occur uniformly across the country but are just as likely to be concentrated in, or to emanate from, particular regions. The structures and processes of 'articulation' within the industrial relations system (the term Crouch (1993) uses to describe the relations of interdependence that bind the different vertical levels of a labour organization together) are thus inherently geographical and, as a result, much more complex than is normally assumed.

But, fourth, the geography of industrial relations is an important factor regulating the *operation of regional and local labour markets*. As yet no comprehensive spatial theory of labour market functioning, adjustment and regulation exists (Martin 1981, 1986; Hanson and Pratt 1992; Peck 1992, 1994), but any such theory would surely have to consider the influence exerted by unions and workplace industrial relations. To the extent that union organization, forms of collective wage bargaining, work practices and traditions of industrial militancy vary across localities, so the impact of unions on the labour market will also vary geographically. Furthermore, that impact may have several different, even opposing, dimensions. For example, on the one hand, trade unions and collective bargaining will tend to impart a tendency towards convergence in the pay and employment conditions of similar workers across different regions. But at the same time, regionally varying union structures and strategies may operate to protect and preserve historically-established differences in pay and working practices between different areas.[5] Economists have devoted considerable effort to theorizing and identifying the effect that unions have on aggregate employment, unemployment and wages. Much of this work has centred on the question of whether unions distort the functioning of the labour market and what the implications of this distortion might be. In particular, a frequent argument is that unions undermine the flexibility of the labour market, especially of wage-setting and job creation processes, and thwart the introduction of new production technologies and changes in work practices.

This contentious issue assumes heightened salience at the regional and local level, for some economists have also suggested that the inferior employment and productivity performance of certain regions and localities can be attributed to union activity. Thus it is argued that unions 'decouple' local wages from local labour market conditions and thereby create local unemployment: by pursuing nation-wide and sector-wide collective wage agreements without regard to local variations in the demand for and supply of labour, unions push local wages above their 'market-clearing' levels and price workers – including union members – out of jobs. That highly unionized regions also often tend to have higher rates of unemployment than less unionized regions is taken as evidence supporting this hypothesis (see, for example, Casson 1983; Minford 1985; Minford and Stoney 1991). Of course, simple correlation is no proof of causation, and quite different and equally plausible alternative interpretations can be constructed to account for this apparent relationship. The basic point, however, is that the geographies of trade unionism and industrial relations form an integral part of the regulatory processes that shape the development and operation of regional and local labour markets. The decline of the unions and the reorganization and decentralization of industrial relations and collective bargaining may be expected, therefore, to carry significant implications for the geography of employment, earnings and socio-economic welfare.

Our view, then, is that an approach that is sensitive to the impress of geography is useful not only in helping to elucidate the changes in trade unionism and industrial relations that have taken place in Britain over the past decade and a half, but also in highlighting the fact that the consequences of those changes, and the constraints and possibilities confronting the unions with respect to reviving their memberships and their role in the workplace, are likely to vary in significant ways from place to place.

---

5   This can happen even in the absence of nationwide or industry-wide bargaining. Local unions are almost certain to use the comparative wages of similar groups of workers in other areas in framing their own wage claims. Of course this may in turn spark off additional retaliatory claims in other, higher wage localities, as unionized workers there attempt to re-establish their customary differentials.

ON METHOD, MEASUREMENT AND PURPOSE

However, if the case for geographical research on trade unionism and industrial relations is easy to make, in practice such research is notoriously difficult. Even at a relatively broad spatial level, which is the main focus of this book, there are problems of data, of methodology and purpose. Some of these issues have already been the focus of intense debate in the geographical literature (see the exchange between Massey (1994) and Painter (1994) on the one hand, and Martin, Sunley and Wills (1994d) on the other). Our main interest here is in three dimensions or manifestations of organized labour: unionism, strike activity and collective bargaining. The latter two are obviously related to unionism, but are also clearly different aspects of industrial relations, and all three may exhibit different patterns through time and across space. The very concept of 'unionism' is itself problematic, since the degree or extent of trade unionism can be measured in three main ways, namely: by the absolute number of trade union members; by union density, that is, the number of members divided by the relevant employment base, or potential membership; and by union recognition, that is, the proportion of firms (or of employees in firms) that recognize unions for negotiation and bargaining purposes. These three indices capture somewhat different aspects of trade union representation, and have different meanings as measures of the 'strength' of organized labour. These differences can be especially significant in a geographical context. How should different regions be compared in terms of the incidence or degree of trade unionism? In terms of absolute numbers of union members, or in terms of differences in the relative presence of union members, as measured by workplace union density or recognition rates? As we shall see in Chapter Three, membership numbers, membership density and recognition each give somewhat different images of the union landscape, especially with respect to identifying core regions of union 'strength'. Indeed, during the course of our research we became increasingly aware of how contentious and political the act of 'mapping' the unions can be.

An additional problem encountered in any attempt to study the geography of trade unionism in Britain is the general paucity of detailed information. There are no regularly published data on British union membership by region. The official annual estimates of trade union membership issued by the Department of Employment (in the *Employment Gazette*, now *Labour Market Trends*) do not include disaggregations by regions or subregions. Nor do the majority of individual unions publish figures for their constituent organizational administrative areas. It is necessary, therefore, to piece together a number of quite different sets of data in order to construct any reasonable geography of the unions. In the following chapters we draw upon six such sources of information. These are discussed in more detail in the Appendix (which also describes the other data sources used at various points of the study), and are only briefly summarized here. The main source of regional union data is that derived from the three Workplace Industrial Relations Surveys (WIRS) undertaken in 1980, 1984 and 1990. The second major source of regional union data is the annual Labour Force Surveys (LFS), which contain very basic information on trade union membership from 1989 onwards, and thus allow analysis to be extended beyond the period covered by the WIRS.[6] Third, these two sets of secondary data were supplemented by our own compilation of regional membership figures and densities for a number of individual unions over the period 1979–1990, using information from those unions' archival records. A fourth and more micro-level data set on trade union membership and industrial relations practices in individual workplaces was obtained using a postal survey of establishments in the north-west and south-east of England. And fifth, a subset of this sample, all engineering establishments, was then selected for further research via interviews with management and union representatives. Certain officials of the Engineering Employers' Federation were also interviewed. Finally, semi-structured interviews were conducted with both head office and regional officials of selected individual unions and the Trades Union Congress (TUC), with the aim of discussing their regional practices, the issue of decentralization, and their membership recruitment strategies. Each of these data sets has its own strengths and weaknesses, but together they allow enquiry to be conducted at various levels of aggregation, and in this respect our study contains elements of both extensive (macro) and intensive (micro) analysis. On the other hand, these different data sets are obviously not directly comparable one with another, as each measures a different aspect of trade union organization and industrial relations. To take one example, the WIRS data are workplace based, but exclude workplaces with less than 25 employees, whereas the LFS data are household based yet do include information pertaining to employees from establishments below this threshold size. Or to take another example, individual unions have different administrative regions, so that geographically different individual unions cannot be compared directly one with another. For these and other reasons, our various data sets provide what in effect are different, though complementary, lenses through which to view the geography of the unions.

Intersecting with these issues is a more fundamental question concerning research orientation and motivation: what is the underlying purpose of our study? Different researchers may study a given phenomenon for different reasons, for different purposes, and such pluralism in academic enquiry is to be encouraged. The recognition of a pluralist dimension to geographical research carries a number of important implications, not least of which is that it behoves us to challenge the 'facticity' of the socio-economy. Different 'purposive interests' or research aims, by shaping what Joseph Schumpeter once called the 'pre-analytic cognitive act', will bring forth different or differently perceived aspects of the system. Thus there can be no singular meanings attached to socio-economic events and processes.

6   The next WIRS is planned for 1997, so that it will not be until 1998 at the earliest that the results will be available for researchers to utilize.

There is no single, 'correct' standpoint from which to measure and interpret the geography of trade unionism.

In her account of why and how geographers should study unions, Massey (1994) suggests that:

> Clearly, at one level, there is the simple fact that geographers map and explain things…so why not trade unions? Yet I suspect that many, if not most, people who choose to take up this subject area do so because they believe that the changing geography of trade unionism is an important component of the shifting contours of the industrial conflict and the political projects of our times. (pp. 96–97)

Her own work on the unions, she argues, was intended to be part of a wide-ranging assessment of the shifting geography of political power and influence on the British Left (Massey and Miles 1984; Massey and Painter 1989). We too are not interested simply in the mapping of the unions as yet one more 'spatial distribution'. Rather, the motivation for our enquiry is essentially twofold.

First, we are concerned to determine what has actually been happening to trade union representation and organization across the different regions of Britain in as precise a way as available data permit. Our analysis is thus intended to complement the industrial relations literature on British union decline by providing an alternative – geographical – perspective on this retreat, and showing how and in what ways the pressures facing the union movement are themselves geographically constituted. In this respect we share Massey's concern to explicate the profundity of the challenge confronting British unionism today, and the ways in which current union strategies are evolving or might evolve to cope with this challenge. Second, our aim is to highlight the geography of trade union decline as an integral component of contemporary uneven regional socio-economic development and transformation. In recent years geographers have directed considerable empirical and theoretical attention to the restructuring of the economic and industrial landscape in advanced countries, but curiously they have given much less emphasis to the spatial restructuring of key socio-economic institutions, and of these, trade unions and industrial relations systems have been all but neglected. Our analysis is meant to remedy this neglect. Furthermore, it is intended as a contribution to what we would like to call the 'geography of industrial relations', a field which we believe should form an integral part of any study of uneven development. Questions of geography, we contend, not only matter for the unions, but also enhance our understanding of them.

We make no claim that the discussion which follows represents a comprehensive account of the geography of union retreat in Britain. However, it is the first attempt to undertake a study of this sort. Given the general lack of research in this field, and the limitations of the various data sources available, our primary interest is in the union landscape as a whole, in the contours of the nationwide canvas so to speak, rather than in detailed portraits of this or that particular place.

Methodologically, our analyis is a rather eclectic one, and draws upon a wide variety of approaches, from the statistical to the qualitative and discursive. In this respect we are conscious that our methodological style may differ from that employed by those industrial relations specialists and labour economists who incline towards more formal models of union behaviour and influence. However, while such differences reflect the disciplinary boundaries of the academy, they do not preclude the exchange of ideas, and we believe our geographical focus has much to contribute to the study of industrial relations and labour economics.

We begin, in the next chapter, by outlining some conceptual issues in thinking about the 'geography of industrial relations'. The aim is not so much to construct a formal theoretical or analytical framework, but rather to suggest how geography enters into the structures and processes of industrial relations, and to link our discussion to regulationist-type ideas of the sort that have become so popular in contemporary geographical research on uneven regional development. Chapter Three then charts the regional contours of the current decline of British unionism, focusing especially on the question of whether and how far this decline has expunged the unions' traditional 'heartland' geography that can be traced back to the historical origins of the union movement in the early decades of the nineteenth century. Chapter Four moves the analysis on by showing how the geography of the unions has remained surprisingly resistent to the uneven regional impact of the various changes in labour market structure and regulation generally believed to have caused union decline. It would seem that the legacy of long-established regional differences in worker and employer traditions still lingers on. Then, in the subsequent chapter, attention is switched to the shrinking landscape of industrial militancy and strike activity. The dramatic decline in industrial action in recent years has itself been a regionally-differentiated process, and this chapter examines the implications of the new 'labour quiesence' for the different regional community traditions and local workplace cultures that historically have been so influential in shaping the incidence and regulation of industrial action. Chapter Six continues this local socio-institutional theme by examining the geography of 'decentralization' and 'localization' in industrial relations, using the British engineering industry as a case study. In the final chapter, and in the light of our various findings, we adopt a more speculative tone, and consider different scenarios for the future development of the landscape of British trade unionism, particularly in the context of what some theorists see as the onset of a general 'detraditionalization' of the socio-economy. We conclude that in the same way that geography has played a role in shaping the development of the unions and the industrial relations system in the past, so it is likely to exert an important influence on the scope for and nature of trade unionism and industrial relations in the future.

CHAPTER TWO

Situating Trade Unionism
Spaces of Regulation and Representation

INTRODUCTION

A sensible starting place for any piece of research is a review of existing literature on the subject. However, when we attempted to review the literature on the geography of organized labour, it soon became apparent that there was a shortage of material devoted specifically to this topic. In this chapter, therefore, we begin to consider why it is that economic geographers have had only a limited amount to say about the geography of trade unionism. In recent years the remit of economic geography has broadened and there is now an increasing interest in the ways in which production intermeshes with other social relations, including labour relations. To date, the most common way of theorizing these interconnections has been to use regulation theory.[1] However, we argue that regulation theory's account of trade unionism is under-theorized and places too much weight on the needs and consequences of production. Our response is twofold. First, we argue for a more autonomous and political conception of 'institutional regulation'. Second, we suggest that in order to understand the geography of trade unionism, it is necessary to view trade unions as shaped by processes of *representation* as well as those of *regulation*. We use the concept of representation to signal the political processes which link trade unions as institutions to their own potential and actual memberships. These processes of regulation and representation are shown to be geographically constituted, and we shall refer to the 'spaces' of regulation and

---

1   Regulation theory was developed in France during the 1970s and became influential in economic geography in the subsequent decade (see Aglietta 1979; Harvey 1989; Amin 1994) There is now a considerable range of regulation schools, Jessop 1992 for example, identifies seven variants). Basically, regulation theories argue that the history of capitalism can be divided into periods of stability and growth, termed regimes of accumulation, and periods of crisis. The alternation between the two is controlled by the relation between a 'mode of regulation' and a 'mode of accumulation'. The mode of regulation refers to the institutional ensemble and regularities (laws, collective agreements, rules, etc.) and the set of cultural habits and norms which co-ordinate and guide capitalist accumulation. When the mode of regulation fails, imbalances intensify and a period of crisis ensues (Nielsen 1991).

representation. In conjunction with the structural effects derived from economic contexts, these processes of regulation and representation form the basis of the spatial regimes, or sub-systems, of industrial relations which we referred to in Chapter One. Finally, we contend that this argument has important implications for the sudy of the contemporary decline of British trade unionism.

ECONOMIC GEOGRAPHY AND LABOUR: THE SHADOW OF PRODUCTION

Economic geographers have long been aware of differences in labour-force characteristics over space. One of the founders of industrial geography, for example, argued that industrial location is not explained by 'pure' economic rules of location. Instead:

> It results, we may say in hinting at the main point, from degrading labour to a commodity bought today and sold tomorrow, and from the ensuing laws determining the labour market and from the local agglomeration of workers created thereby. (Weber 1929, p.13)

However, when Weber drew up his simplified theory of location he confined himself to considering labour as a 'factor of location' (Clark 1989). He wrote:

> These labour costs can only have been factors in location by varying from place to place. That is self evident. But it is important to realize that, since we are still investigating the regional development of industry, such local differences of labour costs concern us only in so far as they are of significance for this problem. (Weber 1929, p.95)

This restricted view of labour was carried over into the subsequent academic development of industrial geography. For much of the post Second World War period, up to the 1970s, this development was based on neoclassical location theory. This assumes that labour is very much like any other commodity, and that labour markets are close approximations to the perfect commodity markets and exchanges encountered in the standard textbook theory: labour is considered homogeneous, information and mobility are costless, atomistic competition prevails between the micro-units of firms and workers, and normal arbitrage processes guarantee the law of equal price, so that differences in wages between firms or locations should be eliminated as workers move from low wage firms and locations to high wage ones.[2] The limitations of this approach were nevertheless apparent to one or two location theorists. Labour costs obviously include indirect wage costs, resulting from variations in efficiency, productivity and organization, as well

---

2   This view of labour goes back, of course, to Adam Smith. It is also found embodied in Lösch's theory of economic location, where it is argued that 'the structure of market areas for labour is exactly the same as that for goods and capital', (Lösch 1954, p.445).

as the direct cost of wages. Thus, even at an early date, Hoover (1948) noted that low labour costs could result not only from low wages, a large supply of labour and a lack of migration, but also from productive advantages. He argued that labour cost advantages were likely to be based on one or more of three things: special skill; a large labour market, providing an elastic supply of all grades of labour; and relative freedom from the restrictions imposed by unions or legislation (Hoover 1937). Indeed, Hoover argued that the causes of spatial variations in labour cost differentials 'is a large subject, to which inadequate scientific attention has been given' (p.70) and he suggested that 'The strengthened bargaining power of skilled and specialised labor in mature industrial centers has often encouraged a search for new locations and new processes adapted to those locations' (Hoover 1948, p.115). Remarkably, however, such insights were largely ignored by industrial geographers, and it was not until the rise of 'radical' industrial geography in the late 1970s that they began to be considered.

As these 'radical' geographical approaches emerged, in part in response to the intense spatial economic restructuring of the 1970s and 1980s, so the significance of capital/labour relations for local and regional development received more attention. At the heart of this move was Massey's (1984) *Spatial Divisions of Labour* which attempted to reconceptualize regional development and the distribution of employment as spatial expressions of relations of production and socially constructed divisions of labour. In her more Marxist-orientated perspective, labour was no longer to be seen as just another commodity. Instead it was emphasized that while labour power could be bought by employers, the actual output of that labour also depended on control and motivation in the labour process. Thus the social and political dimensions of employment were highlighted. Moreover, the complex interactions between labour organization and location began to attract interest (Massey and Miles 1984). Morgan and Sayer's (1988) influential study of the electronics industry in Britain also demonstrated how variations in labour/management relations are a central component of the social and institutional forms that shape national and regional competitiveness. Subsequently, economic geography's interest in labour has broadened and deepened.

Storper and Walker (1984, 1989) gave labour even more prominence in their geography of industrial capitalism. One of their key arguments is that as other factors of production – especially capital and technology – become increasingly mobile and malleable, labour remains unique as a location factor because of its relative immobility and the peculiarities of labour performance, control and reproduction in particular places. Both labour supply and labour demand are social processes depending on institutionalized practices and together these processes mean that labour remains highly geographically differentiated. Storper and Walker's explanation of the geographical differentiation of labour is based on a dynamic employment model and is in many ways still the most comprehensive account formulated to date. They argue that the employment relation between capital and labour, which is at the core of their theory, can be subdivided into two types of relations: production relations and exchange relations. Production relations describe the relations of co-operation and conflict which occur between capital and labour in the workplace; while exchange relations are those processes of purchase, negotiation and segmentation set within local labour markets. In addition, however, Storper and Walker insist that the employment relation is also at the centre of an interplay between industrial and sectoral development on the one hand and the social reproduction of labour and community development on the other. The uneven trajectory of sectoral and industrial development sets limits on the nature of the employment relation and, at the same time, the reproduction of workers in distinct communities with distinct histories shapes the social character of the labour supply. It is this tension that is at the heart of the spatial division of labour: 'Over time the intersection of labour and capital in space, as a critical dimension of employment, feeds back into the fortunes of capital, the evolution of technology and, of course, the history of working class communities' (Storper and Walker 1984, p.41).

Although they do not discuss industrial relations as such, Storper and Walker's dynamic employment model highlights many of the complex conjunctures which help to shape the geography of trade unionism. However, in their subsequent treatise on the territorial development of industry Storper and Walker (1989) made much more use of ideas derived from regulation theory. They used regulation theory's concept of a 'regime of accumulation' to refer to a set of political-economic relations that arise with, and sustain, periods of capitalist growth. In their account, regulation refers to the maintenance of 'the institutional fabric of growth in a dynamic and contradictory setting through state interventions and class compromises' (Storper and Walker 1989, p.203).[3] Class relations are defined as central to these territorial regulatory regimes. But although regulation theory has since become the predominant way in which economic geographers describe the correspondence between economic activity and the surrounding institutional contexts, it has had a mixed set of consequences for economic geography's theoretical and empirical analysis of labour.

Typically, regulationist approaches have focused on the contemporary transition between the old 'Fordist' regime of accumulation and the emerging new 'post-Fordist' regime. Fordism, it is argued, involved a compromise between capital and labour, in which high real wages were granted in return for high productivity growth, thus facilitating the buoyant economic expansion of the long post-war

---

3   This argument is also similar to the 'social structure of accumulation' approach developed by certain American labour economists. This again argues that long periods of rapid and stable economic expansion require a complex mix of supporting institutions called a 'social structure of accumulation'. These include domestic arrangements, such as labour- management relations, work organization, financial institutions, as well as international frameworks in trade, money and investment. Central to this approach is the view that these institutions control investment via their effect on capitalists' expectations. For a useful summary and comparison with regulation theory see Kotz, McDonough and Reich (1994).

boom. Furthermore, a tacit 'social contract' between the state and labour involved an exchange of publicly-funded social wages for co-operative behaviour on the part of the unions (Harvey 1989). In some countries, such as Sweden and to some extent the United Kingdom, this mode of regulation also promoted the creation of corporatist or tripartite institutions involving the state, the unions and the representativies of private capital.[4] Certainly the 'Fordist compromise' encouraged an expansion of collective bargaining and the development of national systems of industrial relations concertation and dispute management (Scott and Storper 1992; Boyer 1988, 1993; Crouch 1993). Regulation theorists have tended to be reticent about what follows the Fordist mode of regulation but they do suggest that the contemporary shift to 'post-Fordism' involves a breakdown of these national regulatory systems and the introduction of more 'flexible' arrangements in the labour market and the workplace (Boyer 1988, 1993).[5] Most accounts of post-Fordism admit a certain degree of indeterminacy in the precise outcomes for labour markets and for organized labour. It is argued that there are alternative routes to flexibility: some based on 'numerical' or external flexibility involving a casualization and contractualization of work; others based on 'co-operative flexibility' and negotiated involvement (Boyer 1988; Leborgne and Lipietz 1988).[6] Nevertheless, despite these alternative scenarios, post-Fordism is usually interpreted as involving the fragmentation of collective bargaining, a dramatic reduction in union membership and a precipitous decline in the power of organized labour. Jessop (1992), for example, suggests that:

> The post-Fordist wage relation could involve a basic recomposition of the collective laborer (with a tendency towards polarization between polyvalent skilled workers and the unskilled, as compared to the Fordist tendency towards homogenization around semiskilled mass labor); the organization of internal and external labour markets around different forms of flexibility (functions and skills, duration and form of labour contracts, wage package etc.); a shift towards enterprise – or plant level- collective bargaining; and new forms of social wage. (p.63)

Yet, while this perspective explicitly stresses that the institutions of labour relations have important consequences for the geography of production, it has not generated much detailed work on the form of these institutions and their specific effects in particular places. This appears to the result of several factors. One is that regulation

---

4   In the United Kingdom, two of the most important institutions of this kind were the National Economic Development Council (NEDC), and the Manpower Services Commission (MSC).

5   Interestingly, both the NEDC and MSC were abolished in the 1980s by the Thatcher government, in part precisely because they were viewed as being associated with the outmoded model of interventionism and institutionalism of the 1960s and 1970s.

6   Some authors dispute these claims and argue that most work practices involve a complex mix of flexibilities and rigidities which cannot be accurately represented by coherent strategies such as 'defensive' or 'innovative' flexibility (see Pollert 1991).

theory takes the national economy as its fundamental unit of enquiry.[7] Theoretically, at least, this allows regulationist theories to investigate the different ways in which accumulation regimes and their associated modes of social regulation, such as Fordism, are constructed in different countries (see Davis 1986; Boyer 1990). But analysis at smaller spatial scales has been rare, and one of the missing links in regulationist work has been an examination of how regulation meshes with uneven development and the possible significance of *local* modes of social regulation (Gertler 1992; Peck and Tickell 1992). For example, in their analsyis of the changing nature and direction of regulation associated with the Thatcher political-economic reforms during 1980s' Britain, Peck and Tickell (1992) argue that local regimes in southern regions of the country did indeed follow a trajectory quite distinct from that of local regimes in the northern regions.

Another factor is that the regulationist approach has also been over-generalized in that it tends to portray the shift from Fordism to post-Fordism as an all-embracing historical break and, as a result, neglects the continuities in production, institutional forms and labour practices in particular areas (Hudson 1989; Sayer 1989; Sayer and Walker 1992; Martin 1994). Furthermore, despite their emphasis on the importance of socialized and institutionalized practices, regulation theorists have given surprisingly little attention to the actual constitution and development of regulatory institutions, or what Clark (1992) refers to as 'real' regulation. Thus even in Sayer and Walker's (1992) recent re-theorizing of the division of labour, in which regulationist-type ideas are a recurring thread, and in which considerable prominence is given to the institutional framework that shapes an economic activity, workplace institutions such as unions and industrial relations systems are not considered at all. To some extent, this omission may be part of a more general lack of theorization of *processes* in regulation theory, and an overriding concern with production (as in the case of Sayer and Walker 1992). However, it is also a result of the implicit reliance on a functionalist explanation of institutional form (Pollert 1991). As Boyer (1993) writes 'Basically, the name of this school of economic analysis derives from the transformation of a concept borrowed from biology: a *regulation* mode describes the set of negative and positive feedbacks in relation to the stability of a complex network of interactions' (p.35). Unfortunately, this analogy means that there is a strong inclination to view institutional forms, like unions and industrial relations systems, as being functionally derived from the requirements of production. The causes of institutions are conflated with their effects in notions such as 'correspondence', 'fit' and 'equilibrium'. There is therefore a paradox at the heart of regulation theory. While in principle it describes the mode of social regulation as *regulating accumulation*, in practice it tends to explain socio-political institutions as being determined by the accumulation regime. In this sense it might be more appropriate to say that regulationist

---

7   In this respect it follows the long tradition of macro-economics, in which the 'national' economic space is assumed to be the critical theoretical and policy entity.

approaches view unions and other social institutions as being *regulated by accumulation*. Consequently, the more autonomous dynamics of institutional change and development have been neglected or reduced to the logic of economic processes. As Lash and Bagguley (1988) have argued, one consequence of this has been that many regulationist accounts go too far in recommending the adaptation of trade union structures and industrial relations to the imperatives of a post-Fordist mode of regulation.

The final, and perhaps the most important, reason why there has actually been only a limited study of the mode of social regulation is the difficulty of delimiting the constituent institutions. In most regulation theory there is little doubt that, theoretically at least, the accumulation system is distinct from the mode of regulation. However, it is not clear whether this distinction serves a useful purpose. If the accumulation system is examined more closely then it is itself made up regulatory institutions such as product and labour markets, firms and corporations. In fact, it is impossible to distinguish a mode of social regulation from an accumulation system. The initial analytical dualism is misleading, as institutions go all the way down to the heart of accumulation itself. As Rubery states 'there is no division between the economic and the institutional as "markets" are formed and shaped through institutions' (Rubery 1992, p.246). Hence it may well be preferable to take a smaller-scale approach and examine specific sets of interactions between unions, labour markets, labour processes and economic change.

While the detailed mechanics of regulation theory are thus open to question, the theory nevertheless does impart a valuable and strong sense of the notion that changes in economic structure, particularly since the 1970s, will have had a substantial impact on the geography of regulatory institutions, including the unions. Indeed, this conclusion is supported by many recent national and comparative studies of union change. It has been argued that this economic impact can be better understood if it is divided into two main types of change: 'structural' and 'conjunctural' (Ferner and Hyman 1992). As we outline in Chapter Four, unions in advanced capitalist countries have been subjected to numerous adverse structural changes in recent years. The restructuring and recomposition of employment have involved the decline of traditionally unionized sectors, such as male blue-collar jobs, and the growth of sectors where unions have been less well-organized (Waddington 1992). In particular, the growth of service employment, women's employment, part-time jobs and a reduction in establishment size have been described as particularly unfavourable to unions. In addition, structural change has involved the growth of international competition and the rise of large multinational companies, many of which have been ill-disposed towards union organization.

But, it is argued, this restructuring has been accompanied by economic change of a more conjunctural type. The deep recessions of the early 1980s and early 1990s presented labour with an unfavourable climate and have resulted in a weakening of the relative power of trade unions. As Kelly argues, the power which unions can exercise in their relations with employers is strongly conditioned by their economic context (Kelly 1990). Thus some authors claim that the high levels of unemployment endemic during the 1980s and the real wage growth of those in work have together added to the unions' problems by weakening the incentive of individuals to remain or become union members (Carruth and Disney 1988; Disney 1990). While such accounts have been heavily criticized for being too compartmentalized, for neglecting the interaction of individual membership and wider issues of union recognition and coverage (Mason 1993), and for assuming an overly instrumentalist view of the individual's decision to join a union, they nevertheless emphasize the complexity and layered nature of the pressures on organized labour.

Hitherto, these arguments have tended to ignore the fact that the changes in both these structural and conjunctural economic contexts are not simply homogenous across the nation.[8] The impact of these trends has a geography even within nation-states, and trade union change has varied between cities, regions and localities. For instance, different places are obviously integrated into the international economy to different degrees, and in different ways, so that the impact of international competition is far from uniform. Moreover, economic restructuring and labour market change have proceeded at different rates across different localities (see Chapter Four). Similarly, both unemployment and real wage growth are frequently regionally differentiated. Hence the economic terrain on which unions organize and operate is highly uneven. It is apparent then, as regulation theorists emphasize, that an appreciation of economic conditions and the organization of production is indispensble to understanding the geography of organized labour. But it does not provide the basis for a complete explanation of that geography. Rather, such an account also needs to consider other more social and political components of regulation and restructuring.

INSTITUTIONAL SPACES AND REGULATION

Clark (1992) provides a more political and autonomous account of regulation which is especially useful in understanding the geography of trade union organization. He criticizes the use of regulationist theory in economic geography on the grounds that the approach subordinates regulation to the needs and dictates of economic accumulation. Regulation is not a process of adaptive feedback but rather refers, in his view, to the administrative manner and style by which states constitute and reproduce society. The form and function of regulation and regulatory mechanisms are derived through the interplay between economics and political

---

8   Nor are they necessarily distinct effects. Severe conjunctural events, such as the deep economic recessions of the early 1980s and early 1990s, can produce profound structural change, so that attempting to separate the two types of effect can be not only difficult, but actually misleading.

culture as mediated through institutional behaviour and practices. Hence, he argues that regulatory responses to the same economic problem will vary according to different historical-geographical cultural milieu and the different institutions within them. This, he argues, provides a context-sensitive understanding of regulation which recognizes that different places are saturated with different customs and subject to different forms of legal adjudication. Furthermore, in Clark's account regulatory cultures and practices in particular places have inertial power, so that re-regulation cannot be enacted at will. In his words, 'If we are to represent the geography of regulation, we must also respect the local ingrained nature of customary modes of decision-making' (1992, p.625). Clark (1989) himself has demonstrated the relevance of this concept of regulation to under-standing the decline of American unionism. He argues that the decline of trade unionism in the United States has been inherently geographical and he explains this geography by following Dunlop's emphasis on the inter-relationships between economic factors and the characteristics of local communities (pp.26–27). Clark interprets this local context as primarily institutional and he endeavours to show how legislative contexts have shaped trade unionism in different states.[9]

Comparative studies of industrial relations have also provided much evidence which supports the significance of this understanding of regulation. States regulate trade unions both directly through legal mechanisms and indirectly through the state's more general influence on labour markets and the economy. Thus similar economic trends at an international scale have been mediated by different national political and institutional contexts (Western 1994). As we noted in the previous chapter, some industrial relations analysts argue that even small differences in these national contexts can have a considerable effect on the level and strength of trade unionism. The most fundamental division is probably between 'inclusionist' strategies, where national states structure economic interests so as to include organized labour in the processes of policy formulation and implementation, and 'exclusionist' strategies where unions are effectively marginalized from the main-stream of economic and political life (Goldthorpe 1984). Ferner and Hyman (1992) argue that these political strategies are often resistant to change. In their view,

> Institutions may be the crystallization of specific class forces and balances of power, but once established they have a life and reality of their own, independent of political (or economic) fluctuations or caprices: they are, in Streeck's term, 'sticky', especially when enshrined in law. This institutional persistence appears to explain much of the variability in countries' responses to common influences in the 1980s. (p.xxxiii)

---

9   This statement is especially appropriate to the federal structure of the United States which allows individual states to implement their own legislation concerning workers' rights and union recognition.

It has often been argued that these institutional conjunctures are very closely related to management decision-making and strategies of managerial control in the workplace. For example, Burawoy's (1985) notion of a 'factory regime' emphasizes the intersection of wider authority structures with workplace management. He argues that there are important variations between nations in the relationship between state structures and the 'production apparatuses' which regulate the labour process. Echoing such concerns, Turner (1991) has recently suggested that the degree of integration of unions into managerial decision-making and the presence of laws and corporatist agreements which encourage and regulate firm-level union participation have a profound effect on trade union fortunes. He writes that 'in contemporary world markets it is precisely the absence of union integration into management decision-making backed up by an appropriate legal and political framework that makes possible the instability in industrial relations and the decline of unions' (p.220).

While this type of regulatory context no doubt has a particular relevance to explaining different national trends, we would also insist that these contexts frequently vary at a regional and local scale within a nation-state. As Clark (1989) argues, this will be especially evident in federal states such as the USA. However, sub-national variations are also apparent in other, ostensibly more centralized, political systems for several reasons. In the first instance, labour markets are not self-regulating commodity markets but are deeply regulated by state policies which often produce spatially uneven effects. Moreover, there are also 'interaction effects' which result from the interplay of state regulation with historically prior uses of space, arising from 'the way in which regulatory processes are realized as concrete events in particular local contexts' (Peck 1994, p.157). Hence, industrial relations systems are typically complex products of practices at different spatial scales. Furthermore, many commentators have suggested that during the past two decades, there has been a trend towards more decentralized industrial relations systems in many advanced capitalist states. As we argued in Chapter One, the territorial structure of the institutions of industrial relations means that different subdivisions of these institutions are able to respond in different ways to national political rules and norms. Moreover, as we hope to show in subsequent chapters, these institutional subdivisions are also characterized by the 'stickiness' or path dependence which Ferner and Hyman invoke.

It is clearly important, then, to incorporate both economic and political senses of regulation into explanations of the geography of unions. However, the politics of trade unionism include not only the national and local regulatory regimes in which the unions operate, but also include the representative politics between the unions and their memberships. The politics of representation are just as geographical as those of regulation and it is to the 'spaces of representation' that we now turn.

SPACES OF REPRESENTATION

Streeck (1992) argues that collective organizations are compelled to operate in two environments or contexts; one formed by state agencies and other organized interest groups, and another formed by their own members. He argues that the second context means that collective organizations are partly governed by the values and interest perceptions of the groups and individuals that they undertake to represent and, in particular, by their sense of collective identity.[10] This is clearly relevant to the relations between unions and their members. Not only do unions reflect their members' values and interests, or they should if they function as democratic organizations, they also represent these interests to others, and this interaction may well feed back to change those interests over time. As Berger *et al.* (1981) argue, *representation* refers to processes of group formation, the identification of collective interests, and the ways in which relations of power within groups and associations are organized. In the few geographical studies of trade unions that have appeared recently, the focus has been on the regulatory aspects of union organization and very little attention has been paid to the role of representation.

In the industrial relations literature, the relationships between unions and their members, and between unions and workers more generally, have long been the subjects of debate. Recent changes in the political and social contexts of trade unions have again given the question of representation a renewed prominence (Fosh 1993). A large number of studies have suggested that workers' propensity to unionize has fallen dramatically in recent years. Indeed, some authors have pointed to a 'crisis of representation' caused partly by a growing belief that unions have become less effective and partly by an increase in other forms of employee representation and involvement within companies. Hyman (1992) summarizes these difficulties under the heading of the 'disaggregation of the working class'. In his account this disaggregation is closely related to the changes in economic regulation which we discussed above. It consists of four factors. First, a shift in employee attitudes from collectivism to individualism, associated with the growth of self-employment, small firms and the redirection of government political ideology in favour of free markets. Second, a polarization of employment into core and periphery, or insider/outsider sectors, as employers adopt more dichotomous labour market strategies. Third, a growing particularity of collective identities in terms of employers, occupations, regions, sectors or industries. And fourth, a fragmentation even within organized labour due to the weakening influence of national leadership authority. Hyman (1992) is critical of some aspects of this disaggregation argument as he suggests that it often invokes a mythical past, a

---

10 Streeck (1992) argues that each of these two organizational environments are governed by distinct 'logics of associative action'. The first is a 'logic of influence' which relates to the surrounding institutional context and the second is 'logic of membership' which concerns the relations between the organization and its own membership. He argues that, if they are to be successful, collective associations must be responsive to both of these logics.

golden age of working-class unity. In his opinion, unions have always organized on very segmented and uneven ground. In our view, this is precisely why the logics of representation in which unions are entangled must be understood as always geographically variable. In the remainder of this section, we illustrate this argument by considering workers' propensity to unionize and by examining the internal organization and representativeness of unions as institutions.

There has so far been very little work exploring spatial variations in the propensity of workers to join trade unions. One of the main reasons for this is that it has traditionally been assumed that membership propensity is simply based on an instrumental and rational decision made on the grounds of potential economic benefits. The classic problem which this assumption generated, of course, was how to account for the problem of free-riders whereby individuals could enjoy collective goods whilst avoiding the costs of membership (Olson 1965). Recently, less reductive approaches have emerged. McLoughlin and Gourlay (1994) have followed Kochan (1980) in arguing that there are three critical determinants of workers' propensity to join unions: their (dis)satisfaction with the economic aspects of their employment; their perception of the positive utility of non-union means of representation to employers, or 'voice' mechanisms; and the instrumental beliefs which they hold about unions. The decision to join a union has thus been rightly described as complex and conjunctural, but there is also evidence that this decision cannot be understood without considering the heterogeneity of labour.

For example, in their study of union membership amongst young workers, Cregan and Johnston (1990) argue that different groups of people join unions for different reasons. For purposes of clarity they classify these groups into core members and non-core members. They argue that core members join a union mainly because they share the interests, values and beliefs of other members of the union but also because they recognize that only by collective action can they achieve their ends or enhance their self-esteem. Subsequently these core members are more active in mobilizing non-members. The decision of non-core members on the other hand is determined by their perception of the relative strengths of employers and unions as well as the availability of alternative actions. These non-core groups are subject to different sorts of pressure: those originating from the unions and employers, and those encountered in the workplace itself. In Cregan and Johnston's words, 'If youngsters who would otherwise be susceptible to union recruitment are in industries or occupations where organisation is weak, or if unions think they are unstable, then there will be less pressure on them to join' (p.99). But in addition to this, the norms and customary practices of the workplace also impact on union membership decisions. These norms are the result of a number of factors, including the density of unionism in the workplace, the legitimizing effect of a co-operative employer and the legislative framework set by the state. The crucial point in this argument, however, is that motivations other than financial instrumentality inspire some employees to join a union. The argument builds on Booth's (1985) proposal of a social custom model of union organization where the paradox of collective action or the problem of free-ridership is answered by the existence of norms and expectations among groups of workers. Yet these studies neglect the fact that these norms and customs, and hence the tendencies to unionization within a workforce, are invariably constructed and reproduced in particular places, and hence in different ways in different locations.

In this sense, geography can be seen as a key determinant of collective organization. As Barnes and Sheppard (1992) suggest, 'Social pressures influencing the perceived rewards to collective action are more likely to create powerful feelings of guilt or injustice in local communities, where individuals have a shared repertoire of daily routines, practical knowledge, and institutional allegiances' (p.15). This is both because individual behaviour can be more easily monitored in such communities and because a strong community has forceful sanctions at its disposal. Individuals can be seen to reach common understandings and construct collective identities through forms of communicative action in dense local social networks (Miller 1992). Indeed there is a wide range of geographical work which shows that the class identities and traditions underlying collective action are constituted though place-specific relations (Cooke 1985; Thrift and Williams 1987). Traditions and identities are always in some sense rooted in the contexts and experiences of specific places, and space sustains differences in social identities, traditions and practices. Furthermore, these arguments are reinforced by an appreciation of the importance of local historical experiences and the cumulative effects of past customs, 'collective memories' and patterns of organization (Massey 1984). For example, the concentration of large numbers of semi-skilled and unskilled workers in large manufacturing plants in post-war Merseyside provided the basis for a distinctive tradition of trade union consciousness and organization in the region (Darlington 1994). Similarly, the geographical isolation and economic specialization of the South Wales coal-mining communities helped to give them a strong sense of collective labourist identity (Cooke 1985). But, more generally, Scott (1994) also emphasizes that labour relations are often encumbered by their history and this historical shadow frequently colours and even distorts both managers and workers' understandings of contemporary changes. Consequently, 'Explaining developments in industrial relations inevitably raises questions about the ways in which past beliefs have co-existed or have been displaced by newer ideas' (p.24).

There is also a considerable body of work which outlines specific formative influences on the production and reproduction of workers' norms and expectations. In recent years, the effects of the labour process itself have been set in the context of the characteristics of labour markets (Warde 1985). To date, no comprehensive spatial theory of labour markets and their functioning has been formulated. Nor is there any adequate detailed typology of local labour markets which indicates what the principal structural and institutional characteristics of different types of market are, or how these characteristics affect the behaviors of employers and employees.[11] As we suggested earlier, labour markets are themselves geographically constituted and formed by types of social networks. Both Peck (1994) and Hanson and Pratt (1992) have examined the place-based processes through which local labour markets and their segmentations develop. According to Hanson and Pratt, 'space is not a *container* of labour market processes but the *medium through which different segments are forged*' (p.404). The intersection of external and internal labour markets may be a central factor behind spatial variations in workers' expectations, preferences and collective action. These variations are not simply the result of production, but also reflect the geography of labour reproduction and spatial differences in socio-political culture (Warde 1987; Storper and Walker 1989). Linked to this, other authors have pointed to the important role played by family socialization in the establishment of individuals' attitudes to unions (Gallie 1990).

It is clear that the characteristics of representation are intimately entwined with those of regulation through these place-specific sets of processes. However, none of these norms or conditions by themselves determine the extent of collective organization. Rather, as Berger *et al.* (1981) put it, and as we argued in Chapter One, they form clusters of resources which provide opportunities for mobilization and organization. Interests are not unequivocally settled by social and economic positions. Whether collective organization actually takes place will also depend on the priorities and internal dynamics of trade unions as institutions, which are themselves geographically structured.

Geography is important to the internal organization and politics of trade unions in several senses. First, the variations in the social and cultural character of labour, discussed above, will clearly be reflected in the relations between members and trade union officials. Consequently these relations will be far from uniform across space. Fosh and Heery (1990) for instance, criticize most theories of union representation and bureaucracy on the grounds that they see members and officers as having fixed interests and attitudes. Instead they insist that:

> The relationship between unions and their members can be highly variable so that any attempt to reduce it to a simple dichotomy of interests, with an associated pattern of conflict between bureaucracy and rank and file, must be judged inadequate. Empirically the goals of union members vary from context to context and over time as does the extent of the gap between the two sets of preferences. Theories of union behaviour, therefore, which start

---

11 An arbitrary and simplistic typology of labour market *models* might distinguish four main categories: (i) the labour market viewed as a straightforward extension of more general market theories; (ii) the labour market seen as a special subcase, subject to special adjustmnent processes and deviations from the orthodox market concept, but nevertheless explicable by conventional market behaviour analysis; (iii) the labour market as an atypical form entailing the introduction of sociological and cultural factors as causes and constraints; and (iv) more general socio-institutional and industrial relations models. All four types could be given different degrees of spatial disaggregation and expression.

from the assumption that officials and members have a limited number of essential interests will only ever possess limited explanatory power. The starting point for a more complete theory of unions, we believe, must be to pose the question *how and why the relationship between unions and their members varies in time and place.* (p.20 emphasis added)

Thus, in their study of contemporary union decline, Kelly and Heery (1994) have recently found that national and local officials within trade unions are often subject to different pressures and influences, and that local officials themselves face different specific circumstances:

> Declining political influence is felt much more acutely by national officers, who therefore have more incentive to adjust union policies in order to restore their influence as well as their finances, and hence the top-down promotion of 'new realism' in its various forms. Local officers, on the other hand, remain subject to pressures very similar to those felt by shop stewards and, where union organization and collective bargaining has been preserved, have less sense of a crisis of trade unionism that requires strategic re-thinking. (p.194)

Second, the territorial differentiation of trade unions into regional subunits (such as branches, divisions, etc.) is both a key cause of these variations and an important organizational response to it. As Streeck (1992) suggests, 'Differentiation of organised interests by subnational territories is almost an omnipresent phenomenon. Nevertheless, it has remained under-studied, due probably to the traditional preoccupation of interest group research with the national (and, incidentally, the inter-sectoral) level' (p.107). On the one hand, he argues that territorial differentiation is shaped by different membership identities and needs and that the services delivered by local offices will be influenced by members' perceptions of what policy should be. On the other hand, however, he notes that organizations use territorial differentiation as a way of managing the heterogenity of members' interests. It is a response to the perennial difficulty of accommodating diversity whilst generating organizational unity. In his view, territorial subunits, whilst also fulfilling other functions, are a key way of generating and absorbing 'requisite variety'.

The role played by territorial differentiation has several significant consequences. Crouch (1993) argues that a key feature of trade unions is their degree of 'articulation'. In his words,

> An articulated organisation is one in which strong relations of interdependence bind different vertical levels, such that the actions of the centre are frequently predicated on securing the consent of lower levels and the autonomous action of lower levels is bounded by rules of delegation and scope for discretion ultimately controlled by successively higher levels. (p.54–55)

What is important to add here is that these institutional layers do not exist in some sort of abstract theoretical space. Rather they are social constructions which interact with many other types of geographical socio-economic differentiation. The local subunits of particular unions may therefore be shaped by their specific contexts and may well develop distinctive responses to similar challenges. Indeed, Painter (1991) argues that this is exactly what has happened in the unions' responses to the privatization of local government services in Britain during the 1980s. Thus he found that trade unions in Newcastle have been much more effective in resisting and preventing the privatization of local government services through 'contracting out' than their counterparts in the London borough of Wandsworth, due to the different traditions of the unions in the two areas, their differing political relations to their local councils, and the varied local circumstances in which the unions' strategies had to be implemented.

Additionally, however, the geographical scale of union organization is itself the subject of dispute and collective conflict. In his study of the role of spatial scale in US labour relations, Herod (1992) puts forward two useful arguments. In the first place, he argues that spatial scales are contested social constructions which are the outcomes of processes of co-operation and competition among social groups. But, second, he argues that scale is not just socially produced, it is also socially producing; that is, the scale of collective action influences the resources which contending groups can utilize and so shapes the eventual outcome. Herod illustrates these points by arguing that the American employers' offensive against unionism during the 1980s depended on a geographical fragmentation of collective bargaining so as to take advantage of local concessionary deals. More generally, there is now a widespread recognition that the larger geographical scale on which capital tends to operate compared to the relative locational fixity of labour often reinforces the unequal distribution of power exercised by the former over the latter (Clark 1989; Cowling and Sugden 1994). In Clark and Johnston's words, 'As unions are the representatives of labour, they must inevitably reflect local labour processes. In contrast, firms are often centralized at much higher tiers of the spatial hierarchy and have no statutory responsibility for sustaining the integrity of local representation' (Clark and Johnston 1987, p.293). In this context, place-specific union organization and campaigns can lead to a defensive and parochial competition between different groups of workers (see Hudson and Sadler 1986, for example). In many cases it has been important for trade unions to widen their scale of representation, not only because this forges identities and shared interests between a wider constituency of workers but also because centralization at a national scale has often allowed unions to have a much greater influence on the strategies of capital, especially large firms, and on the national government's decision-making. In this way, the spatial construction of representation again proves to be inseparable from uneven processes of economic and political regulation.

CONCLUSIONS AND IMPLICATIONS

So far then we have made a general case that unions are integrated into dynamics of regulation and representation and that both these sets of processes are inherently geographical. Indeed these processes form the bases of the spatial sub-systems of industrial relations which we referred to in Chapter One. As we also argued, it is now widely agreed that the last decade and a half has been a period of traumatic decline and dramatic restructuring for British trade unions. It is clear from many accounts that, as far as the unions are concerned, there have been significant discontinuities in the processes of regulation and of representation. Once again, most analyses of these discontinuities have been focused at a national scale and have talked about changes in the economy as a whole, in the national political environment, or in the relationships between different national unions (particularly mergers). If, as we have argued, regulation and representation are both inherently spatial, then aggregative studies at a national scale are at best partial and at worst misleading. Such explanations have neglected the way that trade unionism grew from regional and local bases and has repeatedly been shaped by complex interactions between the different spaces of regulation. Likewise, little is known about how regional and local representation has responded to national regulatory changes. But the existence of spatial sub-systems in industrial relations means, first, that national aggregative studies may obscure the different trends taking place in different regions and, second, that changes in particular local areas may in turn be shaping the evolution of industrial relations at a national scale. At a time of profound discontinuity in economic and political life the need for a disaggregated regional perspective is intensified.[12] Our intention in the following chapters is to begin to develop such a perspective.

---

12 Our argument is analogous to that made for a regional perspective on the first Industrial
    Revolution. In recent years several economic and social historians have argued that the
    economic and social changes set in motion by an uneven pattern of industrialization are better
    understood by means of a regional perspective (see Hudson 1992; Pollard 1981).

CHAPTER THREE

The Contours of Decline
Union Retreat and Resilience in the Regions

INTRODUCTION

Trade unionism, we have argued, is an integral part of the process of uneven regional development, of the geographies of economic accumulation and social regulation. Given that unions are institutions which organize workers in their place of work, we would expect unionism to reflect to some extent the spatial division of labour, that is, how production and employment are organized and regulated across space. At the same time, as part of the system of social and workplace regulation, the geography of trade unionism in its turn influences the evolving geography of production and employment. The history of economic accumulation in Britain over the past two hundred years has consisted of successive waves or phases of uneven regional development, each of which has added a new spatial division of labour to the economic landscape inherited from previous phases (see Massey 1979, 1984; Dunford and Perrons 1983; Marshall 1987). As this process has unfolded, so it has shaped and reshaped the spaces of worker representation and labour regulation referred to in the previous chapter. Although all of the main accounts of British trade union movement pay surprisingly little attention to the role of geography (for example, Clegg 1979; Pelling, 1992), the evolution of the British trade unionism has been moulded in significant ways by this episodic and uneven development of the space economy.

By the time the British trade union movement had reached its zenith at the end of the 1970s, at least a century and a half of worker struggle and collective organization had produced a complex geography of union membership and representation. It is against this historically sedimented configuration that the decline and retreat of recent years has taken place. As the space economy enters yet another phase in its evolution, and new structures of 'post-Fordist' or 'flexible' accumulation and regulation confront the old, 'Fordist' structures, so the system of trade unionism is also being recast.[1] A new map of trade unionism is being forged, a map which is itself the outcome of the interaction of new economic and political forces with the old terrain of union representation built up in the past. Our aim in this and the subsequent chapter is to identify and explicate the main features of this new union map. Here we focus on charting the contours of union decline; and then in the next chapter we examine the role played by the contemporary economic restructuring process in carving these contours. We begin by outlining the development of the union landscape on which the current decline is being inscribed. The purpose of this brief excursion into history is to highlight the way in which, despite the progressive extension of the trade union movement across the country, certain features of the union map — specifically, the existence of significant regional differences in unionization, especially between the highly unionized northern 'heartland' regions, on the one hand, and the less unionized regions of the south, on the other — have displayed a remarkable degree of overall persistence. One of the questions we seek to address in this chapter is whether and to what extent the present process of union decline is obliterating this historical legacy.

THE EARLY GEOGRAPHICAL DEVELOPMENT OF THE UNION MOVEMENT

It was only from the 1830s and 1840s onwards that the modern British trade union movement began to emerge (see Pelling, 1992).[2] Its precursor was the numerous craft guilds, journeymen clubs and trade-friendly societies that had developed in the previous century. These were highly localized institutions, associated with particular trades in particular towns and cities: for example, cotton textile workers and mechanics in the towns of Lancashire; carpenters in London; shipbuilders on Merseyside, Tyneside and London; iron founders in the major towns of Lancashire, Yorkshire and the Midlands; and miners in the coalfields of Yorkshire and Durham (see Southall 1988). From about 1800 an increasing number of these local societies 'came into union', establishing formal reciprocal relations between cognate trade societies in different towns, especially towns clustered in the same region of the country. In this way the origins of the trade union movement were quintessentially geographical, based on the formation of industry- and occupation-specific unions in the leading industrial centres of the period, in particular in the core industrial areas situated in the North East, North

---

1   As we noted in the previous chapter, we use the terms Fordist and post-Fordist here because they have become part of the standard lexicon in discussions of contemporary economic, social and political change. However, we are only too well aware of the problems and debates that surround these concepts.

2   In this and the following section the aim is not to rehearse the historiography of the development of the trade union movement, but rather to highlight some of the main geographical features of that development.

West, Midlands and London regions of England, together with South Wales and Central Scotland (see Langton and Morris 1984). The product of the Industrial Revolution and the subsequent wave of Victorian economic development, these areas formed a distinct industrial geography organized in terms of a particular type of spatial division of labour, namely a pattern of regional sectoral specialization in which craft work and subsequently the fast-developing factory system were central (see Massey 1979, Marshall 1987). Localized key natural resources and external economies (particularly the accumulation of local pools of skilled labour and the growth of specialized suppliers), and rapid export growth, fuelled the geographical clustering of the country's key industries (coal mining, textiles, steel, shipbuilding, and mechanical engineering) (Dunford and Perrons 1983). Whole areas became dominated by and dependent on these propulsive sectors and their allied activities. Perhaps not surprisingly, these were the areas which many of the first trade unions were born and from which subsequently the union movement progressively emanated.

The fact that these local labour markets were dominated by particular industries and labour processes imbued their workforces and communities not only with particular types of employment and skills, but by the same token with the social foundations for emergent collective class identities and politics, which although often highly sectional helped fuel the development of regionally based, work-place radicalism and union traditions. The North West region played a particularly formative role in the trade union movements of the 1830s and 1840s. As early as 1810 in fact, spinners in the region had organized a four-month strike from a base in Manchester, and despite defeat by the employers, the seeds of future collective action and organization had been sown. The first attempt at unionization came in 1818, when the Lancashire spinners set up a 'union of trades', a loose federation of workers' societies whose members were 'recommended' to support each other from their funds in time of need (Pelling 1992). Despite the short life of this initiative, workers in the region continued to organize, and in 1829 cotton spinners in Manchester established the Grand General Union of the Operative Spinners of Great Britain and Ireland, followed a year later by the National Association for the Protection of Labour (NAPL). The latter consisted of numerous local unions of trade clubs, and although its main strength was in Lancashire, from there it spread into other industrial areas such as Huddersfield and Birmingham, and its influence was also responsible for the formation of a union among the Staffordshire potters. By the 1840s the North West had in fact become a leading centre for the emerging trade union movement, as Engels noted in his *The Condition of the Working Classes in England*:

> The factory operatives, and especially those of the cotton districts, form the nucleus of the labour movement. Lancashire, and especially Manchester, is the seat of the most powerful unions, the central point of Chartism, the place which numbers most socialists. (Engels 1973, p.244)

Meanwhile, the rapid growth of the coal industry promoted the formation of unions in the country's main coal-mining areas. A few attempts at organization had been made in the Scottish and South Wales fields as early as the 1820s, but these proved largely unsuccessful. However, by the 1840s 'county unions' had been formed in the coal-mining communities in Durham, Northumberland, Lancashire, Yorkshire, and Staffordshire as well as in Scotland. In 1842 delegates from these areas formed a Miners' Association of Great Britain and Ireland, which by 1844 claimed to represent some 70,000 miners, about a third of the total labour force in the industry at that time. As in the case of textile workers, however, union organization in the mining industry was then set back by economic slump and unsuccessful strikes. By the late 340s the Association had all but collapsed, although mining unions survived in several of the coal-mining counties. During the 1850s the movement recovered again, especially in the coalfields in the North East and Scotland, where, in 1863, the National Miners Association was eventually established.

In the textile industry, as in mining, unions developed intermittently in this mid-century period, and tended to be localized (regional and urban) rather than national institutions. Partly because the mining and cotton industries were regionally concentrated, for some time the struggles of the mining and cotton worker unions had only a limited impact on labour organization elsewhere in the country. But the development of trade unionism in the engineering industry was to have wider ramifications: the union structure evolved by workers in this industry became the pattern other craft workers sought to imitate. Again workers in the North West played a leading role. Following the repeal of the Combination Laws in 1825, several societies of millwrights, machinists, and other engineering craftsmen were formed in the north of England, especially in the Manchester region, and in the 1840s workers in the industry endeavoured to amalgamate all the skilled engineering societies into a single over-arching organization. The result was the Amalgamated Society of Engineers (ASE), the first national union, created in 1851 from more than a hundred local associations. Apart from its formation by the amalgamation of numerous local associations, the ASE also combined a central financial administration based in London with a devolved organizational structure of local branches and districts. This fusion of many local unions into a single, nationally centralized but regionally organized structure, was hailed by Sidney and Beatrice Webb at the time as a 'new model' of trade unionism (Webb and Webb 1894), an institutional and organizational form that other unions should follow.

As Lane points out, the move towards amalgamation and national organization had became a widespread trend over the second half of the nineteenth century:

> Throughout the period 1850–90 there was a strong, persistent and irreversible tendency for [union] powers to be concentrated at the centre. Tenaciously held popular views that power properly belonged to the locality,

and attempts to enforce those views, were progressively overcome. (Lane 1974, p.80)

By the time of the Board of Trade's Report on Trade Unions in 1894, perhaps as many as half of all union members were in unions with national organizational structures (Southall 1988). Yet, Lane argues, this trend towards national centralizaton nevertheless retained strong elements of a locally and regionally based membership. This was even the case for the 'model' national union of the Amalgamated Society of Engineers, in which regional loyalties remained particularly strong, especially in the early historic core areas of Lancashire and Scotland (Jeffreys 1945; Lane 1974), and, unlike the situation in many other unions, the institutionalization of regionally elected officials and representatives was a prominent organizational feature. These loyalties reflected not only regional differences in industrial structure, but also differences in the socialized attitudes of workers, differences that were in part rooted in the specific historical experiences of each region. Indeed, although several unions underwent centralization, membership nevertheless remained concentrated in the industrial and mining communities of Northern England, Central Scotland and South Wales.

From mid-century on, several factors combined to promote the growth of the union movement. The increasing scale of industry, the widening of the market for labour and goods, and the greater mobility of workers, and, later, the growth of employer's associations, were all factors which increased the scope of trade unionism. By 1869 membership of unions affiliated to the newly established Trades Union Congress (TUC) had grown to an estimated 250,000, and by 1873 numbers had expanded to 509,000 as a result of the economic boom of the early 1870s and a series of legislative measures which extended the legal rights of unions in the workplace (Friedman 1977).[3] According to the Webbs in their *History of Trade Unionism*, membership at the beginning of the 1890s had reached an estimated 2 million.[4] Their work also contained one of the first attempts to map the geographical distribution of aggregate union membership, and this shows that despite the expansion of the trade union movement and its national organization over the second half of the nineteenth century, and the growth of unionization amongst semi-skilled workers, trade unionism was still largely confined to the original historical core or 'heartland' regions (Webb and Webb 1894). Union densities in the north of Britain were more than three times greater than those in the south and east, ranging from over 16 per cent in the North West and Northern

---

3   Such as 1867 Master and Servant Act and the 1875 Employers and Workmen Act, which made it easier for workers to strike without fear of imprisonment for breach of contract; the 1871 Trade Union Act, which helped to secure the legal status of unions; and the Conspiracy and Protection of Property Act of 1875, which legalized peaceful picketing.

4   The precise source of their data is unclear, but is almost certain to be based on the information for 1889, 1890 and 1891 collected by the Board of Trade and published in its *Fourth* and *Fifth Reports on Trade Unions*.

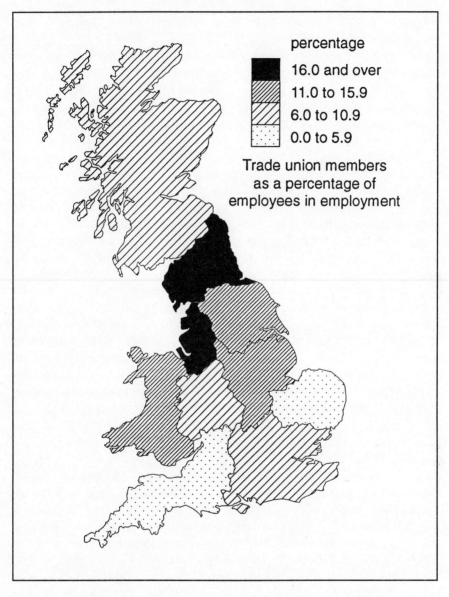

Source: Webb and Webb, 1894

Figure 3.1: Regional trade union densities, 1892

regions to less than 5 per cent in the Outer South East, East Anglia, and the South West (Figure 3.1).[5]

With the advent of the twentieth century, trade unionism began to grow much more rapidly. By 1912 total membership had increased to 3 million, and over the next eight years it rose dramatically, reaching 8.2 million, or some 44 per cent of the employed workforce, by 1920 (see Cronin 1979). Furthermore, union organization had now reached every major sector of industry. The formation of the Labour Party in 1906, in which parliamentary candidates were supported by individual unions, meant that trade unions now had a direct impact on the course of national politics and governance in Britain. This new influence, in combination with the spread of the shop steward movement, a succession of fierce industrial disputes, and deep economic recessions that afflicted all of the traditional industrial regions of the country, imparted a new sense of national purpose and unity to the labour movement. Nevertheless, geography continued to play a central role. With the onset of high unemployment in the 1920s, the trade unions went on the defensive. Union leaders accepted drastic wage cuts in the traditional export sectors and, partly out of disaffection, trade union membership plummeted, from 8.3 million in 1920 to 5.6 million just three years later. The subsequent defeat of the unions in the General Strike of 1926 and the collapse of employment in the Great Depression of 1929–32 ensured that the fall-out of trade union membership continued into the early 1930s. Much of this decline was concentrated in the old industrial regions specializing in the traditional heavy industries and export staples. At the same time, employers used the economic slump to dismantle national institutional structures that had been established in the inter-war period, forcing the unions to rely on their traditional regional strongholds. By 1934 total membership had fallen back to 4.2 million, a decline of 4 million or 50 per cent in fourteen years.

The 1920s and 1930s were in many ways years of economic transition between one phase of economic development and another, as the locus of economic growth and employment shifted away from the nineteenth-century sectors towards new mass production industries (particularly motor vehicles, armaments, and household and electrical goods), in which the demand was primarily for less-skilled labour. Much of the recovery in union membership during the late 1930s was bound up with these new forms of employment, and with the expansion of nationwide mass utilities such as transport, electricity and gas. The main unions to grow in this period were general workers' unions, which were better able to penetrate the new sectors of industrial growth. Thus membership of the Transport and General Workers Union (TGWU), formed in 1922 by a merger of some 23 separate unions,

5   This map has been derived by converting the Webbs' county estimates to the present-day standard regions, and expressing union members as a proportion of the employed workforce (using data from Lee 1979), and not as a proportion of the total population, as in the Webbs' figures.

had grown to 650,000 by 1937, making it the largest union in the country. The other main union was the National Union of General and Municipal Workers, which also grew quickly in the 1930s: from 269,000 members in 1934 to 467,000 by 1939.

However, a new geography of trade unionism was forged during this period. The new sources of employment did not in general overlap geographically with the old, but instead tended either to be more evenly spread across the country or to be biased towards the large consumer and labour markets of the South East and Midlands (Dunford and Perrons 1986; Marshall 1987). In addition, the 'war economy' between 1939 and 1945 gave a massive boost to the union movement. The tight labour market conditions associated with full employment, explicit Government pressure on employers and employers' associations to recognize unions, and the setting up of joint production committees in key industries, all gave an enormous boost to the union movement and had a lasting impact on membership expectations (Beaumont 1990). Whereas union membership had fallen to 4.2 million by 1934, by 1948 it had more than recovered to 9.4 million. The geographical effect of this growth was to reduce somewhat the marked regional differences in union membership and density that had been so characteristic of the nineteenth century. The early heartland pattern was still an important feature of the union landscape, but the contours of union density had become more evenly spaced, a process that was to continue after the Second World War.

THE GEOGRAPHICAL 'DISPERSAL' OF POST-WAR TRADE UNIONISM.

Two phases can be distinguished in the post-war development of the union movement up to its peak in 1979. For the first two decades or so after the war, trade union membership in the UK remained relatively stagnant, and even by 1966 had only increased to 10.2 million, while density remained more or less unchanged at 45 per cent. This was true also for each of the main sectors of the economy: density in public services remained static at about 70 per cent, that in manufacturing at just over 50 per cent, and that in private services at around 15 per cent. As we noted in Chapter One, virtually all of the post-war growth in unionism took place in the following decade, between 1968 and 1979. During this period, the largest single union, the Transport and General Workers (TGWU), passed the 2 million mark, the Amalgamated Engineering Union (AEU) with almost 1.5 million was not far behind, followed by the General and Municipal Workers Union (now the GMB) with just under a million and the National and Local Government Officers' Association (NALGO) with 753,000. The fastest-growing unions were those catering for white-collar staff.

According to Massey and Painter (1989), these trends in the development of the unions were associated with important shifts in the trade union map. More specifically, they suggest that a number of key forces produced a progressive 'flattening out' or 'dispersal' of the landscape of organized labour from the late 1950s onwards. First, a process of manufacturing employment decline undermined trade unionism in the old industrial cities where the traditions of labourism had been deeply rooted. As Fothergill and Gudgin (1982, 1986) point out in their analysis of the geography of post-war employment change in Britain, the regions where employment growth was slowest over the 1950s, 1960s and 1970s were those that contained major conurbations. Thus the North West (Manchester and Merseyside), Central Scotland (Clydeside), Yorkshire and Humberside (Sheffield and Leeds), West Midlands (Birmingham) and the North (Tyneside), all grew less in employment terms than the national average. In contrast, the less-urbanized regions of East Anglia, the South West, the East Midlands and the Outer South East all grew much more rapidly. Moreover, the conurbations were the first areas to experience the de-industrialization that began in the 1960s (see Martin and Rowthorn 1986). Between 1959 and 1975 the number of manufacturing jobs in Britain's conurbations (including London) fell by 16 per cent whereas in rural areas manufacturing employment increased by as much as 77 per cent (Fothergill and Gudgin 1982, p.22). Not only did the major cities lose significant numbers of unionized industrial jobs but, as Lane (1972) has argued, this decline seriously affected the urban-based networks of union activists and campaigners that, historically, had helped to sustain these centres of union membership concentration.

In addition to this process of urban industrial decline, Massey and Painter argue that a second factor promoting the more even geographical spread of trade unionism from the late 1950s onwards was the trend for new manufacturing plants to be located in the smaller centres of population, in new towns, rural areas and 'greenfield' sites, and for some older urban-based plants to relocate to new premises in such areas. Indeed, they suggest that this (re)locational bias towards rural areas – what in some circles of industrial geography became known as the 'urban-rural shift' (Fothergill and Gudgin 1982) – was in part a reaction by capital to the rigidities of the Fordist landscape, a desire to escape the combative unionism and entrenched working practices of urban labour forces. Third, they suggest that that by the 1970s the spatial reorganization of economic activity was accompanied by various changes in the production process itself, including the dismantling of old craft and skill divisions, thus disrupting and undermining the traditional collective identities, workplace solidarity and union allegiance of factory labour within manufacturing. This process is also believed to have contributed to union decline in the heartlands of many of the old industrial unions.

Finally, Massey and Painter point to the growth of public service unionism over the 1960s and 1970s as a factor behind the flattening of the union map. Given that public sector employment is much more evenly distributed across the country than is industrial employment, the expansion of union membership that accompanied the growth of employment within the public services also fuelled the shift away from a heartland-based geography of union organization. Thus, they argue, as a result of these various processes and trends, by the late 1970s a 'new geography of trade unionism' had emerged which was

> ...more widely distributed, both overall and within individual trade unions. The heartlands of the trade union movement have declined relatively and absolutely. There has been decentralization to new areas. The growth of new sectors in the economy has produced threats and opportunities for the unions. It has enabled the development of new, more widely dispersed trade unions and it has seen the rise of non-unionism in particular areas, industries and secions of the workforce. (p.134)

In their view, by the late 1970s the relative significance of the traditional union heartlands had been substantially eroded, in some cases expunged altogether, and the historical map replaced by a much more even regional distribution of membership numbers.[6]

However, although containing some measure of substance, particularly with respect to growth of public sector white-collar unionism, this picture should be viewed cautiously (see Martin, Sunley and Wills 1993, 1994d). In the first place, Massey and Painter's account is based on a rather limited set of data. In fact only three unions, the National Union of Tailors and Garment Workers (NUTGW), the Amalgamated Union of Engineering Workers (AUEW) and the National Association of Local Government Officers (NALGO), are analysed in any detail, and the desciptions of various other unions are much more superficial. Thus it is difficult to judge how representative their results are. Indeed, their argument tends towards synecdochism, in that a few specific instances are taken as indicative of general tendencies. The extent of 'greenfield' relocation as a 'union avoidance' strategy by employers is a case in point. No doubt instances of this can be found (for example, Mulhearn 1984), but there is little evidence that was it a significant or widespread geographical phenomenon. For example, Fothergill et al. (1986) give other plausible reasons for the decentralization of industry away from the conurbations, including floor space constraints, outmoded factory premises, high rental costs, problems of accessibility, and rising wage bills in city sites. And in any case, many branch-plant relocations in the 1960s and early 1970s were from the South East and Midlands into the heavily unionized areas of the north of the country, including such long-standing bastions of trade unionism as Merseyside.[7] There is little evidence that unionization rates in the branch plants in these regions were significantly different from those in nearby older urban-based workplaces.

Second, as Massey and Painter themselves are aware, the growth of membership in what they call the union 'peripheries' was not necessarily the same type of

---

6   As we shall see later, they go on to argue that this flattening or dispersal of the trade union map has continued into the 1980s and 1990s.

7   Merseyside, and the North West region more generally, developed a substantial branch-plant economy during this period, in part the result of inward moves of firms and plants taking advantage of regional policy assistance.

organization as had been developed in the traditional heartlands, and was often far less deeply rooted amongst the workers and employers in the areas concerned (Price and Bain 1983). The engineering union illustrates this. The rapid growth in membership of the AEEU after the Second World War allowed the unionization of new spaces and places in the engineering economy, particularly in the south and Midlands of the country.[8] For example, over the period 1970–79 whilst membership grew by 5 per cent in the union's traditional stronghold regions of the North West and Scotland, it expanded by some 19 per cent in East Anglia and the East Midlands, two of the union's 'peripheral' regions (see Martin, Sunley and Wills 1994a). However, the type of engineering unionism found in the southern regions of the country has long differed from that found in the older centres of the union (Marsh and Coker 1963; McCarthy 1966). As McCarthy points out, the differential geographical origins and regional development of trade unionism in the engineering industry has played an important role in shaping the form of unionism that was established:

> In the ninteenth century trade unionism was at its strongest in the North and in the Industrial belts of Scotland and Wales. Indeed, the office of shop steward first developed there, mainly on Tyneside and Clydeside, towards the end of the century. But in these areas, it was essentially a supplement to the existing vigorous institutions of branch life. In contrast, trade unionism in London and the South was to a much greater extent a product of the twentieth century, and branches were for the most part built up contemporaneously with the institution of shop steward imported from the North. Here, therefore, there was no long-standing tradition of branch life and shop stewards played a larger part from the beginning. (p.56)

The dispersal of union membership into new geographical areas, therefore, does not necessarily map into a corresponding dispersal of union power and organization away from traditional heartland areas. The *form* of unionism in the older geographical centres is likely to differ in significant ways from that in the new locations, not only because of differences in production organization, employment conditions or management strategy in establishments in the old and new regions, but also because of differences in the historically constituted and locally embedded socio-political traditions of those areas.

---

8   The main engineering union has undergone several changes of name and industrial coverage since its origin in 1851 as the Amalgamated Society of Engineers (ASE). It became the Amalgamated Engineering Union (AEU) in 1920, the Amalgamated Engineering and Foundry Union (AEF) in 1967, and the Amalgamated Union of Engineering Workers in 1971. It then reverted to the Amalgamated Engineering Union (AEU) in 1986, but subsequently changed its name to the Amalgamated Engineering and Electrical Union (AEEU) when it merged with the Electrical, Electronic, Telecommunications and Plumbing Union (EETPU) in 1992. The names used in the text thus vary according to the historical period being referred to.

Third, Massey and Painter confine their discussion to regional membership *shares*, and do not discuss regional trends and patterns in union membership *recognition* or *density*. While these latter two measures of unionization are obviously related to membership numbers, they can give quite different maps of the geographical incidence of trade unionism from that based on absolute numbers of union members. As a consequence, they can also lead to different definitions – and meanings – of union 'heartlands', and hence of the notion and measurement of union 'dispersal'. We return to this important issue later, but it is important to stress that we are not arguing that no dispersal or flattening out of the union map took place during the 1960s and 1970s. There can be little doubt that as union membership expanded in the 1960s and 1970s, a diffusion of trade unionism across the regions took place, resulting in the 'infilling' of the union map. However, this levelling of the geography of trade unionism should not necessarily be equated with the demise of the traditional union 'heartlands', and still less with the disappearance of the historical north/south divide in unionization. Evidence from the National Training Survey in 1975 (Booth 1984), just before the peak in union membership was reached, shows that while regional convergence in unionization rates had certainly taken place over the post-war period, and regional union densities had become much more uniform compared to the situation at the end of the nineteenth century, union density in northern England, Wales and Scotland remained noticeably higher than in the south and east of the country. Even by the end of the 1970s, when union membership had reached its historical peak in the UK, the north/south divide was still a prominent feature of the union landscape (Figure 3.2). Despite considerable change, then, the geography of trade unionism had also displayed a significant degree of continuity.

THE REGIONAL IMPACT OF CONTEMPORARY DECLINE

What then of the most recent phase in the evolution of the union movement, of the decline that has taken place since 1979? How far and in what ways has this involved a reshaping of the union map? To begin to explore this question, we first use the data from the three Workplace Industrial Relations Surveys of 1980, 1984 and 1990, together with information from the Labour Force Surveys of 1989 and 1994, to chart the retreat in unionism across the British regions. In the following section we then examine the experience of a number of individual unions, using their archival membership records.

As we noted in Chapter One, the Workplace Industrial Relations Surveys (WIRS) provide two basic measures of regional unionization: a *density* measure, calculated as the proportion of employees in each workplace who are members of a union, and two *recognition* measures, calculated either as the proportion of employees who are in establishments where unions are recognized, or the proportion of establishments that recognize unions. Unfortunately, because of the way questions were posed in the 1980 WIRS, it is not possible to calculate overall

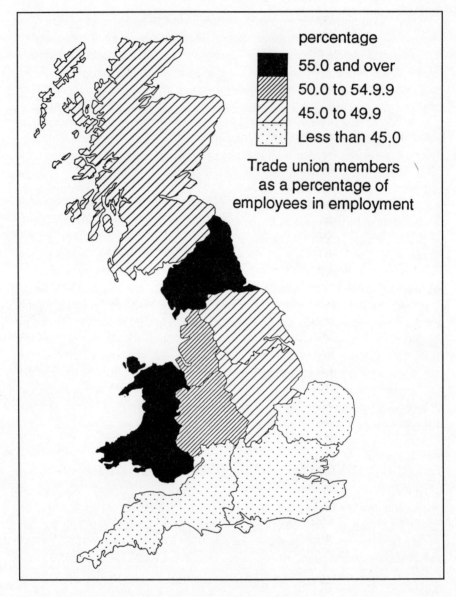

Source: Based on survey data contained in Booth, 1984

Figure 3.2: Regional trade union densities, 1975

regional union densities from that survey, and only the recognition measures can be derived for that year. Union density and union recognition are two different but related indices of union representation in the workplace. In the broadest sense the potential for an employee to be represented by a trade union in his or her dealings with management in the workplace is created by the act of joining a union. Since 1980, there has been no legal obligation on the employer to meet with or accept communication from union officials attempting to act on behalf of employees, so that the actual role of unions in workplace industrial relations will depend on how far and in what ways employers *recognize* unions.[9] The WIRS data refer to 'full union recognition', that is, where management recognizes unions for the purpose of collective bargaining and negotiation (see Millward 1994). Whether employers recognize unions in their workplaces is an important determinant of workers' propensity to join unions, and hence the extent of union membership amongst employees, that is, union density. For this reason, many industrial relations analysts prefer to focus on recognition rather than density in their discussions of the decline of the unions: relatively few, if any, confine their attention to absolute membership numbers alone.

Union recognition, whether measured by the proportion of workplaces which recognize unions or the proportion of employees working in establishments where unions are recognized, has fallen sharply since the late 1970s. The industrial relations literature suggests that union recognition status is a component of the historically determined management or industrial relations 'style' of the individual establishment, and typically represents a long-term decision made at or near the set-up date of the establishment. Developing this proposition, Disney, Gosling and Machin (1993) have used the WIRS data to estimate national trends in the proportion of workplaces recognizing unions over the 1970s and 1980s.[10] Their results suggest that union recognition has declined for all workers apart from those (especially non-manuals) in the public sector. The decline has been most pronounced among manual workers in manufacturing, where the percentage of workplaces with recognized manual unions fell from 71 per cent in 1980 to 48 per cent in 1990. The same sharply downward trend also holds, however, for the employee-based measure of recognition. In the private sector, the proportion of

---

9   The 1980 Employment Act removed trade union rights to contest any employer which refused to recognize unions in the workplace. In essence, the Act made union recognition by employers voluntary.

10 These estimates are calculated by forming a three-year moving average of the proportion of plants 'born' between 1970 and 1990 which currently recognize unions. As Disney *et al.* stress, the assumption that the recogniton decision occurs at or around the time the establishment is initially set up is critical to this procedure. In fact the age question in WIRS asks how many years the establishment has been operating at its current address. Hence if establishments have changed their address, the response does not measure age but simply the number of years since they moved. Disney *et al.* argue that if the recognition decision is made at the time of the move – as might be expected if a (largely) new workforce was installed after the move – then their estimates remain valid.

manual employees working in establishments recognizing unions fell from 84 per cent in 1980 to 57 per cent in 1990, while for non-manuals recognition fell from 61 per cent to 41 per cent.

This decline in union recognition has exhibited some distinctive patterns geographically (Tables 3.1 and 3.2). In 1980, the proportion of private sector manual workers in establishments recognizing unions was high almost everywhere, although there was a discernible difference between the four southern regions of London, the Outer South East (that is, the South East excluding London), East Anglia, and the South West, in which union recognition rates were all below the national average, and the remaining regions of Britain where recognition rates were all above the national rate: recognition was lowest in the Outer South East (69%) and highest (over 90%) in the two Midlands regions and the North (Table 3.1). Although by 1990 union recognition had fallen throughout the country, the relative differential between the southern and the northern regions had actually widened substantially: the proportion of private sector manual employes working in establishments recognizing unions had dropped to around 40 per cent in the south but remained above 60 per cent in the northern half of the country, and almost 70 per cent in Wales. A similar, if less systematic, pattern is also evident in the case of private sector non-manual workers. Recognition rates for this group are consistently lower than those for manual employees. In 1980 they were lowest in London, the Outer South East (the lowest, at 44%) and Yorkshire-Humberside;

Table 3.1: Union recognition by region, 1980–1990, manual workers private sector

	Percentage of employees in workplaces recognizing unions			Regional recognition rate relative to national rate (as %)	
	1980	*1984*	*1990*	*1980*	*1990*
London	76	68	41	90.5	71.8
Outer South East	70	49	43	82.9	76.4
East Anglia	82	50	41	98.1	72.0
South West	79	64	56	94.6	99.3
East Midlands	93	63	60	111.1	105.3
West Midlands	91	86	62	108.6	108.4
Yorks-Humberside	87	86	62	103.3	109.0
North West	89	85	64	106.8	113.2
North	92	85	65	104.8	111.8
Wales	86	73	69	102.4	121.3
Scotland	85	67	62	102.0	109.2
Great Britain	**84**	**70**	**57**	**100.0**	**100.0**

Source: Authors' analyses of WIRS, 1980, 1984 and 1990: Private Sector Workplaces.

Table 3.2: Union recognition by region, 1980–1990, non-manual workers, private sector

	Percentage of employees in workplaces recognizing unions			Regional recognition rate relative to national rate (as %)	
	1980	*1984*	*1990*	*1980*	*1990*
London	55	40	29	89.4	71.9
Outer South East	44	43	36	72.4	87.9
East Anglia	68	39	47	111.4	114.2
South West	67	51	36	110.4	87.2
East Midlands	74	65	52	121.0	128.5
West Midlands	68	59	50	111.1	122.1
Yorks-Humberside	57	56	43	93.3	106.1
North West	69	67	55	111.9	135.6
North	72	65	54	115.9	133.2
Wales	73	72	42	119.1	102.7
Scotland	63	47	52	101.9	126.8
Great Britain	**61**	**52**	**41**	**100.0**	**100.0**

Source: Authors' analyses of WIRS, 1980, 1984 and 1990. Private Sector Workplaces.

and highest in the Northern region, Wales (the highest, at 73%) and the East Midlands. Thus while a broad north/south pattern was evident, it was much less clear-cut than for manual workers. By 1990, however, as in the case of the manual group, in relative terms a more pronounced division in recognition had opened up between the north and south of the country (Table 3.2). Thus, while union recognition has fallen in every major geographical area of Britain, it appears to have been noticeably more resilient in the older, traditionally unionized northern regions of the country than in the traditionally less unionized south.

A broadly similar story emerges for the incidence of union density decline across the regions. In 1984 overall union density among full-time workers varied from lows of 47 and 48 per cent in East Anglia and the Outer South East respectively, to highs of 75 and 76 per cent in Wales and the Northern region.[11] Although by 1990, nationally union density had fallen by 12 percentage points, from 62 per cent to 50 per cent, regional differentials in union density remained substantial, ranging from 36 and 37 per cent in London and the Outer South East to 63 and 64 per cent in Wales and the North. The WIRS data for 1984 and 1990 reveal that for manual, non-manual, full-time, and part-time workers, the division between the less unionized south and east of the country and the more unionized

---

11 Recall that it is not possible to calculate estimates of union density for the regions from the 1980 WIRS.

North, Scotland and Wales, persisted through the 1980s into the beginning of the 1990s (Tables 3.3 to 3.6).

Again, in common with union recognition, in the case of manual workers this regional division not only persisted, but in relative terms actually widened over the period (Table 3.3). The same is broadly true for non-manual workers, except for this group union density actually increased slightly in East Anglia and fell particularly rapidly in the West Midlands, with the result that the north/south division is less consistent. Nevertheless, the gap between the extremes of the North, Wales and Scotland on the one hand, and London and the Outer South East on the other, did also increase for this category of worker (Table 3.4). East Anglia experienced the most rapid expansion in employment (including industry) of all of the regions during the economic boom of the second half of the 1980s (see Martin and Townroe 1992; see also Chapter Four), and this may partly explain the rise in union density for non-manuals in this region. Likewise for part-time workers, the sharp fall in union density in the North region is the major exception to an otherwise continuing gap between the north and south-east of the country (Table 3.6).

The WIRS data provide an indication of trends over the 1980s, but (as yet) not beyond. Nationally, the unions have continued to decline into the 1990s. Some 1.7 million members were lost during the recession of 1990–94, and overall density fell from 43 to 38 per cent (see Table 1.4 in Chapter One). For information on the geography of this decline, we turn to Labour Force Survey data, using information from the 1989 and 1994 surveys. As we have already noted, these data are household based rather than workplace based, and tend to give lower estimates of union density than those derived from WIRS. Estimates of regional union density based on the LFS are not, therefore, directly comparable with WIRS estimates. Nevertheless, the LFS figures also indicate a clear division between a more unionized north and a less unionized south of the country. Furthermore, it would appear that this regional division remained more or less intact into the mid 1990s, despite the continuing retreat of the unions (Table 3.7 and Figure 3.3).

Two features of the geography of contemporary union decline stand out from these analyses. First, although the traditional union regions, namely the North, the North West, Wales, Scotland and the West Midlands, have experienced large falls in union density and recognition, except for the case of the West Midlands these falls have not been disproportionate. Indeed, relative to national trends, workplace density and recognition in these regions have actually been remarkably resilient. At the same time, while union density and recognition have also held up well in the region that has traditionally had the lowest degree of unionization, East Anglia, they have fallen quite sharply in London, the South East and the South West, also regions with historically low rates of unionization. Thus, despite regional differences in the incidence of decline over the 1980–1994 period, the historical division between the more unionized north and the less unionized south and east of the country has persisted as a central feature of the landscape of organized

Table 3.3: Union density by region, 1984–1990,
manual workers, all sectors

	Union density (union members as % of employees in employment)		Regional density relative to national density (as %)	
	1984	1990	1984	1990
London	65	45	97.0	84.9
Outer South East	47	39	70.1	73.1
East Anglia	52	30	77.6	56.6
South West	62	51	92.5	96.2
East Midlands	66	54	98.5	101.8
West Midlands	71	56	105.9	105.6
Yorks-Humberside	73	56	108.9	105.6
North West	80	64	119.4	120.7
North	83	62	123.9	116.9
Wales	79	71	117.9	133.9
Scotland	67	58	100.0	109.4
Great Britain	**67**	**53**	**100.0**	**100.0**

Source: Authors' analyses of WIRS 1984 and 1990.

Table 3.4: Union density by region, 1984–1990,
non-manual workers, all sectors

	Union density (union members as % of employees in employment)		Regional density relative to national density (as %)	
	1984	1990	1984	1990
London	37	31	72.5	72.0
Outer South East	41	35	80.4	81.3
East Anglia	35	46	68.6	106.9
South West	47	40	92.1	93.0
East Midlands	56	51	109.8	118.6
West Midlands	59	41	115.6	95.3
Yorks-Humberside	61	52	119.6	120.9
North West	65	50	127.4	116.3
North	61	55	119.6	127.9
Wales	66	60	129.4	139.5
Scotland	60	57	117.6	132.6
Great Britain	**51**	**43**	**100.0**	**100.0**

Source: Authors' analyses of WIRS 1984 and 1990

Table 3.5: Union density by region, 1984–1990,
full-time workers, all sectors

	Union density (union members as % of employees in employment)		Regional density relative to national density (as %)	
	1984	1990	1984	1990
London	51	36	82.2	72.0
Outer South East	48	37	77.4	74.0
East Anglia	47	45	75.8	90.0
South West	58	47	93.5	94.0
East Midlands	64	59	103.2	118.0
West Midlands	70	51	112.9	102.0
Yorks-Humberside	69	56	111.3	112.0
North West	77	60	124.2	120.0
North	76	64	122.5	128.0
Wales	75	63	120.9	126.0
Scotland	67	59	108.1	118.0
Great Britain	**62**	**50**	**100.0**	**100.0**

Source: Authors' analyses of WIRS 1984 and 1990.

Table 3.6: Union density by region, 1984–1990,
part-time workers, all sectors

	Union density (union members as % of employees in employment)		Regional density relative to national density (as %)	
	1984	1990	1984	1990
London	24	21	55.8	63.6
Outer South East	27	20	62.7	60.6
East Anglia	25	16	58.1	48.5
South West	34	33	79.1	100.0
East Midlands	49	38	113.9	115.5
West Midlands	48	35	111.6	106.1
Yorks-Humberside	58	44	134.8	133.3
North West	57	42	132.4	127.3
North	58	36	134.8	109.1
Wales	63	58	146.5	175.7
Scotland	52	40	120.9	121.2
Great Britain	**43**	**33**	**100.0**	**100.0**

Source: Authors' analyses of WIRS 1984 and 1990

labour. In fact, in some respects the relative gap between these two geographical 'halves' of British unionism has widened. Furthermore, the ranking of the regions in terms of overall rates of unionization and recognition has not dramatically altered. While there has been some narrowing of regional differences in unionization in the case of non-manual workers, the reverse is true for manual employees.

In aggregate terms, there is little evidence, therefore, to support Massey and Painter's (1989) argument that the spatial dispersal of trade unionism that they document for the 1960s and 1970s has continued into the 1980s and early 1990s: no dramatic 'flattening out' or 'levelling down' of the map of aggregate trade unionism has taken place over this period. To be sure, their argument was couched in terms of the regional distribution of membership *numbers*, not regional union *densities* or *recognition rates* and, as they have subsequently acknowledged, their claim that dispersal has continued from the 1960s and 1970s into the 1980s and 1990s was in any case based less on systematic evidence and more 'on a "feel" for what was going on in the trade union movement at the time' (Massey 1994, p.96). Nevertheless, the regional trends in overall union decline discussed in this section at least raise questions over Massey and Painter's claim that the geographical heartlands of British unionism have all but disappeared. Unlike Massey and Painter's analysis, which was based on a sample of individual unions, the aggregate regional trends described above give a more comprehensive picture of the map of union decline. However, although charting the geographies of aggregate trade unionism along the lines we have just discussed provides a useful overall picture

Table 3.7: Union density in the regions, 1989–1994 all workers and sectors

	Union density (% of respondents who are union members)		Regional density relative to national density (as %)	
	1989	1994	1989	1994
London	34	28	87.1	86.1
Outer South East	29	25	74.3	75.7
East Anglia	30	27	76.9	81.8
South West	33	28	84.6	84.8
East Midlands	40	32	102.5	96.9
West Midlands	43	36	110.2	109.1
Yorks-Humberside	45	36	115.4	109.1
North West	47	40	120.5	121.2
North	52	43	133.3	130.3
Wales	48	46	123.1	139.4
Scotland	46	39	117.9	118.2
Great Britain	**39**	**33**	**100.0**	**100.0**

Source: Authors' analysis the household-based Labour Force Surveys, Spring 1989 and Autumn 1994.

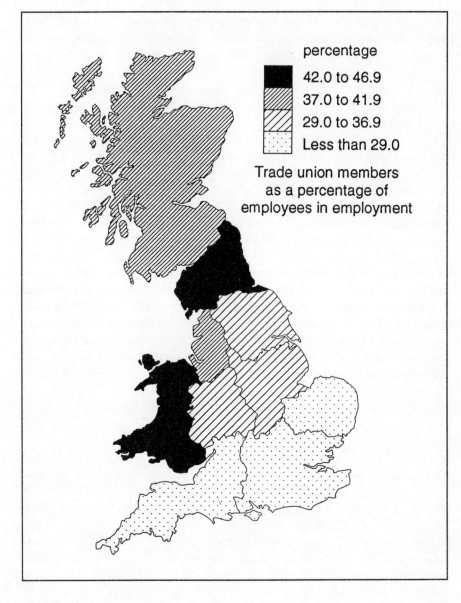

Source: Labour force survey

Figure 3.3: Regional trade union densities, 1994

of change and continuity in the landscape of organized labour, it clearly smooths over and conceals the particular experiences of individual unions.

THE HEARTLANDS ISSUE:
THE EXPERIENCE OF INDIVIDUAL UNIONS

We now turn attention, therefore, to the changing spatial configuration of specific unions, thereby linking our analysis more directly to that by Massey and Painter (1989) referred to earlier.[12] However, constructing individual union geographies is fraught with difficulties. In the first place, surprisingly few unions seem to have kept comprehensive archival records of their memberships by region. Only since the introduction of legislation making 'check-off' compulsory (whereby the unions have to keep detailed records of members to enable employers to deduct membership dues at source), have such data become more widely collected and collated. Although some twenty national unions were approached, only ten were able or willing to provide consistent and usable regional membership data. Nonetheless, these ten unions are representative, and cover a wide range of economic sectors and employment types. Together they had a combined membership of 6.7 million in 1979, 50 per cent of all union members at that time, distributed across manufacturing, private services and the public sector. By 1990, their total combined membership had fallen to 4.9 million, a decline of 27 per cent (see Table 3.8). It is immediately apparent that membership trends have varied considerably between different unions since the beginning of the 1980s. The unions associated with traditional industries and economic sectors have experienced the most rapid rates of membership loss, in some cases approaching or even exceeding falls of 50 per cent since 1979: for example, the Amalgamated Engineering Union (AEU), the Iron and Steel Trades Confederation (ISTC) and the Transport and General Workers' Unions (TGWU). In contrast, in other service-orientated sectors membership has actually expanded, for example the Fire Brigades Unions (FBU) and, especially, the Banking, Insurance and Finance Union (BIFU).[13] These different unions will tend to have different membership geographies, reflecting not only the specific locational distributions of the industries and occupations with which they are associated but also regional differences in the unionization rates within these industries and occupations, differences that may derive – in part at least – from long-standing spatial variations in local labour and

---

12 The following discussion draws on the analysis presented in Martin, Sunley and Wills (1993). That analysis generated considerable discussion and debate, including the critical commentaries by Massey (1994) and Painter (1994), and our response (Martin, Sunley and Wills 1994d). That exchange also informs this section.

13 Since 1990 membership of BIFU has declined, as a result of the large-scale shake-out of staff from the finance sector, due both to the severe recession of the early 1990s and a wave of new technologies in banking.

Table 3.8: Membership change in selected unions, 1979–1990

Union	1979	1990	Change 1979–1990	
			Numbers	Per cent
BIFU	125,025	171,087	46,062	36.8
FBU	40,533	47,801	7268	17.9
NALGO	753,226	744,414	-8812	-1.2
NUPE	691,770	592,663	-99,107	-14.3
GMB	967,383	810,391	-156,992	-16.2
USDAW	470,017	361,789	-108,228	-23.0
UCATT	334,026	251,213	-82,813	-24.8
TGWU	2,076,466	1,218,241	-858,225	-41.3
AEU	1,217,593	660,938	-556,655	-45.7
ISTC	112,075	40,439	-71,636	-63.9
Total	**6,675,114**	**4,898,976**	**-1,776,138**	**-26.6**

Source: Individual Union Records.

Notes: Key to Unions:
AEU (Amalgamated Engineering Union) (Engineering only)
BIFU (Banking, Insurance and Finance Union)
FBU (Fire Brigades Union)
GMB (General, Municipal and Boilermakers' Union)
ISTC (Iron and Steel Trades Confederation)
NALGO (National and Local Government Officers' Association)
NUPE (National Union of Public Employees)
TGWU (Transport and General Workers' Union)
UCATT (Union of Construction, Allied Trades and Technicians)
USDAW (Union of Shop, Distributive and Allied Workers).

employer traditions and cultures (an issue we take up in more detail in the next chapter).

Herein lies a second difficulty, of how best to measure or portray the (changing) geography of an individual union. This is by no means as straightforward as it might seem, and has an important bearing on the whole question of whether (as Massey and Painter, 1989, argue) union 'heartlands' are withering away. For while the data in the Workplace Industrial Relations Surveys (WIRS) and the Labour Force Surveys (LFS) allow us to estimate regional union recognition rates and densities, but not overall numbers of union members, in the regions,[14] individual union records only provide details of regional membership numbers. Thus these data only allow us to map a union in terms of the absolute numbers of its members

---

14 Since both WIRS and LFS are based on samples. Likewise the TUC does not keep records of trade union membership numbers on a regional basis.

per region or the regional shares of its total membership. This is the method used by Massey and Painter in their work. They argue that regional membership shares provide a meaningful indicator of differences in union 'strength', that is 'cultural and political presence', between regions. Moreover, they go on to suggest that to the union concerned 'the most important region politically and industrially, is likely to be where the largest number of its members live and work' (Painter 1994, p.100). Such regions are the union's 'heartlands', and are defined as those areas having the largest percentage shares of a union's national membership. Areas with low numbers of members, and hence low shares, are referred to as union 'peripheries'. There is an undeniable logic to this approach to the definition and interpretation of union heartlands. The more a given industry is regionally concentrated, the more obvious the spatial link between its employment and union membership is likely to be. Moreover, the larger the number of union members in an area, the greater the potential for the development of local labour networks, organization and social solidarity. Some of the early industrially specialized areas of the country, such as the coalfields and the original iron, shipbuilding and textile centres of the country where, as have seen, the trade union movement was born, fit this schema. However, there are also problems with using membership shares.

Different unions have different regional organizational structures and the regional administrative divisions used by any given union, and to which its regional membership numbers refer, often vary significantly, both in terms of areal coverage and, more fundamentally, in terms of employment size. This makes the use of membership numbers or shares potentially misleading as a device for comparing regions and defining union heartlands, since the regional units themselves may not be directly comparable. A given region may have a large number of union members and be designated a 'heartland' area simply because it happens to contain a large workforce, *irrespective* of the degree of workplace organization and 'political strength' of the union in that region. To use absolute numbers, or shares, alone to measure and compare the regional strength of unions would to be ignore the arbitrariness of the regional divisions involved and the *degree* of organization of the workforce within them (see Martin, Sunley and Wills 1993, 1994d). Thus, mere numbers of members may not necessarily be the most meaningful indicator of differences in union 'strength' or presence between regions. Such a definition takes no account at all of the regional distribution of the workforces – the 'potential' memberships – that unions could in principle organize, or of how far a union has actually organized the workforce in a given region. If absolute membership numbers or shares are used to measure union strength and political presence, then a union whose members were equally distributed across regions would be deemed to have no geographical heartland, even though the workers in certain regions may have much stronger traditions of political activism and industrial militancy than those in other regions. For even if membership numbers are equally distributed regionally, membership density – the relative *degree* of organization – may well vary significantly between regions. By definition, regional union density, the proportion of the relevant potential workforce the union has successfully organized in a region, takes the geographical distribution of that workforce directly into account. It provides a surrogate measure of the extent of workplace organization by the union in question, of the cultural–political solidarity within the relevant regional workforce. However, this measure may produce a map of regional unionism that differs substantially from one based on membership shares. A region may have a large absolute number of union members, but also a very large workforce, so that union density there may be only moderate or even quite low. On the other hand, by comparison, another region may have a small absolute number of union members but also a small workforce, so that density there is actually high.

It is important to emphasize these points, given the dominance of the British space economy by the South East region. This single region alone contains some 35 per cent of the country's employment. Not surprisingly, for many unions this region also contains large (in some cases the largest) numerical concentrations of members. However, these trade unionists tend to be either spread relatively thinly across the regional workforce, or else concentrated in a small proportion of workplaces where the unions have been recognized for bargaining purposes. Recognition is the key determinant of union membership in the workplace (Millward *et al.* 1992). If management in an establishment does not recognize unions in the workplace, membership is likely to be low or non-existent. As we have seen, overall union recognition is markedly lower in the southern half of the country, including the South East, than in the northern regions. Thus, despite the large absolute number of union members in the South East, as a result of lower recognition by employers and low rates of worker organization, union density is lower than elsewhere. In addition, culturally, overall levels of worker militancy and strike activity in the region have also tended historically to be significantly below the national average (see Chapter Five). Of course, this is not to deny that particular groups of workers have long been strongly unionized in the South East, public sector workers and the printing industry being notable examples: but these tend to be the exceptions to the rule. Painter (1994) argues that if potential memberships are small there can be very high densities in regions where the union has virtually no cultural or political impact. Equally, however, it can be argued that if the potential membership (employment base) is very large, as in the South East region, there can be a substantial number of union members but a low overall density and little relative power or political impact. In a regional context, the sheer number of union members does not translate automatically into union 'strength' or political presence, nor does it necessarily equate with a well-developed or solidaristic union culture within the local workforce.

These arguments (which are developed in more detail in Martin, Sunley and Wills 1993, 1994d) suggest that a density measure provides a meaningful alternative way of mapping a union and its regional heartlands. Certainly the local 'strength' of a union depends on the degree of its organization within local workplaces, and density is crucial to this. As recent institutionalist research has suggested, the scope for, and goals of, union action are shaped in part on the union's 'encompassingness' (Crouch 1993), that is its extent of representation in the workforce, at plant, industry, regional or national levels. Obviously, this is not to imply that a high union density within workplaces naturally or automatically translates into political activism: such activism is always dependent on a host of specific and contingent factors.[15] Nevertheless, without the significant penetration and organization of a given workforce, and a high degree of organization at workplace level, a union may be able to do very little, regardless of its absolute numbers of members or the traditions in a given region.

But this debate is not meant to suggest that the use of density indicators to measure and map regional unionism is without its own limitations and drawbacks. Calculating union-specific densities on a regional basis is itself problematic, both empirically and conceptually (see Martin, Sunley and Wills 1993). First, there is the question of defining the 'relevant' sectoral employment base that a given union can reasonably regard as its 'potential membership'. If the employment base is too narrowly defined the estimated density will be exaggerated; while if its definition is too broad this will result in an underestimation of the union's density and workplace presence. Indeed, Painter (1994) argues against density measures on the grounds that the use of 'potential membership' as the denominator gives rise to what he terms 'double counting', that is the inclusion of employment groups which are largely irrelevant to the calculation of the organizational strength of the union concerned in a particular region:

> 'Non-members' may not be non-members at all, but members of another ('rival') union. As such, while they may be technically part of the potential membership, in practice the union concerned may never see them as such, or feel itself to be weakened by their non-membership. A region with many unions represented in a particular sector might in density terms seem marginal to them all, while being a heartland region for trade unionism in political terms. (Painter 1994, p.101)

Painter's argument seems to be that the potential membership of any given union should be defined so as to exclude any workers who are members of other unions, even if those other unions are rivals. But this could result in a problem of 'under-counting'. For if two or more unions are indeed rivals in a particular sector of a region's employment base, it would seem reasonable to view that sector's workforce as each union's potential membership, even though it includes members of other unions, since they are in competition with one another for members. The effect of such overlapping potential memberships, as Painter implies, will be to lower the estimated densities of the individual unions involved, although it does

---

15 See Martin, Sunley and Wills (1994b) for a discussion of this issue in the case of differential trade union responses to plant closures.

not necessarily mean that their presence is therefore 'marginal' in the region. And provided the potential memberships are defined in the same way across all regions, the resultant regional densities for any one of the unions involved will be consistent and thus indicative of that union's geographical organization within the sector concerned.[16]

Clearly, then, the definition and meaning of union heartlands are not straight-forward issues. There is probably no single comprehensive measure (recall our methodological comments in Chapter One). Much depends on the purpose of the enquiry for which the concept of heartlands is being used. Membership shares and densities represent different ways of demarcating and conceptualizing the geo-graphical bases of individual unions, and each has its advantages and disadvan-tages.[17] Painter suggests that his and Massey's measure – membership shares – is the more appropriate for discerning the 'symbolic and political importance of key regions…in permitting the invention of traditions' (1994, p.101). However, Massey and Painter concede that relative membership (that is, density) is a better measure of the industrial role or workplace power that unions exercise in different regions. In our view, density of membership shapes the effective 'political reach' of a union in a region, and this may be just as important or even more important than the simple number of members in influencing the invention and formation of union traditions. A union is likely to have a greater degree of 'industrial muscle' in those areas where it has a high membership density than in those areas where, even if its absolute membership is high, its density is low. Thus a given union may have quite different traditions of militancy and strike activity in different regions of the country.

What is also evident is that it is important to distinguish between three different forms of union 'heartland': regional heartlands defined as the geographical centres of aggregate union presence, of the sort discussed in the previous section; regional heartlands or core regions specific to a given union; and regional union heartlands specific to a given industrial sector. These three conceptions represent different 'cuts' across the union landscape, three different ways of looking at the geography of trade unionism, and the relationships between them (statistical, conceptual and 'political') can be complex. It is entirely possible for some unions to be only marginally represented – to have low densities – in a region that is a heartland in an overall, aggregate trade union sense. However, the fact that union density is

---

16 In any case, the problem of double counting may not in fact be as great as Painter implies, since, contrary to popular perception, the majority of unionized establishments are in fact single- rather than multi-union (Millward 1994; see also the next chapter).

17 As Martin, Sunley and Wills (1994d) point out, the notion of union 'heartland' involves several layers of metaphor. The precise meanings of any metaphor are difficult to establish. Indeed, part of the very attraction of metaphors is their lack of definitive boundaries. The union heartland idea is no exception. For a full and frank debate over the heartland issue see the papers by Massey (1994), Painter (1994) and Martin, Sunley and Wills (1994d) referred to above.

generally high in a region may give a low density union in that area a 'political strength' it would not otherwise enjoy, by virtue of support from and coalitions with other far more organized unions in the region. Likewise, of course, workers in a highly unionized industry in an otherwise low density region may find their potential political strength undermined by the weak presence of other unions. It is not possible, therefore, to read off political presence, workplace power or industrial muscle, directly from either absolute membership numbers or density of membership. Again we are led to emphasize the role of history in shaping the place-specific traditions and routines of union presence and organization.

Given these problems, we use both membership shares and relative membership density measures to examine our sample unions. With respect to the first of these, for each union we calculated the shares of its total national membership accounted for by its constituent administative regional divisions in the two years 1979 and 1990 (both the number and precise geographical boundaries of regional divisions vary substantially from union to union). The regional shares in 1979 were then used to identify each union's 'membership heartlands'. In the absence of any existing theoretical guidelines for determining the critical membership share size needed for a region to be designated as a heartland (Massey and Painter's work provides no help here), a very simple procedure was followed. For each union a region was designated as a 'heartland' area if its membership share (in 1979) was above the share that each region would have if the union's membership was equally distributed across its regions.[18] The remaining regions, with shares below the hypothetical equal-distribution value, were then designated as the union's 'periphery'.

This method yielded two or three heartland regions for each of our sample unions (see Table 3.9). The proportion of membership accounted for by these heartlands varies significantly from union to union. It is lowest (around 28–30%) in those unions which are associated with economic sectors that in employment terms are distributed fairly generally across the country, such as public sector services (NALGO and NUPE) and retail and distribution (USDAW), or those unions which cover more than one economic sector (GMB). It is much higher (around 50%) in those unions associated with economic sectors that tend to be more localized, such as banking and finance (BIFU) and construction (UCATT), both concentrated in the more urbanized, metropolitan regions of the country, and iron and steel trades (ISTC). Although the different unions have different membership heartland areas, certain regions (or groups of regions) tend to recur, especially London, the North West (including Manchester), the Midlands, the North East, and Scotland (the precise definitions of these areas obviously vary

---

18 The arithmetic difference between the cumulative sum of shares of the heartlands defined this way and the corresponding cumulative sum of shares these regions would have under the assumption that the union's membership was equally distributed across its regions, would be equivalent to a Gini coefficient of geographical concentration.

**Table 3.9: 'Heartland' regions of various unions,
based on membership shares 1979**

Union	'Heartland' regions: defined as regions with largest membership shares (see text)
AEU (Engineering Only)	Manchester and West Midlands, East Midlands
BIFU	London, South and Western, Scotland
FBU	London, Yorkshire, Scotland
GMB (All Sectors)	London, Northern, Scotland
ISTC	Midlands, North East, North
NALGO (Local Government)	London, North West
NUPE	London, North West
TGWU (All Sectors)	London and South East, Midlands
UCATT	London, North West, Scotland
USDAW	Midlands, North East

Source: Authors' calculations.
Note: Regional definitions are based on each union's own areal divisions,
and hence vary from union to union.

from union to union). These are all regions dominated by large metropolitan–industrial centres.

Defined by membership shares, in 1979 London was a heartland area in seven out of the ten unions (BIFU, FBU, GMB, NALGO, NUPE, TGWU, UCATT). As argued above, this is not surprising since the London area contains the largest single concentration of employment in the UK, and thus it is to be expected that this region also contains large absolute numbers of union members. In the case of the banking, insurance and finance union, BIFU, for example, London accounts for some 25 per cent of national membership. But this region also contains some 30 per cent of the UK's employment in this sector.

Table 3.10 shows the membership trends in each union's heartlands and periphery over the 1979–1990 period. The degree of resilience of the heartlands is striking. In four of the unions, BIFU, FBU, ISTC and USDAW, the relative significance of the heartland regions remained unchanged or even increased marginally. Although for the other six sample unions the rate of decline in membership in their respective heartland areas did exceed that in their peripheries, the decline in the membership shares of their heartlands was typically very limited, at most three or four per centage points (in AEU, GMB, NUPE and TGWU). Moreover, there is no consistent correlation between the relative importance of a union's heartlands, in terms of the proportion of its total membership they contain, and the scale of membership decline experienced over the period. The evidence in Table 3.10 suggests that for our sample unions at least, using Massey and Painter's own preferred measure of heartlands, there is no sign of any dramatic collapse or disappearance of the core areas of union membership. These results

**Table 3.10: Changes in membership 'in heartlands'
and 'peripheries' of various unions, 1979–1990**

	Heartlands			Peripheries		
	Shares of total national membership		Per cent change in membership	Shares of total national membership		Per cent change in membership
Union	1979	1990	1979–90	1979	1990	1979–90
AEU	35.7	32.7	-62.8	64.3	67.3	-24.2
BIFU	49.1	49.6	38.0	50.9	50.4	35.7
FBU	35.3	35.5	18.8	64.7	64.5	17.9
GMB	35.0	32.7	-21.9	65.0	67.3	-13.2
ISTC	50.3	52.3	-62.5	49.7	47.7	-65.3
NALGO	28.6	26.6	-7.4	71.4	73.4	13.1
NUPE	28.4	27.7	-22.2	71.6	72.3	-16.3
TGWU	47.1	43.3	-46.1	52.9	56.7	-37.4
UCATT	49.7	48.6	-26.4	50.3	51.4	-23.1
USDAW	29.9	31.0	-20.2	70.1	69.0	-24.2

Source: Based on individual union records.
Notes: 1. Heartlands defined as Table 3.9
   2. Period refers to 1979-1990 in all cases except the AEU, which is for 1979-92.
   3. Regional shares are proportions of total UK membership, except for GMB
      and TGWU where GB total is used.

appear to differ, therefore, from the trends found by Massey and Painter (1989) for the 1960s and 1970s, which they argue continued into the 1980s. Even by the early 1990s, after a period of intense decline in British trade unionism, the membership geographies of our sample unions had changed only marginally, and by no means in a consistent direction.

Thus far we have ignored the relationship of a union's membership to the underlying employment base from which that union customarily seeks to recruit its members. In order to investigate the geographies of union densities, we first consulted with our selected unions in order to delimit, as closely as possible, the sectors of employment that they themselves regard as their principal fields of organization.[19] Most of our unions are more or less sector specific, such as BIFU (banking, insurance and finance) USDAW (retail and distributive trades), UCATT (mainly construction), NALGO (primarily Local Government), and NUPE (National Health Service and Local Government). The main problems concerned the GMB and TGWU (both spread across much of manufacturing and the utilities), and the AEU (several different branches of engineering and manufacturing).

---

19 By interviewing the chief research officers or equivalent officials in the unions concerned.

Fortunately, the TGWU has customarily monitored its memberships on a sector by sector basis, and it was possible to identify three industrial groups where the union is concentrated: namely, automotive industries; chemicals, oil and rubber; and passenger transport. (We were unable to obtain regional membership numbers for the AEU or GMB on a sector by sector basis, and so these unions were excluded from this aspect of our analysis.)

Unfortunately, none of the unions keep information on their potential memberships in the different regions of the country. To complicate matters, the regional administrative or organizational divisions used by individual unions rarely coincide with the standard economic regions (as used in the previous section) for which detailed employment data are readily available. It was necessary, therefore, to construct our own estimates of these regional potential memberships by aggregating local employment data (see Martin, Sunley and Wills 1993). More specifically, we utilized 1981 and 1991 Census of Employment data compiled at the level of the 485 Local Authority Districts across the country.[20] For each union these 485 Districts were matched as closely as possible with the union's organizational regions, and the data for the relevant employment categories aggregated accordingly. Regional union memberships (M_r) were then divided by these estimated potential memberships or relevant workforces (E_r) to obtain regional densities (U_r) for each union. As far as we are aware, regional membership densities for individual unions have not been available hitherto, and our estimates (as also used in Martin, Sunley and Wills 1993) represent the first such measures to be calculated.

One way of using these densities to map the changing geography of the individual unions is to express them relative to the national density of the union concerned, that is (U_r/U_n). This is equivalent to calculating regional location quotients, since

$$(U_r/U_n) = (M_r/E_r)/(M_n/E_n) = (M_r/M_n)/(E_r/E_n) = LQ_r.$$

The location quotient expresses a region's share of national membership for the union in question relative to that region's share of the union's total national potential membership (relevant employment). If a region has the same union density as the nation as whole $(LQ_r = 1.0)$, its share of union membership is equal to its share of potential membership. Thus regions with location quotients well above unity indicate a significant degree of geographical concentration of union membership relative to the distribution of potential membership, and in this respect may be regarded as constituting union density 'heartlands'. Defined in this way, such heartlands indicate areas with particularly high *rates* of workforce organization. This simple approach also provides a useful means of establishing whether there has been any prevailing trend towards spatial dispersal or levelling in unionization. If spatial flattening of the union map is a predominant trend, the

---

20 These data are held by the National On-Line Manpower Information System (NOMIS).

regional location quotients for a given union should show convergence towards unity over time.

The regional location quotients for our sample unions (excluding the AEU and GMB) for 1981 and 1991, together with the respective regional union densities for 1991, are charted in Figure 3. 4. For almost all of the unions (except the FBU and the passenger transport section of the TGWU) regional variations in membership density are far greater than those in membership share. Taking into account the regional pattern of potential membership (relative workforce) into account results in a much more uneven geography of union strength. Defining those distinct sub-groups of regions with the largest location quotients above unity as 'heartland' areas yields a different configuration from those based on membership numbers alone (Table 3.11; compare with Table 3.9). One obvious feature is that in *density* terms, the London region (as variously defined by individual unions) is not a major core area of union workplace strength. Whereas at the beginning of the 1980s, London figures prominently as an area of membership concentration for BIFU, FBU, NALGO, NUPE, TGWU and UCATT, only for the FBU and ISTC was it also the region of highest membership density. In the other unions, London's share of each union's total membership was in line with, or typically less than, what would have been expected on the basis of its share of the relevant workforce. For these unions, the majority of the regions with location quotients greater than unity are located in the north and west of Britain (the North West, North, Wales and Scotland). Furthermore, the plots of location quotients indicate that the regional patterns of density change in our sample unions over the 1980s were quite varied. While the heartland regions of NUPE, UCATT, BIFU and ITSC have lost ground,

Table 3.11: 'Heartland' regions of various unions, based on membership density 1981

Union	'Heartland' regions: defined as regions with highest relative densities (see text)
BIFU	North and South Wales, Scotland
FBU	(No clear heartland)
ISTC	South Eastern, South Western, Wales
NALGO (Local Government)	North East, Yorkshire-Humberside
NUPE	Northern, Yorkshire-Humberside
TGWU Automotive	Midlands
Passenger Transport	(No clear heartland)
Chemicals, Oil, Rubber	Eastern, North-Eastern, Wales
UCATT	Northern
USDAW	Manchester

Source: Authors' calculations.

Note: Regional definitions are based on each union's own areal divisions, and hence vary from union to union.

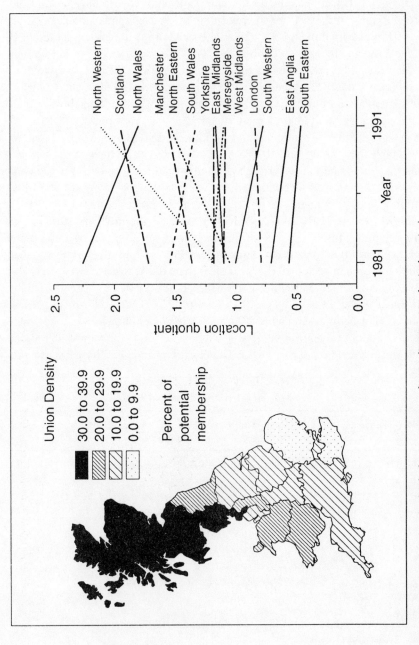

Figure 3.4i: Regional densities for selected individual unions, 1981 and 1991 (BIFU: 1991 density by region)

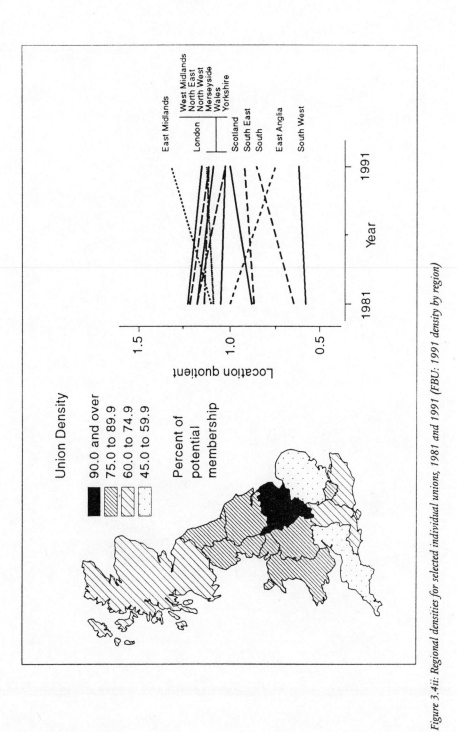

Figure 3.4ii: Regional densities for selected individual unions, 1981 and 1991 (FBU: 1991 density by region)

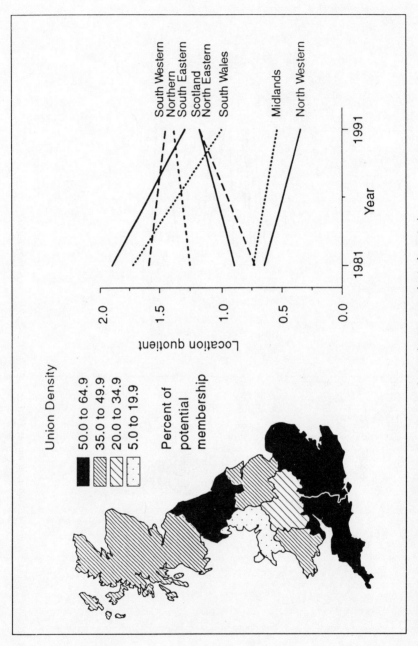

Figure 3.4iii: Regional densities for selected individual unions, 1981 and 1991 (ITSC: 1991 density by region)

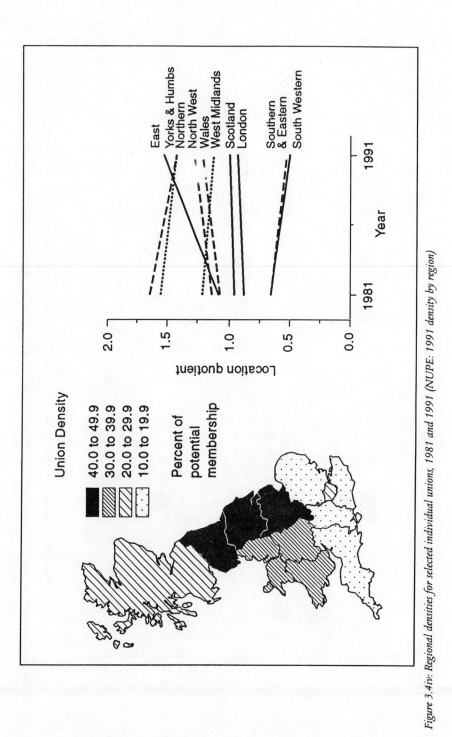

Figure 3.4iv: Regional densities for selected individual unions, 1981 and 1991 (NUPE: 1991 density by region)

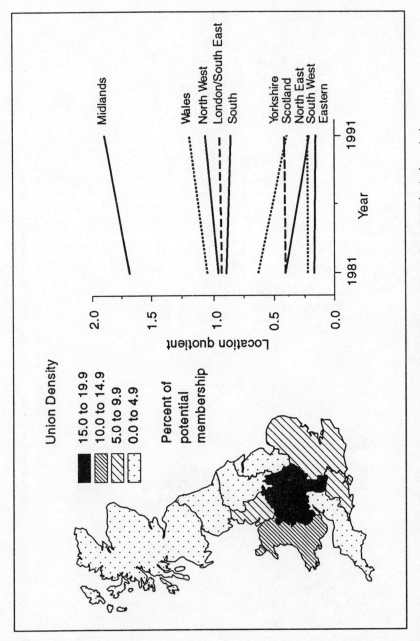

Figure 3.4v: Regional densities for selected individual unions, 1981 and 1991 (TGWU Automotive sections: 1991 density by region)

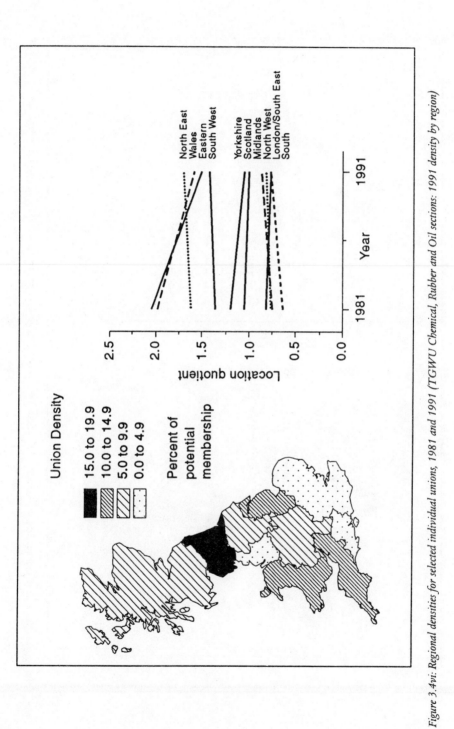

Figure 3.4vi: Regional densities for selected individual unions, 1981 and 1991 (TGWU Chemical, Rubber and Oil sections: 1991 density by region)

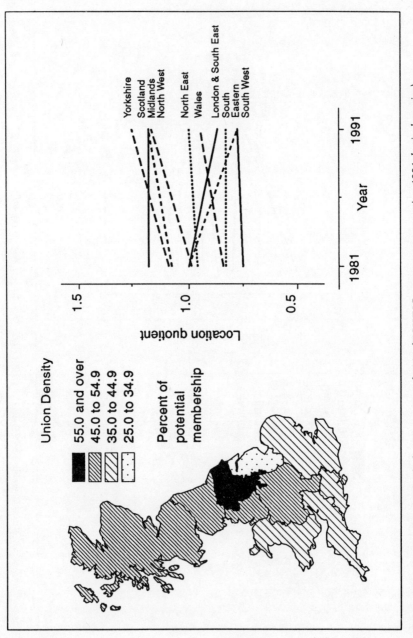

Figure 3.4viii: Regional densities for selected individual unions, 1981 and 1991 (TGWU Passenger transport section: 1991 density by region)

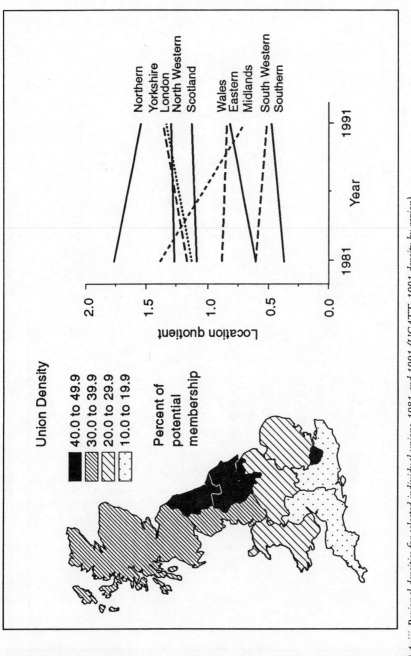

Figure 3.4viii: Regional densities for selected individual unions, 1981 and 1991 (UCATT: 1991 density by region)

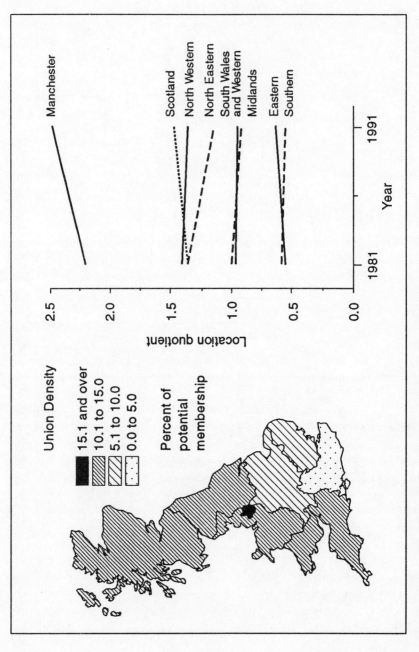

Figure 3.4ix: Regional densities for selected individual unions, 1981 and 1991 (USDAW: 1991 density by region)

those of USDAW, NUPE, NALGO and both the automotive, and chemicals, oil and rubber, sections of the TGWU have retained their relative position. Finally, as mentioned above, if spatial flattening has been the predominant trend since the early 1980s, the location quotients should show strong convergence towards unity over the period. In fact, there is very little evidence of any widespread or consistent spatial levelling. These results are thus generally consistent with the aggregate trends highlighted in the previous section.

CONCLUSION: RESILIENCE AMIDST RETREAT

The question we posed at the beginning of this chapter was whether and to what extent the decline of British trade unionism since the end of the 1970s has erased the regional pattern of union organization that has dominated the development of the union movement since the middle of the nineteenth century. By the early 1990s trade union membership and density had fallen back to what they were in the late 1940s. Few if any areas of the country have escaped this dramatic retreat. A priori, it might have been expected that the impact of decline would be most intense precisely in those areas where trade unionism was concentrated, and that as a result by the early 1990s regional differences in unionization would have all but disappeared. The evidence we have marshalled, both on aggregate union recognition and density, and for a number of individual unions, suggests that geography has exercised a tenacious hold on the shape of the union map despite the scale of decline in union membership.

Whether we define union heartlands as those regions having the largest numbers of union members or as those regions where workplace organization (membership density) is strongest, the same general conclusion is reached. There appears to be no prevailing trend towards the collapse of the unions' heartland areas or any marked tendency towards spatial dispersal. While a 'flattening' of the union map may have taken place during the years of expansion during the 1960s and 1970s, it would not be a valid description of trends during the recent period of union decline. A more accurate depiction of the geography of the contemporary retreat would be one of comparative resilience and retrenchment within the majority of the historic heartlands (the exception being the West Midlands). Despite the retreat of the unions nationally, the evidence points to an enduring north/south 'divide' in trade unionism. To be sure, the union movement has shrunk in these areas, but for the most part no faster than in the 'peripheral' union regions, and in several instances noticeably slower. In relative terms, northern Britain remains the organizational stronghold of the labour movement as represented by the density of union membership and the degree of union recognition. Although much reduced from their historical levels, workplace recognition and density rates there were still quite high in the early 1990s, typically still in excess of 50 per cent. Certainly by contemporary international standards, the Northern region, the North West, Wales and Scotland remain as economic spaces where unions continue to exist as key elements of the mode of workplace regulation. Furthermore, in these regions, unions are still significant local actors shaping and influencing economic and political affairs. In southern Britain, on the other hand, union recognition and density have fallen to levels which may be approaching the threshold at which unions find it difficult to exercise workplace influence and membership support. In this sense the legacy of history lingers on in the landscape of unionization. Of course, if the general haemorrhage of membership from the union movement continues, the relative resilience of the northern heartland areas may well wither away and regional differences in trade unionism disappear. But thus far the degree of persistence in these areas appears to have been surprisingly high. This raises some interesting questions as to how the processes generally believed to have promoted the decline of British trade unionism have operated across the regions, and the ways in which employers and the unions in different parts of the country have reacted to them. These are the issues we take up in the following chapter.

CHAPTER FOUR

Labour Market Restructuring and Regional Unionism

INTRODUCTION

The decline of the unions has taken place against a background of intense change in the economy. The British labour market in the 1990s is vastly different from what it was in the 1970s, when the trade union movement enjoyed its heyday. Of course, changes in the economy and in employment occur all the time, and the labour movement has always faced shifting contraints and opportunities with respect to its membership and influence. Indeed, for much of its history, the British labour movement has proved surprisingly successful in reinventing itself as socio-economic conditions have changed. But since the mid to late 1970s, several fundamental developments have combined to promote particularly rapid and far-reaching shifts in the structure and organization of the economy, a process of 'restructuring' or, to use Schumpeter's phrase, 'creative destruction'.[1] It is now widely agreed that, as part of this restructuring process, the labour market in the advanced industrial countries is undergoing an historic transformation, in its employment composition, its operation and its institutional organization and regulation (see, for example, Offe 1985; OECD 1994). In Britain, as elsewhere, the adjustment strains posed by this transformation have been intense and uneven:

---

1   The term 'restructuring' has become something of a catchword in the social sciences. There is now a large and diverse literature on the topic, and the term itself has come to be used in various ways, and with multiple meanings, to discuss structural and organizational change at all scales, from the individual firm to the national socio-economy and even the international economic system. At one level it is used descriptively, to distinguish the various dimensions of contemporary socio-economic change. At another, it is used theoretically, to conceptualize the main restructuring processes behind those changes. A third usage is political, to denote the restructuring strategies pursued by governments, and the different underlying political ideologies of how the socio-economic system *ought* to be re-organized. Given these different, but interrelated and often conflated uses, the term has developed into a 'chaotic concept', lacking in definitional and analytical precision. However, notwithstanding this polysemy the term is now the standard lexicon for summarizing the upheavals and changes in economic structure and organization of the past two decades.

the 'gales of economic destruction' have afflicted certain workers and communities much more than others, and likewise the 'creative benefits' have been unequally distributed (Martin 1988a, 1988b). As far as the unions are concerned, the outcome thus far would appear to have been distinctly unfavourable. The world of work and employment is changing in ways that are inimical to organized labour. In contrast to the period from the 1940s to the 1970s, the structural and regulatory bases of trade unionism are in decline, while those of non-unionism are in the ascendant.

While industrial relations analysts have been attempting to unravel the detailed impact of this restructuring of the labour market on the unions, geographers have devoted considerable attention to the ways in which restructuring is transforming the space economy. Not only is the labour market changing, so is its geography. Since the 1970s, the geographical patterns of regional and local economic development built up over previous decades have been progressively dismantled, and new landscapes of production and employment are emerging in their place. Restructuring – 'creative destruction' – is not a spatially neutral process, but impinges on different areas in different ways, if only because of differences in the inherited socio-economic structures and roles of individual regions and localities. But equally, regional and local labour markets are not merely passive canvases on which the logic of general (system-wide) processes of economic change are inexorably inscribed, mediated only by the circumstances of local structural particularity. Regions and localities can stamp their own autonomous imprints on such processes: as Massey (1991, p.26) puts it, 'the relation between political, cultural and economic changes may have an important local level of operation'. Thus although the changing geography of trade unionism will reflect the geography of restructuring, the relationship is likely to be far from straightforward. In addition, geographers are far from agreed as to the precise direction in which spatial restructuring is leading. Even though the majority see it as a shift from a Fordist 'spatial division of labour' to a post-Fordist or 'flexible accumulation' one, opinions differ over the exact shape of a post-Fordist economic landscape. Some claim that the post-war geographical centres of industry and employment are being replaced by a much more diverse and locally fragmented pattern; others believe we are witnessing a reconcentration of activity into new regional agglomerations of high technology industry and small-firm based flexible specialization; and still others see the shift as one towards a general convergence of regional economic and employment structures. Such competing visions obviously carry different implications for prognoses of the changing geography of trade unionism.

Geography thus complicates the 'restructuring' view of union decline in two crucial ways. First, regional patterns of union change and resilience will be shaped, to some extent at least, by regional variations in the restructuring process itself, and these variations will reflect regional differences in economic structure, such as industrial mix, firm size and organization, and employment composition. But, second, the precise impact on the unions will depend on the locally specific responses of individual employers, unions and workers to restructuring, and these responses may well be influenced by non-economic factors, including local socialized and institutionalized traditions and cultures and the locally contingent politics of labour/capital conflict (Herod 1991; Hudson and Sadler 1986; Massey 1991; Painter 1991; Martin, Sunley and Wills 1994a, 1994b, 1994c, 1994d; Wills 1996a). Apart from the study by Massey and Painter (1989), little attempt has been made to determine whether, in the British case, economic restructuring has eroded local variations in employment, social traditions and work cultures across the country, or whether and to what extent local contextual features have been resilient to the forces of change. In Massey and Painter's view, the net effect of restructuring has indeed been to remove geographical differences in structural context and, as we saw in the previous chapter, they claim this has resulted in a more uniform geography of trade union membership. Since our findings indicate that the map of union retreat in Britain has been more complex, and the geography of unionization less convergent, than these authors suggest, the impact of restructuring on the unions in the regions is an issue requiring more research and analysis. This is the aim of this chapter.

UNIONS AND THE CHANGING EMPLOYMENT STRUCTURE

Industrial relations accounts of the impact of labour market restructuring on the British unions have tended to focus on three main themes: the recomposition of employment, the recasting of employment legislation, and the reconfiguration of workplace and workforce management systems. A fourth type of explanation rejects these restructuring accounts and instead attributes the decline of the unions to macro-economic conditions, in particular persistent high unemployment (which has effectively removed many workers from trade union membership while disciplining the influence of organized labour) and rising real incomes (which are argued to have reduced workers' perceptions of the need for and benefits of trade unionism). But such macro-economic factors, though having some role, are far from adequate as an explanation. Britain's mass unemployment problem is largely a manifestation of the economic restructuring process, so that many of the effects attributed to the former are inextricably bound up with the latter. Also, the unemployment argument implies that should national employment conditions improve, union membership and organization will recover. The fact that union membership and density continued to fall during the 1983–90 employment recovery suggests that no such simple relationship exists. This is not to argue that mass unemployment has not formed part of the unfavourable context surrounding trade unionism over the past decade and a half, but rather that it is only one of several, interacting, causal factors behind union decline. Similarly, real incomes also rose between the mid 1950s and the late 1960s, but union membership and density did not fall in that period, so that of itself this factor is also insufficient as an explanation.

Table 4.1: The restructuring of employment in the United Kingdom:
the shift from industry to services, 1979–1993

	Millions (mid-year)				Change (millions)			
	1979	1982	1990	1993	1979 –82	1982 –90	1990 –93	1979 –93
Employment								
Manufacturing	7.3	5.9	5.1	4.4	-1.4	-0.8	-0.7	-2.9
Production	9.2	7.6	6.7	5.6	-1.6	-0.9	-1.1	-3.6
Services	13.6	13.4	15.9	15.7	-0.2	2.5	-0.2	2.1
Total Employees	23.2	21.4	22.9	21.6	-1.8	1.5	-1.3	-1.6
Trade Unions								
Membership (Millions)	13.3	11.6	10.4	8.7	-1.7	-1.2	-1.7	-4.6
Density (%)	57.3	54.1	44.5	40.5				

Source: Department of Employment.

Note: Manufacturing defined as SIC Divisions 2–4: Production as Manufacturing plus Energy and Water Supply (SIC 1) and Construction (SIC 5); Services as SIC Divisions 6–9.

The wave of economic restructuring and reorganization that has swept through the British economy during the past two decades has been the most intense since that of the inter-war years (see, for example, Green 1989; Martin 1988a). There has been considerable debate over the nature of the process, its causes and its consequences. The fact that economic restructuring has not been confined to Britain but has been a feature common to all of the advanced industrialized nations suggests that the process is a generic one, induced by the systemic onset of economic slowdown and crisis during the 1970s (Allen and Massey 1988; Glyn *et al.* 1990; Lash and Urry 1987; Martin 1989b).[2] However, it is also generally accepted that in Britain's case this crisis has been superimposed on and compounded by a further process of deep-seated long-term relative economic decline and dwindling competitiveness that, according to many commentators, can be traced back to the end of the nineteenth century (Feinstein 1988; Overbeek 1989; Gamble 1990). As a result, the economic crisis in Britain has been much more acute than in many other countries, and both the need for and stimulus to

---

2 Regulationist theorists, of course, see this slowdown, and the restructuring it has promoted, as the exhaustion ('crisis') of the Fordist techno-economic paradigm and the search for a new (post-Fordist) regime of accumulation and regulation. Whatever the interpretation, capitalism has undergone similar episodic restructurings in the past, with equally transformative consequences.

wide-ranging restructuring and modernization of the economy have been considerably greater than elsewhere.

The implications of this restructuring for the composition of employment have been considerable. Many of the country's older production industries and firms, where trade unionism was well established, were precisely those that had fallen behind in international competitiveness, technological advance, productivity and profitability, and thus were in most need of thoroughgoing reconfiguration. For these activities restructuring has meant deindustrialization: corporate 'de-layering' and 'slim-down', the rationalization of productive capacity, and, above all, large-scale job loss. Employment in the UK's production industries (manufacturing, energy, mining, water supply and construction) reached its historical peak of 11.5 million in 1967 and had already been declining throughout the 1970s (see Thirlwall 1982; Rowthorn 1986): by1979 it had fallen to 9.2 million. But during the economic upheavals of the 1980s, the pace of deindustrialization accelerated, and by 1993 employment in production had slumped to a mere 5.6 million (Table 4.1).

Most of the jobs that have gone have been those held by male manual workers in industries with traditionally high union densities, especially energy and mining, metals and chemicals and engineering (see Table 4.2). Moreover, a significant proportion of these losses have been the result of the closure and 'downsizing' of large plants and firms. Manufacturing establishments employing over 500 employees have experienced the most substantial falls in employment, and it is these workplaces where union densities amongst male manual workers have traditionally been highest (Table 4.3). Since 1979, therefore, the restructuring of the industrial base has involved a dramatic shake-out of unionized labour from the workforce. In Rubery's (1986) view this collapse of industrial employment has been the primary factor behind the decline in union membership:

> A large part of the fall in membership has occurred because of the elimination of jobs, not because of a retreat from trade union membership by employed workers. Union membership as a proportion of employed workers (instead of the traditional measure, which includes the registered unemployed) has held up remarkably well in the post–1979 period. (p.83)[3]

At the same time as the number of industrial jobs has shrunk, employment in the UK service economy has expanded, from 13.6 millon in 1979 to 16.0 million by 1990 (Table 4.1). Although some retrenchment then occurred during the recession of the early 1990s, service employment in 1993 was still 15.7 million, some 2.1 million higher than it was in 1979. Almost all of this job growth has been

---

3   Underlying Rubery's argument is the assumption that most unionized workers drop their union membership upon becoming unemployed. Empirical evidence supports this contention. However, Rubery's claim that union density has held up well is inaccurate: density did fall during the 1980s (including the period of employment expansion between 1983–90) and has continued to decline during the 1990s.

Table 4.2: Employment change and union density by industrial sector, Great Britain.

| SIC Division (1980) | Employment change 1979–1993 | | Union density | | |
	000s	%	1984	1990	% change 1984–1990
Energy, Water	-366.3	-51.5	87	75	-13.8
Mineral Extraction, Metals and Chemicals	-597.5	-52.9	64	56	-12.5
Metal Goods and Engineering	-1483.9	-44.5	59	46	-22.0
Other Manufacturing Industries	-822.3	-31.0	52	47	-9.6
Construction Industry	-388.8	-32.3	36	46	27.7
Transport and Communication	-219.3	-15.0	89	73	-17.9
Distribution, Hotels, Catering and Repairs	335.8	8.0	31	19	-38.7
Banking, Insurance and other Business Services	1041.2	64.2	29	29	0.0
Public Admin, Health, Education, Other services	909.8	15.2	67	61	-8.9
All Industries and Services	-1627.5	-7.2	58	48	-17.2

Sources: Department of Employment; WIRS 1984 and WIRS 1990.

Table 4.3: Establishment size and union density

| Establishment size band by number of employees | Employment (% change) | Union density (%) | |
	1984–90	1984	1990
25–49	14.7	31	19
50–99	5.4	46	36
100–199	-0.7	52	47
200–499	-2.9	64	56
500–999	-13.0	87	73
1000 and over	-22.8	89	75

Sources: Census of Production; Authors' analysis of WIRS 1984 and WIRS 1990.

Table 4.4: Union density and recognition, by employment group, Great Britain, 1989 and 1994

	Union density			Union recognition
	1989	1992	1994	1994
All Employed	34	32	30	
All Employees	39	36	33	48
Men	44	39	36	49
Women	33	32	30	47
Full-time	44	40	38	51
Part-time	22	22	21	40
Manual	44	38	35	46
Non-manual	35	34	33	50
Self-employed	9	10	9	

Source: Labour Force Surveys.

Table 4.5: The shift towards female work, part-time jobs and the self-employed, Great Britain

		Millions		Change
		1978	1994	1979–94
Total Employees		22.27	21.01	-1.26
of which:	Full-time	17.88	15.06	-2.82
	Part-time	4.40	5.95	1.55
	Males	13.10	10.63	-2.47
	Females	9.17	10.37	1.20
Production		9.00	5.30	-3.70
of which:	Males	6.72	3.83	-2.89
	Females	2.28	1.47	-0.81
Services		12.89	15.36	2.47
of Which:	Males	6.09	6.53	0.44
	Females	6.80	8.83	2.03
	Of which: Part-time	3.11	4.54	1.43
Self-employed 1.84		3.06	1.22	
of which:	Services	1.12	1.88	0.76

Source: Department of Employment and Labour Force Survey.
Notes: 1. Employment data refer to Great Britain, not United Kingdom and are mid-year estimates.
2. Self-employed data refer to 1978 and 1991, not 1994.

concentrated in the private service sector, where new job creation during the second half of the 1980s was particularly strong, especially in business services, banking, finance and insurance (Table 4.2). The unions have always it found notoriously difficult to organize workers in the private services sector where, compared to manufacturing, there is a much greater 'fragmentation' of employment amongst numerous small firms, labour turnover rates are often high, and significant numbers of workers are women, part-timers and self-employed, groups of people whom the unions have typically had limited success in recruiting (Table 4.4). Some 80 per cent of the 2.4 million new jobs created in services in Britain over the period 1978–94 were for females, and nearly two thirds of these in turn were part-time. And over half of the 1.2 million increase in the number of self-employed between 1978–91 were in private services (Table 4.5). In addition, the nature of the work process in many private services, often involving a high degree of worker autonomy and direct, reflexive, contact with individual customers tends to inhibit the formation of collective worker identities and the scope for workplace organization.[4] Thus while in theory the growth of employment in the private service economy has provided new opportunities for the relevant unions to expand their memberships, in practice the unions have largely failed to penetrate this sector. This challenge of a changing labour market is acute in the minds of trade union officials:

> The traditional difficulties for unions in seeking to achieve recognition in areas such as small firms, those with a high labour turnover or a high proportion of part-time workers, foreign-owned firms, the service sector and white-collar workers, have intensified. Unions are finding it difficult to recruit and bargain in the fastest growing parts of the economy. (Trades Union Congress 1988, p.5)

Almost all accounts of the decline in British trade unionism assign some role to the recomposition of employment. Thus in its review of union trends during the 1980s, the Confederation of British Industry (CBI) concluded that:

> Firstly, most of the opportunities (at that time) arose in areas of activity which have traditionally proved unfruitful recruiting grounds for trade unions: self employment; part-time work in smaller enterprises and private sector services. Few larger enterprises, with their traditionally higher levels of union density, increased their recruitment. Secondly, many of the new jobs were taken by women who have generally been less inclined to join unions. Recent labour market developments point to a continuation of these trends. Many

---

4   Of course private sector service employment covers a wide range of occupational cataegories and types of job, from unskilled manual work at one end (for example, cleaners) to highly skilled professional work at the other (for example, solicitors). Although these different forms of employment obviously vary considerably, very few are characterized by the sort of work conditions or environments that promote large-scale collective organization.

parts of the trading sector with relatively high union densities are continuing to shed labour: coal, steel, the railways, the utilities, post and telecommunications amongst them. Contracting out, market testing and the general need for more cost-effective service provision may be reflected in real reductions in public sector employment overall. (CBI 1994)

Similarly, according to Bassett (1986) the growth in

non-unionism...tends to be associated with the following characteristics: smaller organisations and smaller establishments within those organisations; relatively high proportions of women workers; relatively small proportions of manual workers;...newer establishments and high technology industry. For British unions the worrying thing about this list is its underlying link: that all these characteristics are now associated with growth in the economy. In every case, the characteristic with which non-unionism is associated is on the increase. (pp.46–47)

There have been several attempts to quantify these effects. Some have found that as much as half of the decline in union density or recognition can be accounted for by employment recomposition (see Beaumont and Harris 1991; Booth 1989; Millward and Stevens 1986; Towers 1989). Thus Booth found that some 42 per cent of national union density decline between 1979 and 1987 could be attributed to the recomposition of the industrial employment structure. Others, however, have found the recomposition effect to be less significant (Carruth and Disney 1988; Disney 1990; Freeman and Pelletier 1990; Green 1992). For example, Green found that the combined effect of several different forms of change in the composition of employment (by industry, gender, full-time and part-time status, size of establishment, and occupation) accounted for no more than 30 per cent of the decline in national union density. Such conflicting results are difficult to reconcile, not least because of differences in the methods, data periods and measures of unionization they utilize.[5] The balance of evidence, however, suggests that employment recomposition has played a role in the decline in union density and recognition, but that it has by no means been the only factor involved.

Regional Employment Recomposition Versus the Unions

While industrial relations theorists continue to debate the impact of employment restructuring on the unions in Britain, few studies have explored the regional dimension of the issue. Yet differences in employment structures across the British regions have long been a topic of recurring interest amongst geographers and regional economists. Characteristically, a region's industrial mix has been seen as

---

5   It is also likely that the impact of recomposition has varied between the recessionary periods of the early 1980s and the early 1990s, on the one hand, and the intervening period of overall employment growth on the other (see Disney 1990).

a key determinant of its economic and labour market characteristics (see Fothergill and Gudgin 1982, and Armstrong and Taylor 1985, for expositions of this idea).[6] What this line of reasoning suggests is that, all other things being equal, regional differences in unionization should be closely correlated with regional differences in industrial composition. Regions with above-average proportions of their employment in industries which nationally are heavily unionized will have high overall union densities and recognition rates; and conversely for regions more reliant on industries which nationally are less unionized. The few industrial relations studies that have examined inter-regional differences in unionization and industrial relations have typically adopted this industrial mix explanation (for example, Knowles 1952; Phelps-Brown 1959; Beaumont and Harris 1988a, 1988b). The implication of this industrial 'structural' view, then, is that, at least to some extent, the map of union decline should reflect the geography of economic and employment recomposition.

As we saw in the previous chapter, the historical evolution of the map of British trade unionism has indeed been closely bound up with the shifting pattern of regional industrial specialization and development. Of course, compared to the late-ninetenth century, by the 1970s the regions were much less specialized industrially and regional labour market structures had become more diversified and less differentiated (see, for example, Chisholm and Oeppen 1973; Fothergill and Gudgin 1982; Dunford and Perrons 1986). As a result, differences in industrial composition as such had become relatively less significant as a determinant of regional labour market performance, while the role of other factors (for example, the age and firm-size characteristics of local capital, the local availability and cost of land and labour, local rates of technological development, and so on) had become correspondingly more important (see Fothergill and Gudgin 1982, for a discussion). Nevertheless, important structural differences still existed (Dunford and Perrons 1986), sufficient for the restructuring of the 1980s and early 1990s to have uneven consequences across the regions.

Geographical accounts of the employment shifts associated with deindustrialization, tertiarization and new technologies have repeatedly highlighted the differential regional dynamics involved (see, for example, Daniels 1986; Fothergill and Gudgin 1986, 1994; Martin 1986, 1989; Hall 1991; Martin and Townroe 1992). Not surprisingly, rates of industrial job loss have been highest in the very regions most dependent on labour intensive branches of manufacturing or the heavy nationalized and energy industries (such as coal mining and steel), namely Wales, the northern regions of the country, especially the old metropolitan centres

---

6   Essentially, regions with a high proportion of their employment in nationally 'unfavourable' industries (i.e. slow growing, unproductive, uncompetitive economic activities) tend to have inferior labour market conditions (such as fewer employment opportunities and higher unemployment); and vice versa for regions with a high proportion of their employment in nationally 'favourable' (i.e. fast growing, productive, competitive) industries and activities.

Table 4.6: Regional employment shifts and union decline

	Employees per cent change 1979–1994			Union decline percentage change in		
	Production	Services	Total	Recognition 1980–1990 (WIRS)	Density 1984–1990 (WIRS)	Density 1989–1994 (LFS)
Greater London	-46.2	0.0	-16.2	-46.5	-23.4	-18.6
Outer South East	-39.5	21.3	5.3	-28.4	-16.2	-12.9
East Anglia	-22.4	40.3	12.2	-39.8	-5.0	-6.9
South West	-32.7	28.7	5.9	-37.7	-18.2	-15.1
East Midlands	-33.5	29.3	-3.3	-32.0	-14.7	-16.3
West Midlands	-43.6	19.7	-13.1	-29.1	-24.6	-20.0
Yorks-Humberside	-43.1	21.3	-8.9	-26.6	-20.8	-20.1
North West	-46.4	9.3	-15.2	-24.1	-19.7	-14.8
North	-43.1	12.9	-13.1	-27.1	-18.8	-18.8
Wales	-37.4	16.7	-7.1	-21.0	-8.5	-4.2
Scotland	-39.2	16.9	-6.7	-22.2	-9.5	-15.2
Great Britain	**-41.2**	**15.8**	**-7.7**	**-32.5**	**-17.2**	**-15.4**

Source: Department of Enployment; WIRS 1980 and 1990; LFS 1989, 1994.
Notes: Separate employment data for Greater London and Rest of South East not available prior to 1982; changes for 1979–1994 estimated from trends, relative to South East total, over the period 1982–1994.

such as Clydeside, Merseyside, Tyneside, and South Yorkshire, together with the Midlands and Greater London (Table 4.6).

With the exception of Greater London, these are precisely the areas where, as we have seen in the previous chapter, workforce union densities and recognition rates have historically been highest. In contrast, industrial job loss rates have been lowest in the less industrialized and less unionized regions of the South West, Outer South East and East Anglia. These are the areas where much of the country's newer consumer goods and high-technology industry is concentrated (see Hall 1991; Keeble 1992). At the same time, all regions, except Greater London, have shared in the expansion of private service sector employment, although the service job boom has been mainly a southern-based phenomenon (Table 4.6). As a result of these differential trends, by the early 1990s regional employment structures had shifted markedly towards services, and had converged somewhat in the process (Table 4.7).[7]

---

7   These comments should not be taken to imply that convergence has also occurred at more local intra-regional scales. In fact there has been much recent discussion which suggests that while regional differences have declined, local intra-regional differences have increased. We are not able to examine union trends at these more local scales.

Table 4.7: The changing economic structure of the regions, by broad sector, 1979-1994

| | Share of total employment | | | | | |
| | Production | | Manufacturing | | Services | |
	1979	1994	1979	1994	1979	1994
South East	31.5	19.1	25.0	14.4	67.5	80.3
East Anglia	36.9	24.8	29.3	20.2	57.2	72.4
South West	34.8	22.4	27.5	18.2	62.4	75.5
East Midlands	49.5	34.6	38.9	30.6	48.3	64.0
West Midlands	50.1	33.6	43.9	28.3	47.8	65.3
Yorks-Humberside	46.5	29.3	41.0	24.8	51.9	69.6
North West	43.8	27.7	38.8	22.4	55.5	71.7
North	45.6	30.5	38.9	24.9	53.2	68.6
Wales	42.9	29.1	36.5	25.0	55.3	69.1
Scotland	39.5	26.5	32.2	20.3	58.2	72.3
Great Britain	**39.8**	**25.6**	**31.4**	**20.2**	**58.6**	**73.2**

Source: Department of Employment.
Note: Manufacturing defined as SIC Divisions 2–4; Production as Manufacturing plus Energy and Water Supply (SIC 1) and Construction (SIC 5); Services as SIC Divisions 6–9.

On the face of it, this convergence of regional employment structures would be expected to have eroded regional differences in the structural bases of trade union organization and representation.

To gain some insight into this issue we applied the procedure used by Green (1992) in his analysis of the role of employment recomposition in national union density decline between 1983–89. In our case we examine the contribution of different dimensions of employment recomposition to the fall in regional union recognition rates between 1980–90 (recall that it is not possible to calculate regional union densities from the 1980 WIRS). The change in union recognition in a region between 1980–90 can be written as:

$$\Delta U_r = \sum_i U_{ir}^{90} N_{ir}^{90} - \sum_i U_{ir}^{80} N_{ir}^{80}$$

where

U_{ir} = the union recognition rate in employment sector or category i in region r (defined as the proportion of employees in workplaces where unions are recognized)

N_{ir} = the proportion of the region's employees in sector or category i, that is, $E_{ir}/\sum_i E_{ir}$

U_r = the overall recognition rate in region r,

and the sums are over the relevant sectors or categories of employment.

This relation may be rewritten as

$$\Delta U_r = \Sigma_i(U_{ir}^{90} - U_{ir}^{80})N_{ir}^{80} + \Sigma_i(N_{ir}^{90} - N_{ir}^{80})U_{ir}^{80}$$
$$+ \Sigma_i(U_{ir}^{90} - U_{ir}^{80}) \Sigma_i(N_{ir}^{90} - N_{ir}^{80})$$

The first term on the right-hand side of this expression measures the decline in union recognition that would have occurred if the employment structure of the region had remained unchanged between 1980 and 1990, but sector-specific union recognition rates had fallen. The second term is the fall in recognition over this period that would have occurred due to changes in the employment structure of the region if sector-specific recognition rates had remained constant. The third term is the interaction of these two effects, and is generally small. This procedure was carried out separately for a number of different aspects of regional employment recomposition: by industrial sector (single digit SIC Divisions), by workplace size (25–99, 100–499, and 500 or more employees), by broad occupational category (manual versus non-manual employees), by gender (male versus female workers) and by status (full-time versus part-time).[8]

The results are presented in Table 4.8, which gives the percentage of the decline in recognition and density in each region due to each type of employment recomposition effect. The most striking feature is that in every region the impact of employment recomposition on trade union decline has been relatively small, and consistently outweighed by within-sector decline. Of the different aspects of the employment structure examined, changes in the industrial-sector and firm-size composition of regional employment appear to have had most impact. In his analysis, Green found that changes in industrial mix, establishment size and occupation structure made the most significant – though still small – contributions to the decline in national union density (of 17, 11 and 14% respectively). Our results suggest slightly larger industrial and workplace size recomposition effects at the regional scale, and this almost certainly reflects the fact that our study period, unlike Green's, spans the deep recession of the early 1980s, when substantial industrial and firm-size shifts in employment structure took place. Thus, notwithstanding the constraints and limitations of the WIRS data used in the analysis, our findings indicate that shifts in the industrial and establishment-size structures of regional employment over the 1980s did account for some of the decline in union recognition in the regions, but that these effects have not been sufficient to erode regional differences in unionization: regional variations in unionization have persisted despite the general tendency for regional employment structures to

---

8   Data limitations in the WIRS surveys, particularly the 1980 WIRS, restrict the degree of region-specific composition analysis that can be carried out. Thus even at the level of broad SIC industrial divisions the sample sizes in some of the regions (especially East Anglia) are very small. The same problem also restricted the establishment decomposition to three size-bands. These points should be borne in mind when interpreting the results.

Table 4.8: The contribution of employment recomposition to the decline in regional unionization

| | *Percentage of decline in union recognition, 1980–1990* | | | | |
| | *Recomposition of employment by* | | | | |
	Industrial sector	*Workplace size*	*Occupation manual/ non-manual*	*Gender*	*Status (full-time, part-time)*
London	22	11	10	8	1
Outer South East	18	13	5	6	2
East Anglia	12	9	3	2	0
South West	24	14	7	2	2
East Midlands	26	17	8	1	1
West Midlands	27	21	11	5	3
Yorks/Humberside	20	16	9	4	0
North West	29	26	4	1	2
North	34	27	12	7	4
Wales	32	22	14	8	4
Scotland	22	18	10	3	2
Great Britain	**22**	**17**	**8**	**4**	**2**

Source: Authors' calculations from WIRS 1980 and 1990.

Note: Contributions of different recomposition effects cannot be summed owing to interrelationships between them.

become more similar. This in turn implies that differences in industrial structure and the establishment-size distribution of employment play a relatively minor role in accounting for regional differences in unionization.

Simple shift-share analyses were used to evaluate this last proposition, by decomposing regional union recognition rates as follows. Let

U_n = national overall union recognition rate

U_{ijn} = national union recognition rate in establishment size band j in industry division i

N_{ijr} = the proportion of the region's employees in establishment size band j in industry division i, that is $(E_{ijr} / \Sigma_i \Sigma_j E_{ijr})$

U_r = actual union recognition rate in region r.

Define the 'expected' or 'rate constant' union recognition rate in a region r as the rate that would be expected if each establishment size band in each industrial sector in the region had the same degree of union recognition as that establishment size band in that industry nationally, that is

$$U^\star_r = \Sigma_i \Sigma_j [N_{ijr} U_{ijn}]$$

where the summations are over the various industrial sectors and establishment size bands concerned. Then, by definition, the difference between a region's recognition rate and the national rate is equal to the sum of a regional 'structural' or composition effect and a residual 'area' effect:

$$U_r - U_n \quad = \quad (U_r - U^\star_r) \quad + \quad (U^\star_r - U_n)$$

Regional	Area	Structural
Recognition	Effect	Effect
Differential		

The 'structural' or composition effect reflects how much of a region's union recognition differential derives from the deviation of its employment structure from the national sectoral and establishment-size mix, while the residual 'area' effect captures the influence of other, 'non-structural' factors. A negative 'structural' or composition effect in this context indicates that a region has a disproportionate share of low-unionized industries or firms; and a positive 'structural' effect the converse. Similarly, a negative 'area' effect indicates that the industries and firms in the region tend to be consistently less unionized than their national counterparts; and again conversely for positive area effects.[9]

Tables 4.9 and 4.10 summarize the results of this analysis for manual and non-manual employees, for both 1980 and 1990. In the case of manual workers there is a clear distinction between the southern, less unionized regions of the country, that is London, East Anglia, the Outer South East and South West, on the one hand, and the traditonally more industrialized and more unionized regions of the North, Scotland and Wales, on the other.

The former group tend to have negative composition effects, that is, above average concentrations of industries that nationally have low union recognition rates. The latter group, in contrast, tend to have positive compositional effects, that is, industrial structures with above average proportions of more highly unionized sectors. However, the shift-share results confirm that the different industrial and establishment-size composition of the regions is of limited importance in account-

---

9   Shift-share results may be sensitive to the degree and type of structural – and indeed spatial – disaggregation employed, although this is an empirical matter. Unfortunately, the levels of industrial/establishment size and regional disaggregation used here are restricted by the data from WIRS and the LFS. The method can also be criticized for its assumption that the structural and area effects are independent, when in fact they may be related since part of an industry effect may be inextricably intermingled with all the other influences operating through the area effect. Finally, the shift-share technique is often criticized for not being amenable to statistical testing. For a discussion of these points see, for example, Armstrong and Taylor (1985).

Table 4.9: Structural versus area effects in regional union recognition differentials, manual workers, private sector, 1980 and 1990

	Percentage of employees in workplaces recognizing unions 1980				Percentage of employees in workplaces recognizing unions 1990			
	Obs. rate	Reg. diff.	Struct. effect	Area effect	Obs. rate	Reg. diff.	Struct. effect	Area effect
London	76	-8	-3	-5	41	-16	-3	-13
Outer South East	70	-14	-6	-8	43	-14	-2	-12
East Anglia	82	-2	-1	-1	41	-16	-4	-12
South West	79	-5	-2	-2	56	-1	0	-1
East Midlands	93	9	5	4	60	3	1	2
West Midlands	91	7	5	2	62	5	2	3
Yorks/Humberside	87	3	1	2	62	5	1	4
North West	89	5	3	2	64	7	2	5
North	92	8	3	5	65	8	1	7
Wales	86	2	1	1	69	12	3	9
Scotland	85	1	0	1	62	5	1	4
Great Britain	**84**				**57**			

Source: Calculated from WIRS 1984 and 1990.
Notes: 1. Decomposition based on procedure given in text.
2. Establishments with no manual workers omitted.

ing for regional differences in unionization. Not only are the residual 'area' effects in most regions substantially larger in magnitude than the composition effects, the 'area' effect is positive in all of the northern regions and negative in almost all of the southern regions. Furthermore, the relative significance of 'area' as against 'compositional' effects appears to increase between 1980 and 1990, as does the division between the northern and southern regions. If industrial structure only partly accounted for regional differences in unionization in 1980, it was even less important by 1990. (Although not shown here, the same overall result was obtained from similar analyses of regional union density differentials over the 1984–90 period, using WIRS, and over 1989–94 using LFS data).[10] While the findings are less clear for non-manual workers, as might be expected, the same basic division between the northern and southern regions is still evident. Although the 'area' effects could, of course, be capturing other aspects of the employment structure, such as differences in gender and status composition, as we have seen, these appear to have had only a minor influence on regional variations in union

10 The LFS data allow only a twofold division of establishment size: fewer than and more than 25 employees.

Table 4.10: Structural versus area effects in regional union recognition differentials, non-manual workers, private sector, 1980 and 1990

	Percentage of employees in workplaces recognizing unions 1980				Percentage of employees in workplaces recognizing unions 1990			
	Obs. rate	Reg. diff.	Struct. effect	Area effect	Obs. rate	Reg. diff.	Struct. effect	Area effect
London	55	-6	-3	-3	29	-12	-4	-8
Outer South East	44	-17	-10	-7	36	-5	-2	-3
East Anglia	68	-7	-2	-5	37	-4	-2	-3
South West	67	6	7	-1	36	-5	-2	-3
East Midlands	74	13	4	9	52	7	1	8
West Midlands	68	7	3	4	50	-9	-5	-4
Yorks/Humberside	57	-4	-2	6	43	2	1	1
North West	69	8	-1	9	55	14	0	14
North	72	11	2	9	54	13	2	11
Wales	73	12	3	9	42	1	-3	4
Scotland	63	2	-1	3	52	11	-2	13
Great Britain	**61**				**41**			

Source: Calculated from WIRS 1984 and 1990.
Notes: 1. Decomposition based on procedure give in text.

decline, which suggests that their role in accounting for regional differences in unionization is relatively insignificant (and, in any case, interwoven with industrial-sector and workplace-size effects).[11] In Chapters One and Two we argued that the geographies of trade unionism and industrial relations practices are shaped not only by spatial differences in industrial composition and labour market structure, but also by regional and local variations in the inherited socialized traditions, customs and cultures that influence the propensity of workers to join unions and employers' attitudes towards collective labour organization in the workplace. Our results in this section would seem to point to the existence and persistence of significant local socio-institutional effects in the map of trade unionism. We return to this issue at the end of the chapter.

---

11 In their analysis of the 1984 WIRS, Church and Stevens (1994) find that union densities in conurbations and large towns are sigificantly higher than those in small towns and rural areas. This suggests that the 'urban-rural mix' of a region's working population might also be a factor in contributing to regional differences in unionization. However, they failed to examine whether urban and rural union densities differ from region to region, and particularly as between northern and southern regions.

NEW REGULATORY SPACES: UNDERMINING THE INSTITUTIONAL BASES OF REGIONAL UNIONISM

The second aspect of labour market restructuring singled out by many industrial relations analysts as having undermined British trade unionism is the barrage of new employment legislation passed by the Conservative government during the 1980s and early 1990s. The express purpose of this overhaul of the legislative framework has been to 'derigidify' the labour market in general and to reduce union power and influence in the workplace in particular. This aim has derived from a fierce right-wing Conservative political belief – espoused especially by Mrs Thatcher and her close supporters – that the unions themselves have been directly responsible for Britain's economic malaise, especially its slowdown in industrial growth, its lack of technological modernization and its endemic inflation. The cultural impact of the labourist tradition, the industrial power of organized labour, and the political leverage exercised by the national trade union leadership, are all seen as having exerted a negative influence on national economic performance. The trade unions, it was claimed, had worked to 'freeze' UK industry and society into its historical structures, locations, technologies and work processes. By assiduously hanging on to attitudes and arguments inimical to industrial change, by persuading their members to retain anti-market goals and values (of social equality and job security, for example), and by adopting a confrontational 'zero-sum' game approach to industrial relations, the unions had 'taught workers to resist efficiency, obstruct management, insist on overmanning, resent profit and ignore customers' (Sir Keith Joseph 1979, p.6).[12] This largely backward-looking and unco-operative culture of the British union movement has frequently been contrasted with the supposedly more market-orientated attitudes of American 'business' unionism and the greater corporate realism and loyalty of Japanese 'company' unionism.

The key problem was seen to be the disproportionate workplace power of organized labour in the UK, not only in manufacturing, where it had allegedly blocked the diffusion and utilization of new technologies and working practices,[13]

---

12 Such views were not confined to right-wing commentators, however. Thus we find Sidney Pollard arguing that by the early-1980s the British unions had come 'to be counted amongst the most irresponsible and destructive unions in Europe' (1982, p.106).

13 Again left-wing readings of this thesis can be found. For example, Kilpatrick and Lawson (1980) argue that even in the 1890s, that is prior to the introduction of Fordist mass production, unions were successfully defending old craft practices and resisting new techniques. The result of this early success, they suggest, was the persistence of skill demarcations, restrictive practices and industrial relations systems that were unsuited to the efficient exploitation of mass production. Williams *et al.* (1983) argue that this continued right through into the post-1945 period, and led not only to low rates of technological modernization within manufacturing but also to high levels of overmanning and sub-optimal utilization of existing machinery. Glyn and Harrison (1980, p.50) make a similar argument: 'The UK working class's strong organization at factory level thwarted many of capital's attempts to increase productivity. New techniques...were often effectively vetoed by unions

but also in the public sector industries and services where the unions had repeatedly exercized their 'unique disruptive ability'. Added to this, the unions had developed a powerful two-tiered mechanism of wage determination, with formal negotiations at a national or multi-plant company level supplemented locally by a largely informal, fragmented and autonomous system of local bargaining between middle management and shop stewards representing well organized work-groups. At both levels, the national and the local, strike action was frequently used to back wage demands. In these various ways, union power was said to have created the 'British disease' – an economic structure in which outmoded work practices, substantial wage drift and widespread strike action eroded productivity, competitiveness and investment. Furthermore, up to 1979 this excessive shop-floor power of organized labour had been protected by a uniquely favourable legislative and regulatory framework within which trade unions wielded their influence and unofficial action could legitimately take place.[14]

There can be little doubt that the tide of employment legislation over the 1980s and early 1990s, including the Employment Acts of 1980, 1982, 1988, 1989 and 1990, the Wages and Public Order Acts of 1986, the Trade Union Act of 1984, and the Trade Union Reform and Employment Rights Act of 1993, has removed much of this protective framework. Unballoted strikes and secondary action have been outlawed; considerable powers have been given to the courts to sequester union funds; and action to preserve the 'closed shop' has been made illegal. Employers with less than 20 employees no longer have to include disciplinary procedures in employment contracts; employment protection has been removed for workers hired for less than two years; and the 'check-off system' (whereby union membership subscriptions are collected directly from employees' pay) now requires the periodic written consent of individual workers. Arguably most significant of all, the legal obligation on employers to agree to workers' requests for union recognition in the workplace has been rescinded.

Alongside these legislative changes, one of the aims behind the Conservative governments' privatization crusade has been to weaken the wage-bargaining position and strike power of the public sector unions, a goal shaped by memories

which did not want to lose jobs. Where new machinery was installed, its effect on productivity was often reduced because unions insisted on maintaining existing operating levels or line speeds'. Several commentators have pointed to the effect of post-war full employment on the workplace power of the unions, arguing that labour shortages enabled organized work groups in new growth industries, especially motor vehicles and light engineering, to consolidate a significant degree of control over pace of work, skill demarcations, manning levels, overtime and introduction of new machinery.

14 According to Hayek, one of Mrs Thatcher's leading sources of ideological inspiration, these 'legalized powers of the unions had become the biggest obstacle to raising the living standards of the working class as a whole...the prime source of unemployment...[and] the main reason for the decline of the British economy in general' (Hayek 1984, p.107). A numbers of right-wing analysts, have pointed particularly to the 1906 Trade Disputes Act, which gave unions immunity from claims for civil damages arising from their industrial action.

of the coal miners' challenge to Edward Heath's Conservative government in 1974 and the national disruption caused by the public sector workers' strikes in the 'winter of discontent' of 1978–79 (see Gardner 1987).[15] The high union densities in the nationalized industries, together with their sheer size and strategic importance, has traditionally given their workers considerable 'industrial muscle'. The tendency has been for privatization – as in the cases of telecommunications, water, gas and electricity – to be used as an opportunity to undertake extensive rationalization and reorganization, usually resulting in substantial job losses. Although union densities amongst the slimmed down workforces have remained relatively buoyant, this post-privatization shake-out of labour has certainly eroded union membership and influence in the activities concerned. Furthermore, given such job losses and, in some cases, the break up of what were nationwide industries into new regional concerns, privatization has seriously weakened the basis for unity and nationwide collective bargaining and industrial action on the part of the workers and unions involved. The government has sought to achieve the same result in the remaining public sector activities, such as health and education, by restructuring their operation and organization along more 'marketized' and 'commercialized' lines; while at the local authority level the Government's legal imposition of compulsory competitive tendering and contracting-out of a range of local services (from refuse and sanitation to school cleaning and catering) has likewise threatened the bedrock of public sector unionism.

Given this historically unprecedented offensive on unionized labour, it is not surprising that 'Nothing so unites Conservatives of all colours than the belief that Margaret Thatcher's assault on the unions was the one unchallengeable achievement of her government' (Cole 1994, p.8). Some analysts (for example, Freeman and Pelletier 1990) attribute nearly all of the 1980s' decline in union membership to the impact of these changes in the regulatory spaces of organized labour. Certainly in the early Thatcher years many union officials were disastrously over-confident of their ability to resist the Conservative Government's legislative

---

15 Faced in early 1974 by the threat of the National Union of Mineworkers (NUM) to call a full-scale strike over its pay dispute with the Conservative government, Edward Heath the prime minister called a general election in February to decide 'who governs Britain'. In the event, only 30 per cent of the electorate voted for the Conservatives, their lowest level of support for fifty years. The 1978–79 'winter of discontent' brought the unions once more into direct confrontation with the government, this time a Labour one under James Callaghan. The National Union of Public Employees (NUPE) had put in a claim for a 30 per cent pay increase, and other unions followed suit. When these claims were rejected, there were widespread public sector strikes. As a consequence, relations between the union movement and the Labour government broke down. One Cabinet Minister observed that 'the trade unions are now the most unpopular institution for a hundred years', and one union leader was quoted as saying' 'if the government falls that's OK, the trade union movement is indestructible' (Barnett 1982, pp.172, 174). The government did indeed fall, to be replaced by the first of Mrs Thatcher's Conservative administrations. As for the claim that the union movement is 'indestructible', this bold prophesy looks far from secure.

onslaught through defensive militancy. In the first half of the 1980s, the government's major struggles with the unions were in the public sector (railways, water, steel, coal, health and education), but later the government gave tacit support to private sector employers who took on the unions. It is not difficult to argue that the confrontations with the unions that the Government initiated or supported during the 1980s and early 1990s had a significant 'demonstration' impact on the conduct of unionized labour, collective bargaining and British industrial relations in general (Brown 1993). By the end of the 1980s, there was a sense that industrial relations had effectively been 'depoliticized' (Farnham and Pimlott 1990).

However, the effect of the new regulatory regime on union membership and workplace recognition has been disputed by others (Batstone 1988; Beaumont 1990; Disney 1990; Deakin 1992, 1988), on the grounds that the precise impact of the legislation is difficult, if not impossible, to quantify or disentangle from the effects of economic and other changes. Much of the 'evidence' is anectdotal. Moreover, as Crouch (1986), McBride (1986) and Gamble (1988) have argued, the Conservative onslaught would not have been possible without the discipline of the early 1980s recession and the underlying structural changes in the economy more generally. Some go further and argue that, instead of leading to the emasculation or elimination of the unions (Kessler and Bayliss 1992), some parts of the new legislation (such as those measures aimed at democratizing the unions through membership ballots) may well strengthen the commitment of rank and file members to their unions (Smith *et al.* 1993; Milner 1994).

But if it has proved difficult to gauge the precise impact of the new regulatory environment on the unions nationally, assessing its effect on the unions in the regions is even more problematic. While the new laws are in principle all-embracing, it is ultimately individual employers who dictate the utilization and implementation of legislation in the workplace. Although there have certainly been some well-publicized examples of 'strong' management exploiting legislation to the full in conflicts with trade unions (such as Timex's bitter conflict with the engineering union AEEU at its factory in Dundee), there is considerable diversity of response to the changes in the legal environment, and no guarantee about how individual employers will use or enforce the latest changes in employment law. Responses will be expected to vary from employer to employer in ways that will reflect the specific circumstances and policies of individual firms and establishments. However, those circumstances and the attitudes adopted by individual employers may also be shaped and influenced by the characteristics of the local labour market in which the firm or establishment is located, including the legacy of local historically rooted workplace experiences, cultures and traditions, of the sort we have already alluded to (in Chapters One, Two and Three). Yet little, if anything, is known about whether and in what ways the responses of employers and workers to the new regulatory regime governing employment relations have actually varied across space.

What is clear, however, is that there has been a strong underlying geographical tone to the Conservative governments' whole approach to reforming the unions. Not only have they seen them as a major cause of national economic decline, they have also blamed them specifically for the economic plight of the country's depressed regions (such as Merseyside, the North East and Clydeside). In particular, the powerful unions in these areas are charged with resisting industrial modernization, hindering productivity growth and above all pushing local wages above their 'market-clearing levels', thereby pricing their members in these areas out of work and into unemployment.[16] One of the stated aims of the Conservatives' general employment laws was to help reduce the power of the unions in such areas and help 'free up' local labour markets as a consequence (see, for example, HM Government 1983). More recently, the Government has also begun to push for locally determined pay negotiation in place of national collective agreements in the public sector (for example in the health service), thereby geographically fragmenting the bargaining power of public sector unions.[17] Other Government attacks on the unions have been even more spatially targeted, as in the banning of unions at its Communications Headquarters (GCHQ) at Cheltenham, its support of News International in the dispute with the printing unions at Wapping, London, and its strategy of geographically policing and 'playing-off' the different coalfields in the National Union of Mineworkers' strike in 1984–85. Arguably, even one of the underlying aims of the Conservative Government's 'regional policy' of overtly courting overseas investment, especially of Japanese multinationals, to locate in the older industrial regions of the country has been to inject into these areas of traditional unionism the more 'flexible' industrial and employment relations practices that tend to characterize foreign firms. In these different ways, either implicitly or explicitly, the Conservative governments have used geography in their quest to 'tame' the unions and to 'localize' industrial action by workers (see Chapter Five).

How far and in what ways the new legislation is reshaping the geography of trade unionism more generally is difficult to judge. The introduction of the new *national* regulatory framework governing trade unions has in effect *fragmented* the organizational and bargaining spaces of the unions, making it more difficult for unionized workers to forge coalitions across space in their attempt to pursue claims or secure improvements in any particular place. Much of the continuing debate

---

16 These views have been influenced by studies such as those by Minford (1985, 1991) one of the leading exponents of right-wing new classical economics, who has consistently maintained that the primary cause of the high unemployment in Britain's depressed regions is the excessive wage bargaining and workplace power of the unions in those areas. He has been one of the main advocates for tougher controls on the unions and for measures to de-institutionalize regional labour markets.

17 The Conservatives' emasculation and eventual abolition of the Wages Councils, which covered several million low-paid workers, and their strong opposition to the idea of a minimum wage, are also indicative of its determination to 'derigidify' the labour market.

about the impact of the new legislative framework has centred on two issues: the extent to which it has all but extinguished strikes and industrial stoppages within British economic life; and the extent to which it has allowed firms to restructure their systems of labour regulation and utilization, and push through new management systems and 'new industrial relations' (Bassett 1986; Millward 1994) in which workforce 'flexibility', single-union arrangements and non-unionism are key features. This move to strike-free 'new industrial relations' (NIR) represents a particular threat to traditional unionism, and especially to the geographical heartlands where traditional unionism has been most entrenched. In the Government's view it was precisely in these heartlands that the power of organized labour needed to be reduced and more flexible workplace relations introduced. We return to the issue of the effect of the new legislation on the use and success of strike action by workers in the next chapter. Here we focus on the impact of the new industrial relations on union organization and recognition with the workplace.

THE 'NEW INDUSTRIAL RELATIONS':
LABOUR FLEXIBILITY, SINGLE UNION DEALS
AND THE GROWTH OF NON-UNIONISM IN THE REGIONS

The pursuit of increased 'flexibility' is seen by many to be at the heart of these new industrial relations. The problem, however, is that the term is used both to describe what *is* happening and what some commentators believe *ought* to be happening in the labour market. Many theorists, especially geographers, view the contemporary drive towards flexibility as the new defining hallmark of economic development, a response to the intense competition, market volatility and rapid technological change that increasingly characterise the economy (see, for example, Piore and Sabel 1984; Harvey 1989; Murray 1989; Boyer 1988; Amin 1994). The general impression given by this literature is that new strategies of workplace flexibility – of production, and of labour utilization and regulation – have already spread across wide sections of manufacturing and services. Others, however, contest this view, and are doubtful of both the actual extent of and the alleged gains associated with the 'new' flexibility (see, for example, Batstone 1988; Elger 1991; Gilbert *et al.* 1992; McInnes 1987; Pollert 1991; Rubery and Wilkinson 1994).[18] While the precise contours and implications of this new 'flexible

---

18 The notion of flexibility has become the central leitmotiv of all of the main theoretical and political accounts of the contemporary restructuring process, whether right-wing or left-wing in orientation. Thus the concept occupies a central position in New Right pro-market political economy at one extreme, and in the neo-Marxist regulationist accounts of flexible specialization and post-Fordism at the other. As Pollert (1988) remarks, the fact that it has been interpreted in such diverse ways, in some cases as a means of securing a much-needed reassertion of managerial control over the production process, in other cases as a means for empowering labour and 'democratizing' economic development, demonstrates the amorphous and confused nature of the concept.

capitalism' continue to be debated, the flexibility of labour has nevertheless been a persistent focus. Indeed, many industrial relations commentators – and many unions themselves – see labour flexibility as a major challenge to unionized workers and as an important factor contributing to the decline of the unions.

Since the claims for the emergence of the 'flexible' firm, with its 'core-periphery' labour force, first appeared in the mid 1980s (Atkinson 1985; Atkinson and Gregory 1986; and Atkinson and Meager 1986), the issue of workforce flexibility has assumed a central and contentious position in labour studies (see Pollert 1991). At one level it is argued that firms are increasingly seeking to improve the *task flexibility* of their workers by reorganizing the labour process away from linear (Taylorist-type) systems involving single-skilled or specialized workers, typically 'machine-paced', towards work configurations requiring small cores of employees who are multi-skilled, adaptable, largely 'self-pacing', often divided into work 'teams' or 'cells', and incorporated into new managerial 'quality circle' and 'inventory control' strategies. Typically, this shift is seen as leading to higher wages and greater autonomy, enrichment and security of employment for such core workers. At the same time, it is argued, many firms are also seeking to increase the *numerical flexibility* of their labour inputs, particularly through the use of more 'peripheral' workers to carry out the less-skilled, usually lower-paid and more cyclically-variable jobs. The growth in part-time employment and temporary work is seen as direct evidence for this move to increase numerical flexibility. Between 1978 and 1994, whilst full-time employment in Britain fell from 17.9 million to 15.0 million, part-time employment increased from 4.4 million to 5.9 million (Table 4.5). Watson (1994) estimates that the proportion of men in employment who are part of the 'flexible workforce' rose from 18 per cent in 1981 to 27 per cent in 1993, while almost half of women employees now work in part-time jobs. For these peripheral workers, 'flexibility' often means less secure employment, indirect employment contracts, reduced employment rights and low wages. Other forms of 'work organization flexibility' that are on the increase include 'flexibility in the place of work' (for example homeworking and teleworking) and 'working time flexibility' (various forms of 'flexitime' in hours and shifts worked). Alongside these developments, firms are pushing for greater *wage cost flexibility*. The shift from full-time to part-time workers, the use of various 'distancing' and 'externalization' strategies to contract out certain work tasks, and attempts to decouple local wages from the national 'going rate' in favour of company bargaining or even individual negotiation; these and other employer policies are all intended to help minimize wage costs and to link wages much more closely to worker performance.

There are two basic questions that complicate any attempt to assess the impact of this new workforce flexibility on the unions, and on regional unionism in particular. The first concerns how far and in what ways the new flexibility has actually changed employment and working conditions in the regions; the second concerns what specific effects these changes have had on the unions. While anectdotal examples of new flexible employment relations exist, there are no systematic accounts of the incidence of explicit flexible labour utilization strategies across the regions of the country. Charting the general geographical incidence of functional (task) flexibility is itself difficult in general terms since empirically it does not translate easily or directly into identifiable changes in readily available employment indices. Measuring the scale of numerical flexibility would, perhaps, seem easier, given that the growth of part-time and self-employment is widely viewed as symbolic of this aspect of work reorganization. However, even here definitional caution is needed; for example part-time workers cannot be assumed automatically to belong to the 'peripheral' flexible workforce, since in many companies a large proportion of employees work part-time and it could be argued that in those circumstances they fc .1 part of that firm's 'core' labour force. In fact, as several critics have pointed out, flexible labour utilization strategies do not appear to be as widespead or formally developed as their protagonists imply (in addition to Batstone, McInnes and Pollert referred to above, see also Hakim 1990; Elger 1991; Hunter and McInnes 1991; McGregor and Sproull 1991). Examples of the fully 'flexible firm' are as yet few in number; indeed, as Hakim (1990) concedes, flexible labour utilization represents as much an ideal type as an accurate description of a general (even if uneven) trend.

Nevertheless, while the flexible workforce model is an exaggeration, and the changes occurring in the deployment of labour and employment relations are far more piecemeal than systematic, there can be little doubt that many of those changes are being driven by a rhetoric and 'politics' of flexibility, and that this politics has major potential implications for the unions. Multi-skilling, team-working, individually-negotiated performance-related pay and other aspects of functional flexibility reduce the traditional rationale and relevance of unions, and weaken the basis for collective worker identities and conventional systems of industrial relations. As we have already noted historically, part-time, temporary and self-employed workers have not historically been fertile groups for union recruitment. The not unreasonable inference is that the new politics of flexibility constitutes a significant structural challenge to established forms of workplace trade unionism.

Much of the thrust towards the 'new flexibility' is alleged to be associated with the spread of the so-called 'Japanese model' of work organization and employment relations first introduced into Britain by the Toshiba Consumer Products factory set up in Plymouth in 1981. The working practices and industrial relations policies introduced there attracted wide publicity and a number of them were adopted, either as a package or piecemeal, elsewhere, not only by other Japanese inward investments but also by British companies, for example Sanyo, NEK, AB Electronics, AVX, Hitachi, Inmos, Irlandus, Lucas, Nissan, Sharp, Shotton Paper, Toyota, Xidex (see Bassett 1986; Rico 1987; Trevor 1988). The basic element of this 'new industrial relations' (NIR) or 'new style agreement' (NSA) model is the comprehensive 'single union no-strike deal' which incorporates, *inter alia*, sole bargaining rights for a single union in the workplace, a 'no strike' agreement with binding 'final offer' arbitration, 'single status' conditions of employment, a broadly-based forum of consultation and employee participation, complete freedom on the part of management to organize the work process, and full labour flexibility (see Millward 1994, p.2). To their supporters, the single union deal 'conjures up an image of modern and progressive industrial relations, allowing for responsible trade unionism within an institutional framework conducive to efficiency and profitability' (Lewis 1990). But such arrangements have aroused considerable controversy amongst the trade union movement, particularly when their introduction involves competition between different unions for the exclusive representation rights in a new site. Some unions, such as the former electricians' union EETPU (now merged with the former AEU into the AEEU), have been much more disposed towards and willing to compete for exclusive union representation than others, which instead have branded the arrangements as 'sweet-heart deals' to 'subordinate the workforce and weaken the unions – strike-free as a transitional stage to union-free' (Lewis 1990).

The Japanese model of the 'new industrial relations' has in turn attracted interest by employers in 'human resource management' (HRM), the series of techniques for managing workplace employment relations in a more consultative and goal-orientated style. In ideal-typical terms HRM includes managerial policies designed to promote employee commitment to the firm's goals and employee flexibility in terms of the work performed. There is a general emphasis on quality in both processes and outputs, integration of the firm's personnel ('human resource') policies with its strategic business planning, regular communication and consultation between management and employees, 'single-status' employment (treating employees in unified harmonized ways), the use of individual wage-employment contracts, and new methods of employee financial participation, including various profit- and share-based schemes. Single status employment has been the most prominent of HRM-type policies. According to some reports it has been particularly associated with newly established Japanese manufacturing plants (Oliver and Wilkinson 1988), and has featured in most of the new 'single union deals' as another way of promoting employee commitment and flexibility (Industrial Relations Services 1993). The intention behind HRM is to manage the work process without the need for unions and old-style forms of collective communication and negotiation. It is basically a strategy for avoiding or attenuating union workplace involvement by co-opting employees more directly and individually into the firm's business goals and performance through various worker benefits and consultative devices.

It is important, however, to distinguish these 'new' single-union systems of industrial relations from the 'old' form of single unionism that has, in fact, long been the dominant form of workplace unionism in British industry and private services. As Millward (1994) has shown, some 61 per cent of unionized establishments in private services, and 50 per cent of those in manufacturing are single-union rather than multi-union. Furthermore, single unionism is highest amongst establishments created in the 1970s, that is prior to the 'new' Japanese-style industrial relations of the 1980s and 1990s.[19] The significance of the new model is its association with Japanese-style human resource management (HRM) policies and flexible production methods. However, although given considerable publicity, the real extent of 'Japanese-style' single union deals (incorporating some or all of the elements listed above) is hard to judge. Recent estimates suggest that there are only about 200 organizations with such single-union deals (Industrial Relations Services 1993b).[20] Nevertheless, it has been argued that:

> The significance of the industrial relations procedures associated with single-union deals is far greater than the number of companies and employees covered would suggest. Their importance is symbolic: arguably, they provide a classic illustration of the style of industrial relations that management would *ideally* like to adopt…companies on existing 'brownfield' sites with more traditional industrial relations machinery may embrace the employment precedents set on single-union sites. We may thus be looking at the shape of the industrial relations agenda of the 1990s. (Industrial Relations Services 1993, p.4)

Unfortunately, there have been hardly any studies of the geography of the 'new industrial relations' (NIR) or 'new style agreements' (NSA), nor even of new flexible work practices. In their original work on the 'flexible firm' Atkinson and his colleagues ignored the question of whether and why there might be spatial variations in the extent of flexibility. Yet the two 'conjunctural' factors they cite as determining the emergence of flexible employment practices, namely unemployment and the pre-existing degree of trade union organization, do indeed vary significantly from one area of the country to another.[21] The question is whether and in what ways corporate strategies on workforce flexibility and their imple-

---

19 Single-union rather than multi-union membership is much more common in smaller and younger establishments, head offices, and those unionized workplaces with a high proportion of part-time employees (see Millward 1994).

20 Also, how 'new' (and 'old') single-union arrangements relate to the provisions of the recent Trade Union Reform and Employment Rights Act (1993) is a topical issue. The Act includes measures to give individual employees greater freedom to join the union of their choice while allowing unions to refuse membership to those who have no commonality of interest with their existing members, for example on the basis of their occupations or geographical location. The new legislation could thus work against single union agreements by facilitating the recruitment of employees by rival unions which might then claim recognition from employers with such agreements. It might also encourage a proliferation of unrecognized unions within some workplaces (Millward 1994).

21 The generic causes are technological change, greater competitive pressure, and greater market volatility and uncertainty. It should be noted that Atkinson's research was based on large firms – small firms were assumed by their very nature to be flexible. Although, as we have seen, the firm size structure of employment has become more even across the British regions, differences still exist, so this also introduces a potential geographical dimension into the flexibility issue.

mentation are conditioned by such locally varying circumstances. At a superficial level, it might be argued that employers in less unionized localities would be more able to push through new employment and industrial relations practices than their counterparts in more unionized local labour markets. Yet the latter are precisely the areas where, some commentators argue, entrenched union traditions and rigid working practices need to be replaced by more flexible arrangements if the industries there are to survive in today's intensely competitive and global market place. Little is known, however, about the empirical extent of such regional and local variations in the adoption of flexible employment strategies.

What few geographically orientated case studies exist have produced contrasting results. Jones and Rose (1986) studied six innovative southern factories from a spread of industrial sectors. They found clear evidence that the specific contingencies of local management and workplace bargaining generated a complex and uneven pattern of workplace reorganization, and that local negotiation played a significant role in shaping the scale and nature of the new workplace practices introduced (though those changes were much less radical than the flexibility literature might suggest). More recently, Penn (1992) has explored the differences in flexible employment practices between more than 900 establishments in six local labour markets with quite different unemployment and labour market conditions, namely Aberdeen, Coventry, Kirkaldy, Northampton, Rochdale and Swindon. Although he found that the extent of flexible employment utilization and flexible management and employment relations practices differed noticeably between localities, these differences were in large part explicable in term of differences in the industrial mix of the localities. When industrial composition effects were removed, there were few independent locality effects in relation to changing patterns of 'flexible' employment. His study thus suggests that, contrary to Atkinson's flexible firm model, local conjunctural factors have little if any role in determining the incidence of new flexible workplace arrangements.

Our own questionnaire survey results from a (random) sample of 455 private sector establishments in the 'north west' of the country (Lancashire and Greater Manchester) and in the 'south east' (Hertfordshire, Bedfordshire and Cambridgeshire) tend to support Penn's findings (see Appendix for details of our survey). We examined both unionized and non-unionized workplaces in each region with a view to determining the incidence of various 'new style' industrial relations practices. Responses to questions about employment relations have to be treated with some caution, since the terms used are open to interpretation and different employers themselves interpret their employment relations practices in different ways. Nevertheless, the results are of some interest (Table 4.11). In line with our previous analyses, union membership density in our sample establishments was considerably higher in the north-western ones (52%) than in the south-eastern (25%). However, fixed-term contracts, performance-related pay and profit-sharing schemes appear to be as common in unionized workplaces as in non-unionized ones in both areas. Similarly, there are no consistent differences between the two

Table 4.11: 'New style' industrial relations: two regions compared

	South east (% of workplaces)		North west (% of workplaces)	
	Non-union	Union	Non-union	Union
Fixed term contracts	14	11	15	23
Performance related pay	44	37	47	50
Profit sharing	23	25	13	22
New redundancy procedures	3	35	3	26
Reduced demarcation	12	56	19	52
Joint consultative committee	3	25	0	18
Single union agreement	–	9	–	14
Single table bargaining	–	12	–	20
Reduced negotiation	–	7	–	8
Withdrawal of recognition	3	5	6	7
No strike deal	–	4	–	1
Number of establishments	147	57	78	90
(% of regional total)	72	28	46	54
Union density (%)	–	25	–	52

Source: Authors' own survey (see Appendix).

Notes: 1. South East refers to the counties of Hertfordshire, Bedfordshire and Cambridgeshire; North West to Lancashire and Greater Manchester.

2. Estabishments classified as 'union' and 'non-union' according to whether management recognizes unions.

3. The percentages are proportions of the respective establishments that provided usable responses to these questions (372 out of 455). The questions were not answered by 40 workplaces in the South East and 43 in the North West.

4. Survey carried out between late 1992 and early 1993.

regions with respect to the relative incidence of these practices nor, within unionized workplaces, of the extent of reduced job demarcation, joint consultative committees, reduced redundancy rights, single union agreements, single table bargaining and reduced negotiation procedures. What differences do exist all but disappear when differences in the sectoral mix of workplaces between the two areas are taken into account.[22] In both regions, the extent of reduced job demarcation, new redundancy procedures and joint consultative committees is noticeably higher in unionized than in non-unionized workplaces. This is as expected since, all other things being equal, traditional skill divisions, rigid redundancy arrangements (such as last in–first out), and collective representation

22 The main difference between the two regions being a higher proportion of sample workplaces in 'other manufacturing' in the north-western group, and a higher proportion in 'other services' in the south-eastern sample.

will have been more widespread in unionized workplaces that in non-unionized ones, and hence more a focus of managerial reform (see also Millward 1994; TUC 1994).

It is perhaps with respect to the spread of new single-union deals more specifically that the role of geography is more evident. Typically, new single-union deals are viewed as a 'greenfield' phenomenon, whereby the creation or relocation of a firm in a less industrialized, usually less urbanized and less unionized environment, provides management with 'what is essentially a *tabula rasa*, an opportunity to start afresh, freed from the constraints of tradition and custom' (Guest and Rosenthal 1992). The fact that many greenfield developments have involved Japanese plants and companies, in which single-union deals and flexible working practices are supposedly central, has given such developments particular symbolic significance. Although the influx of Japanese industrial plants began in the early 1970s, including Sony's television plant in South Wales, it was during the 1980s that Japanese inward investment changed from a trickle to a rush and began to have a more significant impact on the industrial landscape. In 1983 only about 3000 workers were directly employed by Japanese industrial establishments; by 1993 this had grown to more than 70,000. Japanese plants are now spread across the country, from Scotland to the South West. New towns like Milton Keynes, Telford, Washington and Livingston, have been particularly successful in attracting new investors. Most discussions of the role of such plants as the carriers of new industrial relations have focused on Japanese electronics plants and especially Japanese car factories (Nissan at Sunderland in the North East, Honda at Swindon, Wiltshire, and Toyota at Burnaston in Derbyshire).

The case of Nissan, in particular, has attracted considerable publicity and academic attention, not least because of its 'greenfield' location within what is otherwise a 'brownfield' region (the North East) with a long industrial history of extensive trade unionism and traditional working practices. If new Japanese-style industrial relations could be implanted successfully by a major employer in this sort of area, it was argued, then they could have a wider 'demonstration effect' on other employers throughout the region. There have been several celebratory accounts of the Nissan model that point to the success of the flexible working practices, employee commitment, high productivity and harmonious industrial relations achieved by Nissan at their Sunderland site. However, other, more critical analyses highlight the way in which the single-union deal there has effectively marginalized trade unionism in the workplace – only about a third of the workforce have joined the union – and the fact that the Nissan model has also meant labour de-skilling, work intensification, and the enhancement of employer power and control (see Garrahan and Stewart 1989, 1992). Such writers see the 'Japanization' of workplace organization and industrial relations as undermining trade unionism and are far less sanguine that the alleged positive benefits of the new model compensate for this erosion.

Recall that Massey and Painter (1989) assign key importance to new greenfield sites as a factor reshaping the trade union map, particularly the use of such sites by management as a strategy for avoiding or escaping strong unionism in established brownfield locations. But it is important not to exaggerate the scale or impact of the greenfield phenomenon. For one thing, outside one or two highly publicized cases (especially the motor manufacturers Rover, Ford, and Vauxhall)[23], examples of the 'Japanization' of employment and industrial relations practices within British industrial plants are markedly uneven and piecemeal (Grant 1994). There is certainly evidence that, especially since 1990, the motor manufacturers are exerting a signficant influence on working practices in their component suppliers. The shift to 'lean production' in the automotive manufacturers has in turn compelled many of the component suppliers to adopt similar techniques themselves. Thus 70 per cent of the component suppliers to the automotive industry surveyed by Industrial Relations Services (1995b) claim to have adopted more flexible work practices. To the extent that the component suppliers are localized around the car manufacturing plants, the latter may well be having a demonstration effect on production methods and working practices in their regions. Yet these changes to more flexible Japanese-style working practices do not appear, thus far at least, to have mapped into a commensurate shift to new employment relations strategies. Less than 50 per cent of the component suppliers reported having single union status (Industrial Relations Services 1995b).

In any case, single-union greenfield developments do not necessarily undermine local trade unionism. In its survey of the UK electronics industry in the early 1990s, Industrial Relations Services (1995) found union densities in single-union establishments varied widely, but still averaged 75 per cent overall. Furthermore, there appeared to be no significant difference between Japanese and British plants. The interesting question, then, is why these new plants have chosen to recognize unions at all, when they could legally have opted not to. Although various reasons were invoked to explain why management opted for a single-union agreement rather than for non-recognition (a single-union deal at least removes the problems associated with multi-unionism; it reduces sectional interests amongst the workers; and it assists in developing single-status employment conditions) there was an underlying realization that:

> ...attempting to adopt a non-union approach would lead to strong union pressure and that ultimately there was a strong likelihood that union recognition might have to be conceded – to one or more unions – on terms less favourable to management than would have been achieved by securing a single union agreement at an early stage. *This was particularly the case for those*

---

23 The 'New Deal' introduced by the Rover Group in 1992 is one such example of 'Japanese-style' employee relations and production arrangements spilling over into 'British' car manufacturers. Interestingly, the Rover agreement still left the old trade union structure for recognition, representation and negotiation in place.

companies establishing new operations in historically strong unionised areas and where it was expected that many prospective employees would be 'union-orientated'. (Industrial Relations Services 1995, p.7, emphasis added)

Geography it would seem has also been important. For those establishments that have located on greenfield sites in brownfield regions, local labourist traditions and workplace cultures have continued to shape even the new industrial relations. As the case of Nissan in the North East and the Japanese firms in South Wales indicate, new greenfield industrial developments by foreign firms in old brownfield regions have typically sought not to avoid unionized labour, but rather to resist *multi-unionism.* Morgan and Sayer (1988), for example, show how South Wales's long tradition of unionization has been carried over, even if under different conditions, into the new, largely foreign-owned electronics industry in the area (see also Rutherford 1991; Wilkinson *et al.* 1993). Single-union deals in these new sites have at least meant new union members for the successful unions involved. And workers in Japanese electronics plants with new style agreements do not appear to relinquish their traditional union beliefs and priorities, although this can give rise to disappointment – and membership loss – if workers feel the union is unable to fulfil those expectations (Grant 1994).

Nevertheless, according to many observers, it is the increasing incidence of explicit policies of non-recognition of unions in the workplace that represents the most serious structural challenge to the unions. There have always been workplaces in which unions are not recognized by management; but since 1980 the extent of non-recognition has increased substantially: recall that nationally between 1980 and 1990 the proportion of manual employees in workplaces recognizing unions fell from 84 per cent to 57 per cent, and the corresponding proportion of non-manual employees from 61 per cent to 41 per cent. There are three possible reasons for this decline: the closure of large workplaces in which recognition rates are high; active de-recognition of existing unionized workplaces; and the establishment of non-union firms. According to Millward (1994) workplace closures were an important factor behind the fall in recognition between 1980–84, a period dominated by economic recession, but were unimportant in the 1984–90 period when far more closures were of small workplaces where union recognition rates are lower. Millward also estimates that active de-recognition within already unionized firms accounted for a notable but still minor proportion of the growth in non-recognition (for example about one fifth of the WIRS panel workplaces that recognized unions in 1984 had de-recognized them by 1990). The primary factor behind the growth in non-unionism, he argues, has been the opening of new establishments in which non-recognition rates have been higher than in new establishments opened in the past. He calculates that only a third of workplaces that opened after 1984 have opted to recognize unions and this marks a major transition from previous experience:

In 1980 the incidence of recognition amongst establishments less than 10 years old was 45 per cent. In 1990 the corresponding figure was 24%. The 1990 figures thus show a much lower rate of new recognition in the 1980s than must have occurred in earlier decades...the drop in the rate of recognition was particularly marked within manufacturing...union recognition was the norm among manufacturing plants created in the 1970s, whereas plants created in the 1980s were no more likely to recogise unions than service sector establishments, whose rate of recognition has always been much lower. (Millward 1994, p.28)

Millward goes on to explain this drop in new recognition in terms of the shifting industrial relations climate, especially the removal of state support for recognition in 1980 and the decline in presumption by the state and employers in favour of collective bargaining. Legally and ideologically, the terrain has moved away from the unions towards management, and this is reflected in the falling incidence of union recognition agreements (see also Disney, Gosling and Machin 1993). However, the geographical aspects of non-recognition have thus far not been examined, and it is this that we want to explore here.

It is significant that, according to the WIRS data, of the new workplaces that have opted for recognition since 1984, over 80 per cent are branches of larger firms where the decision to recognize a union frequently rests with non-local managers. Such decisions have been made either through choice or pressure in order to standardize practices across the organization, and in the majority of cases have been made at head office. Thus despite recent moves to decentralize industrial relations practices, particularly with regard to pay bargaining, in multi-site companies the actual decisions about union recognition have tended to remain centralized. In this sense geography might be assumed to be less significant for recognition purposes than is the company policy of the firms themselves. Yet the 1990 WIRS shows that of the stand-alone establishments that have also opened since 1984 almost a third have likewise opted for recognition, unencumbered by any pre-existing corporate policy (Millward 1994, p.27). Despite the shift in industrial relations climate, a considerable minority of newer companies are still recognizing trade unions, and it is here that the neglected effects of geographical location might be most important. In our analysis of the WIRS data, we have found major differences in union recognition rates in newer firms across the British regions.

Table 4.12 shows the percentage of employees in each region who are employed in private sector establishments which recognize unions, and in the younger workplaces (less than 10 years old), there is a 38 percentage point difference between the most strongly organized region, Wales, with a recognition rate of 56 per cent, and the least organized, London, with a rate of 18 per cent. This variation is virtually the same when we look at the incidence of newer workplaces that have opted for union recognition (Table 4.13). In both cases, employees and workplaces, new recognition rates in the northern and industrial

**Table 4.12: Union recognition and age of establishment
in the regions, by per cent of employees, 1990**

	Per cent of employees in recognized workplaces by age of establishment		
	0–10 yrs	*11–20 yrs*	*Over 20 yrs*
London	18	20	55
Outer South East	21	38	62
East Anglia	21	48	57
South West	35	26	68
East Midlands	44	56	68
West Midlands	23	47	84
Yorks/Humberside	39	57	71
North West	46	52	74
North	43	67	73
Wales	56	70	67
Scotland	39	57	71
Great Britain	**31**	**47**	**68**

Source: Authors' analysis of WIRS 1990.

**Table 4.13: Union recognition and age of establishment
in the regions, by per cent of workplaces, 1990**

	Per cent of employees in recognized workplaces by age of establishment		
	0–10 yrs	*11–20 yrs*	*Over 20 yrs*
London	17	20	51
Outer South East	12	30	56
East Anglia	14	15	37
South West	22	18	56
East Midlands	22	45	60
West Midlands	15	56	63
Yorks/Humberside	30	37	56
North West	30	37	49
North	24	31	57
Wales	49	51	23
Scotland	32	48	49
Great Britain	**22**	**34**	**53**

Source: Authors' analysis of WIRS 1990.

areas of Britain are more than twice those in the south and east. The effect of the changing national industrial relations climate upon union recognition would thus seem to be mediated by location, despite the obvious break between older and younger establishments at a national level. It would appear that even amongst the newer workplaces union recognition is still much more likely in traditionally more strongly organized areas, such as Wales, Scotland and the North, than it is in the weakly unionized regions in the south of the country. This might be due to the expectations of the workers or the accepted practices of managers, or some combination of both.[24] Gaining new recognition often involves union members and activists in the workplace recruiting and organizing their fellow workers prior to making a request for negotiating rights. Such activity depends upon previous knowledge of the union movement and support from other members and officials. It is likely, therefore, to be easier in regions where union organization is already more deeply embedded in cultural practices.

The persistence of regional practices is neither inevitable nor permanent, however: local socialized norms are not immutable, and if subjected to sufficiently strong social, economic or political shifts may change substantially. The West Midlands illustrates this. The recognition rate in this region has declined very dramatically over recent decades. Some 84 per cent of employees who work in establishments that have been operating for more than 20 years have union recognition agreements compared to only 23 per cent of those in establishments formed in the 1980s. Unionization in those firms that are less than ten years old has fallen below the national average in a region that was always seen as a stronghold of manufacturing trade unionism. This represents a major decline for the unions in a traditional area of strength and demonstrates that the reproduction of behaviour in respect of trade unionism in the workplace is by no means automatic or inevitable. The local reproduction of institutionalized practices depends on active social agency and the presence of key actors, but even these may not succeed in prevailing against new economic and political imperatives.

Given these regional differences in union recognition amongst new workplaces, it is clear that the geography of new firm formation is now a crucial factor influencing the current strength and future prospects of trade unionism. New firms setting up in the northern regons are much more likely to recognize unions than those setting up in the south. At the same time, it is in the south and east of the country that new firm formation has been concentrated (Keeble 1992; Mason 1992). The 1980s saw a major wave of new firm formation, with 1.5 million new business registrations and a net increase in the stock of businesses of nearly a third of a million between 1984–90. The South East region alone accounted for almost 50 per cent of this net increase (Table 4.14), compared to around 3 per cent in Wales and the Northern region. Together, the four southern regions (South East,

---

24 Shift-share analysis reveals that these differences do not appear to be due to regional variations in industrial composition.

Table 4.14: New business registrations, by region, 1984–1990

	Registrations	Deregistrations	Net change	Per cent share
South East	601,291	448,304	152,987	48.5
East Anglia	55,380	42,364	13,016	4.1
South West	135,030	103,245	31,785	10.1
East Midlands	97,406	76,989	20,417	6.5
West Midlands	122,918	99,422	23,496	7.5
Yorks/Humberside	108,244	90,843	17,401	5.5
North West	142,827	123,601	19,226	6.1
North	52,939	44,450	8489	2.7
Wales	63,320	52,439	10,881	3.4
Scotland	96,350	78,692	17,658	5.6
Great Britain	**1,502,000**	**1,181,000**	**315,356**	**100.0**

Source: Small Business Research Trust (1993).

East Anglia, South West and East Midlands) generated nearly 70 per cent of net new business registrations over this period. These regional disparities in new firm formation and the propensity of new firms to recognize unions go some way to explaining the widening north/south gap in recognition found in the previous chapter. The task of retaining, let alone increasing, membership and workplace organization in the southern part of Britain would thus seem on the face of it to be particularly challenging for the unions.

THE ROLE OF REGIONAL TRADITIONS

As the analyses in this chapter have revealed, the geography of employment recomposition has had only a limited impact on the unions' fortunes in particular regions. In fact there appears to be a substantial degree of stability in the regional pattern of trade unionism despite the marked industrial and labour market restructuring of recent years. Even allowing for industrial, establishment size, and other forms of employment recomposition and structural convergence across the regions, the configuration of regional unionization differentials has shown a surprizing degree of persistence. We are led to conclude, therefore, that this persistence is in large part the product of *geographically based traditions and cultures* (what Beaumont and Harris (1988b) label as local 'externalities') which, although established in the past, still continue to underpin *spatial subsystems* of trade unionism and industrial relations.The sharp differences in new recognition as between the northern and southern regions of the country support this view.

The argument here is that the union and industrial relations traditions of key groups of workers, firms and industries in a region are not self-contained, but rather generate spillovers to other workers, firms and industries in the region through the course of time. Although the specific mechanisms involved are complex and are themselves influenced by the process and path of local economic development, the result is that the attitudes, expectations and behaviour of employees and employers in other industries in the region are influenced by the historical traditions and contemporary proximity of these locally dominant industries and their workforces. Hence the whole employment structure in the region becomes characterized by the forms of industrial relations systems, traditions and conventions found in the (once) leading or dominant sectors(s), thus producing high (or low) levels of union density, recognition, collective bargaining, shop steward representation, industrial militancy and community activity relative to the average levels found in these other industries nationally.

Once this regional externality effect begins to develop, it becomes self-reproducing though a process of local institutionalization and socialization, thereby generating a regionally embedded set of industrial relations traditions and cultures (disposed either towards, or against, trade unionism), which are perpetuated over time, and which may survive long after the original industrial developments and structures around which they evolved have disappeared. It is in this sense that we may argue that there is 'path dependency' or 'collective memory' in unionization and industrial relations practices in the regions. By 'path dependence' we mean a situation in which, historically, a socialized institutional ensemble of knowledge, customs, conventions, ideologies and behavioural norms alters the incentives of actors and causes organizations to become dependent on, and to operate in ways that tend to reproduce, that ensemble (see North 1990). Such local institutional ensembles, or contextual 'settings of interaction' (Giddens 1984), do not, of course, mechanically or rigidly determine worker and employer behaviour, but rather structure the material and cultural 'resources' that enable or constrain individual and collective action. Local 'traditions' of unionism (and anti-unionism) are not, therefore, unchangeable: they are continuously remade. But how they are remade is likely to be strongly influenced by the form and content of existing traditions. The differential regional response and resilience of trade unionism to the pressures of geographically uneven restructuring and governmental employment policies partly reflects these region-specific socio-cultural effects. Our previous research on the main British engineering union, the AEEU, confims the existence and significance of such contrasting regional traditions and institutionalized cultures (Martin, Sunley and Wills 1994a, 1994c), and we explore them further in Chapters Five and Six below.

In the light of our findings we would argue that the main reason the long-standing spatial pattern of unionization, itself the historical product of differential regional economic development and associated region-specific socialization and institutionalization, has so far survived the contemporary contraction of the union movement to the extent that it has is not simply the persistence of inter-regional differences in employment structure but the relative resilience of institutionalized regional workplace cultures, traditions and expectations. Penn and Scattergood (1990), for example, attribute much of the resilience of trade unionism in the northern town of Rochdale during the 1980s to the strength of local traditions:

> If there is a crisis within local trade unionism, it is not characterised by significant membership loss, increasing inter-union conflicts nor systematic de-unionisation. Rather it is the conservativism and traditionalism inherent within the institutional structures that have 'held the line' during the 1980s'. (p.48)

But while this conservatism and traditionalism may have been a strength, it is arguably also a weakness. It may have restrained the loss of membership in well-organized areas but, at the same time, it may have intensified the difficulties of organizing new ones, especially in the southern regions of the country, where the unions desperately need to transform local 'negative' traditions into positive ones. And even in their regions of relative strength, the unions may not be able to rely on their historical 'structural conservatism' (Mahnkopf 1992) indefinitely.[25]

---

25 In discussing the options for unions on workplace change, Mahnkopf (1992) uses the term 'structural conservatism' to refer to the form of union strategy that attempts to defend 'Fordist achievements' such as existing technical and social divisions of labour and traditional shopfloor rights, typified by the stance of British unions in the 1980s. He contrasts this response to that of 'active modernization', involving either 'price-orientated' adaptability, for example keeping wage settlements below the rate of productivity growth in different sectors and regions, exemplified by US unions; or 'skill-orientated modernization', which focuses on shifting employer flexibilization strategies away from numerical to functional flexibility, as in the case of German unions.

CHAPTER FIVE

Striking Out The Past?
Geographies of Industrial Action

INTRODUCTION

The landscape of industrial action has been fundamentally recast in recent years.[1] Strikes in Britain are at their lowest levels since records began, and, as we pointed out in our introductory chapter, this pattern of decline is mirrored across other advanced capitalist economies. Economic realignment, new management strategies and changes in the legislative regime of industrial relations have undermined the scope and collective capacity of British workers to take industrial action. For some commentators, this decline is terminal, irreversibly reconfiguring industrial politics by squeezing collective class confrontation out of popular experience. It is argued that mass organization and mobilization on the part of the industrial working class is being superseded by a 'post-Fordist' experience of employment in which workers are more firmly tied to the interests of their employers, without access to, or even interest in, collective channels of dissent (Casey 1995). Such developments are, however, uneven. Recent industrial action by British railway signal workers, train drivers, dockers, bank staff and postal workers is testimony to the fact that strikes are still part of the collective repertoire of organized labour, even if the general level of industrial stoppages is at an historical low. While strikes have declined, they have by no means disappeared, and current change needs to be set in geo-historical context.

Industrial action has always been spatially differentiated, and while such geographical variations might be expected given the uneven distribution of economic activity, our analysis suggests that the spatially differentiated histories of workers' experiences, their cultures and traditions also shape the map of collective action and strikes. Geographical location mediates workers' experiences, interests and priorities, influencing collective attitudes to, and capacities for, industrial action. This is not to imply that location determines strike activity, but

---

1 Following common practice, the terms 'industrial' action, 'industrial' conflict and 'industrial' stoppages are used in this chapter in a general sense to refer to strikes and stoppages in any sector of the economy, not just in industry narrowly defined.

rather that place is often a key factor in moulding the incidence of grievances on the one hand, and union resources, collective experience, shared interpretations and beliefs on the other. The detailed map of industrial action has expanded and contracted many times in the past, reflecting the shifting geography of economic and political change. Yet there have also been prominent and significant continuities in that map: the historical pattern of strikes in Britain indicates that certain places and regions have consistently been more prone to strike than others. How far the collapse of strike activity during the 1980s and 1990s has been shaped by this entrenched geographical unevenness in strike propensity is the focus of this chapter.

Despite the significance – and visibility – of strikes in Britain's post-war socio-economic landscape, geographical studies of this aspect of the capital/labour relation are few and far between. As in the case of trade unionism, the study of strikes has been the preserve of industrial relations analysts, labour economists and economic historians, and only very recently has the topic begun to attract the attention of geographers (see for example Ellis 1992; Gilbert 1995a; Wills 1995, 1996b; Charlesworth et al. 1996). Our analysis is conducted at a variety of spatial scales, from the nation to the region, the community and the workplace. This multi-layered approach makes the case for a geographically-focused perspective on industrial action.

DISCONTINUITIES IN INDUSTRIAL ACTION

Records of industrial action indicate a dramatic decline in British strike activity during the 1980s and the 1990s, and whilst commentators debate the long-term significance of this trough (see Edwards 1995), we focus here on its geography. In 1993, only 0.6 million days were lost in 211 strikes in the UK, a figure that appears truly insignificant when compared to the 29.5 million days lost in more than 2000 disputes during 1979. In only 15 years, industrial action has declined from its post-war peak to its lowest level since records began in the 1890s, and the downward trend shows little sign of reversal (see Figure 5.1). Such cycles and fluctuations in strikes are one of the most enduring features of industrial action in industrialized countries (see Shorter and Tilly 1974; Hobsbawm 1964; Cronin 1979; Jackson 1987). The incidence of strikes can vary enormously from one year to the next, and strikes have tended to occur in waves rather than consistent trends over time. Indeed, Bain and Price (1980) suggest that this wave-like pattern is also reflected in the movements in union membership in Western economies during the nineteenth and twentieth centuries. Economic change and industrial militancy are registered in the cyclical patterns of trade union membership itself, and they suggest that 'union growth is characterized by cyclical fluctuations and that these vary in amplitude and duration both within and between countries' (p.163).

For Shorter and Tilly (1974, p.140), strike waves amongst French workers 'march as exclamation marks in labour history', as periods of intense class conflict

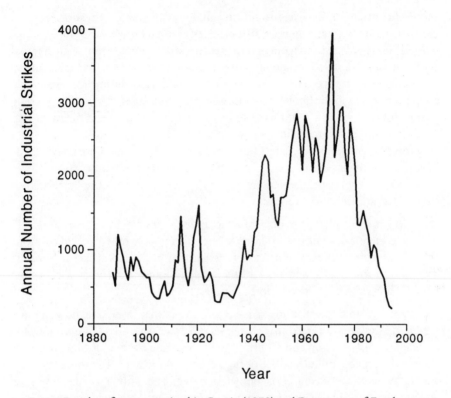

Sources: Based on figures contained in Cronin (1979) and Department of Employment
Figure 5.1: Strike trends in the UK, 1888–1993

have been interspersed with downturns in industrial action. Similarly, in his explorations of twentieth-century strike data from five industrialized countries (France, Germany, Italy, Britain and America), Screpanti (1987) identifies peaks in activity which were common to all. Strike waves erupted across the advanced economies between the late 1860s and the early 1870s, from the early 1910s to the early 1920s, and again, between the late 1960s and the mid 1970s. In each case, these periods of intense class conflict were followed by a decline in trade union activity, a fact that Screpanti (1987, p.110) links to 'the sharp and severe defeats with which big international strike waves have usually been closed'. Historically, these political and emotional defeats have been cemented by economic recession, unemployment and increased managerial control, all of which have typified the current downturn in industrial action in the UK.

Linking strikes to Kondtratieff 'long waves' of capital accumulation, Screpanti argues that industrial action is closely associated with cycles of economic growth. Whilst there tends to be an increase in workers' propensity to take industrial action during periods of economic expansion, Screpanti argues that major upheavals and strike peaks generally break out around the upper turning points of long-term economic cycles. Likewise, using the analogy of the combustion engine, Hobsbawm (1964) has suggested that class tensions and grievances will accumulate over time, only breaking out in response to intense compression, or an external spark, at the end of an economic upturn. Hobsbawm argues that trade union organizational practices and expectations which develop during the favourable conditions of economic boom will be threatened by the onset of recession, thereby pushing union members into taking strike action in order to defend their working conditions and rights to trade union organization.

Processes of economic change thus have a direct effect upon historical trends in industrial action. As Cronin (1979, p.38) explains, the nature of economic activity is closely related to workers' political practices, even if the latter are not strictly determined by the former:

> The uneven character of economic growth lies behind the comparable unevenness of industrial conflict… The effect upon workers…is to confront them with a different complex of problems and grievances at each major shift and to stimulate a 'remaking' of their consciousness and forms of collective organisation every two or three decades.

This approach to understanding strike trends is less than complete, however, for although scholars are agreed that economic processes have direct implications for trade union organization and industrial militancy, the direction of these relationships is uncertain, and difficult, if not impossible to predict.[2] The role played by unemployment, for example, is hotly contested, and although low levels of unemployment can raise workers' bargaining power and thus reduce the need for strikes, high unemployment can do likewise, as workers fear jeopardizing their jobs by taking any form of action (see Edwards 1995). Whilst Mayhew (1979) and Shalev (1980) have found evidence that low unemployment reduces strike action, Davies (1979), in contrast, argues that it is rapid increases in unemployment which have the most significant impact on reducing strikes. In practice, then, understanding the effects of economic processes such as employment change, restructuring, inflation and changes in remuneration, upon strikes, is only possible in context. None has a systematic or predictable effect on workers' propensity to strike in isolation from the operation and effect of other factors and events.

It is partly for these reasons that Shorter and Tilly (1974) attribute greater importance to the political determinants of strikes. For them, historical strike waves are a result of particular political conjunctures, arising

---

2 For example, econometric studies have generally not been successful in explaining the temporal variability in UK strike activity during the 1960s and 1970s (see *inter alia*, Pencavel 1970 and Shorey 1977). Cross section studies of inter-industry differences in strike activity have been more fruitful. For example, Geroski *et al.* (1982) and Shorey (1976) suggest that workplace and industry structure account for some, but by no means all, of the variation of strike activity across industries.

when it becomes apparent to the working classes as a whole that a point of critical importance for their own interests is at hand in the nation's life, and when the latticework of organisation suffices to transform these individual perceptions of opportunity into collective action. (pp.344–5)

In their analysis, Shorter and Tilly usefully bring the importance of workers' organizations to our attention, suggesting that political questions are also central to trends in industrial action (see Jackson 1987). Existing industrial relations practices and institutions influence both the power and inclination that unions and union members have to respond to economic change. Thus, without attention to the politics of trade union organization, explanations of strike propensity tend to be rather one-dimensional, neglecting the non-economic determinants of collective organization and activity (see also Gallie 1983; Lash 1984).

Despite the importance of national political institutions and labour traditions across the industrialized world, however, it is significant that strike propensity has declined in all the major OECD economies since the early 1980s. National political institutions and procedures have mediated the outcomes of economic change, but, as discussed in Chapter One, rates of industrial action have tended to fall across almost all of the advanced economies (see Table 1.2). Processes of economic change have left their legacy upon strike rates, and the combined effects of high unemployment, low inflation, management hostility and economic restructuring have dampened levels of strike activity throughout much of the Western world. In the British context, what is more significant, for Gilbert (1995a) at least, is the way in which since 1979 successive Conservative governments have claimed this reduction in strike activity as their own achievement. Mrs Thatcher, in particular, drew attention to her success in solving industrial stoppages and conflict, a central component of what she termed the 'British Disease':

They used, when I first came in, to talk about us in terms of the British Disease. Now they talk about us and say 'Look, Britain has got the cure. Come to Britain and see how Britain has done it!' That is an enormous turnaround. (Margaret Thatcher, quoted in Gilmour 1992, p.76)

In contrast, Gilbert argues that:

...although Conservative governments of the 1980s and 1990s claimed that their trade union reforms and economic policies had cured 'the British Disease', comparison with the record of other countries suggests that Britain's relative position has not improved greatly, and that the most important causes of the decline in overt industrial conflict are general economic factors common to all advanced countries. (Gilbert 1995a, p.3)

Gilbert is suggesting that although there has been a sharp fall in strikes, the relative positions of different national populations have not altered significantly during this process of decline. International disparities in strike propensity have persisted, indicating that the effects of economic change are mediated by political institutions

Table 5.1: Working days lost in industrial disputes, selected nations, 1982–1991

| | Days lost per thousand employed | | | | Change in rate |
| | 1982–86 | | 1987–91 | | |
	Rate	Rank	Rate	Rank	
Netherlands	20	14	10	13	-10
Germany	50	13	10	13	-40
Sweden	60	12	100	8	40
France	80	11	50	10	-30
USA	120	10	70	9	-50
Norway	170	9	30	12	-140
Denmark	250	8	40	11	-210
Australia	280	7	220	4	-60
UK	**420**	**6**	**132**	**7**	**-288**
Ireland	450	5	190	5	-260
Canada	490	4	360	2	-130
Spain	520	3	650	1	130
New Zealand	550	1	230	3	-320

Source: Bird (1992, p.610).

and cultures, and that these non-economic concerns have remained important. Table 5.1 indicates that whilst the UK ranked sixth in terms of strike days per thousand workers when compared with thirteen other nations during the early part of the 1980s, by the latter part of the decade, the comparative position of the UK had improved by just one place, to number seven. In short, geographical differences in strike propensity at an international scale have persisted despite the widespread trend toward labour quiescence and the impact of severe economic change.

These international differences are replicated at the sub-national scale, as national strike statistics mask significant regional and local disparities in strike propensity. Even in a country the size of Britain, which has an over-arching legislative regime, in which trade union organizations are nationally organized, and across which economic structures are now much more uniform, considerable spatial variations in trade union organization and industrial activity have persisted. In the remainder of this chapter we focus on this uneven geography of strike activity across the country, moving down the spatial hierarchy from the region to the workplace, putting strikes very firmly in their place.

THE GEOGRAPHY OF BRITISH STRIKE WAVES

In Britain, peaks in industrial action occurred during the 1830s, 1870s, between 1880–90, 1910–1913, 1919–20, and in 1968 and 1972 (Hobsbawm 1964;

Cronin 1979) (see Figure 5.1). But whilst the parallel movement of strike trends across different industries during these periods suggests that these waves might have had common historical causes, workers' responses to, and involvement in, industrial action differed in each case. Reflecting the uneven distribution of collective grievances and capacities for resistance, and variations in the social and political development of institutions amongst different groups of workers, each historical strike wave has involved certain segments of the workforce more than others. As Cronin (1979) points out in his superb historical analysis of British strikes, workers have not always displayed the same interest in or capacity for strikes:

> Textile workers were the prototypical strike prone workers in the nineteenth century, but strike rates in that industry fell to very low levels after 1932. Miners, notorious for high strike rates at all times, were not noticeably more prone to strike than other workers before 1920, and since 1957 their level of activity has decreased markedly. Likewise the dockers, whose reputation for militancy seems to have been largely a product of the years since 1945, or thereabouts. (p.28)[3]

These fluctuations in strike propensity within and between industries over time are, of course, inherently geographical in their manifestation. As new groups of workers developed the resources to take industrial action, or experienced the grievances to which strikes are deemed a necessary response, strike patterns have taken on a new and expansive cartography. Strikes in the 1870s, for example, accompanied the growth of trade unionism amongst agricultural workers in East Anglia and industrial workers in the North East and South Wales. The 1889–90 strike peak saw the growth of new unionism amongst the unskilled and unorganized urban working class, most particularly the dockers and gas workers in London. In contrast, miners, dockers and railway workers accounted for the majority of strike days lost during the years before and after the First World War (the strike waves of 1910–13 and 1919–20). But by the late 1960s, strikes were more commonly associated with manufacturing operatives and white-collar employees in public services. Regions such as the West Midlands were severely affected by industrial action for the first time after the Second World War, as new forms of organization were created in the large (Fordist) factories and offices of the region. Industries that had been a weak point for the unions during the 1930s, such as the motor vehicle plants located in areas such as Longbridge, Luton, Oxford and Dagenham (see Tolliday 1987), were in the forefront of the strike wave of the late 1960s and early 1970s. Workers in these locations took time to develop their

---

3   Cronin's analysis of historical discontinuities in strike propensity needs updating with the experience of the coal-miners' union during the mid 1980s. The national miners' strike between 1984 and 1985 was the most significant dispute in post-war Britain and had an enormous effect on the union movement as a whole and on the political climate more generally (Beynon 1985; Samuel *et al.* 1986; Gilbert 1995a).

collective capacity for industrial action. As Gilbert (1995a) remarks, the cinematic films of industrial conflict which were made during the late-1950s were no longer set in the industrial heartlands of the coal-mining regions, but rather in the engineering workplaces of the Midlands and the industrial South. While *Love on the Dole* (1941) was set amid the coal heaps and the declining localities of the North, *I'm All Right Jack* (1959) and *The Angry Silence* (1960) were played out in very new industrial environments. In Hobsbawm's view, strike waves:

> ...mark qualitative as well as quantitative changes. They are, in fact, generally expansions of the movement into new industries, new regions, new classes of the population; they coincide with a clustering of new organisations, and the adoption of new ideas and policies by both new and existing units. (Hobsbawm 1964, p.127)

This expansion of industrial militancy to new groups of workers and new places does not mean that 'old' groups and areas are rendered unimportant, however, and whilst it is true that the map of industrial action has been re-configured a number of times, as new groups of workers have been brought into the ambit of labour organization, existing organizational strengths have proved remarkably persistent. Just as in the case of trade union membership and recognition (see Chapters Three and Four), industrial action has historically been concentrated in specific regions, particularly the North, Wales and Scotland (see Figure 5.2 illustrating the earliest published records of strike geography from the nineteenth century).

Trade union organizational resources and traditions (including those associated with industrial militancy) have proved to be strongly embedded in particular places. Despite recent economic restructuring, and the dramatic fall in strike activity, the map of industrial action still reflects these different local and regional histories. In the vein of Massey's (1995) argument, that at any given time the socio-economic geography of a country is composed of different historical 'layers', reflecting the economic roles of individual places and regions in successive spatial divisions of labour, so both old and new communities have been combined in the changing geography of strikes. The geographical pattern of industrial action tends to reflect both traditional trade union membership strengths and newer groups of employees in locations less associated with the industrial action of the past. So although strike incidence in the West Midlands grew significantly during the 1950s and 1960s, Wales still recorded the highest incidence of strikes in the UK (see Durcan *et al.* 1983; Smith *et al.* 1977). Indeed, as is discussed in the next section, Wales is a region which has been associated with above average strike incidence throughout the twentieth century. Continuity and change have co-existed, and necessarily so, for as the geography of production has altered, trade unions and industrial organizations have had to expand their boundaries to survive. In so doing, the labour movement has itself been changing, taking on new ideas, new groups of workers and an evolving geography, with new patterns of organization constantly being overlaid on those inherited from the past.

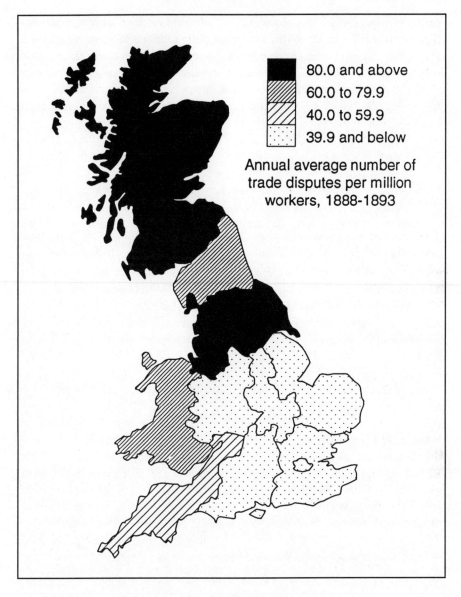

80.0 and above
60.0 to 79.9
40.0 to 59.9
39.9 and below

Annual average number of
trade disputes per million
workers, 1888-1893

Source: First report of the Board of Trade Labour Department

Figure 5.2: The geography of strike activity in the late nineteenth century

From the vantage point of the mid 1990s, with strike activity at historically low levels, it is difficult to assess the relative balance of older and newer geographies of industrial action in the UK. For some commentators, the current downturn in strike action is emblematic of a shrinking working class and a 'new politics' based upon individualism and issue-based social movements rather than class divisions (Eder 1993; Maheu 1995). Industrial action on the scale of the notorious years of 1968–74 is now regarded by many as inconceivable, particularly as increasing numbers of workers are no longer members of trade union organizations. It is also significant that the legal framework in which unions now operate has made the organization of industrial action much more difficult. As detailed in Chapter Four, wide-ranging changes in employment law have been enacted by successive Conservative governments since 1979. Legislation has been devised to kerb trade union influence and, in particular, the legal framework regarding strikes has been significantly rewritten making it more difficult to take action without breaking the law (Marsh 1992; Coates 1989; Smith and Morton 1994; Taylor 1994; Elgar and Simpson 1993). The 1982 Employment Act, in particular, removed much of the unions' legal immunity in the realm of strike action, restricted 'legal' action to the 'pursuit or furtherance' of a 'trades dispute', and substantially narrowed the definition of the latter so that 'political' strikes were outlawed.[4] The argument that the new employment and trade union legislation has depressed strike activity in the way the Government has claimed is not easy to test, however, given that other economic, political and social changes have been taking place simultaneously.[5] However, some studies have found evidence for such an effect. Thus in an econometric analysis of industry strike rates between 1977–87, McConnell and Takla (1990) conclude that the 1984 Trade Union Act (which compels trade unions to hold pre-strike ballots amongst their memberships) has had a discernible negative impact; while in their study of bargaining group strike activity over 1979–89, Ingram et al. (1993) find clear evidence of a negative influence of successive legislation throughout the 1980s. They see this as being consistent with what labour economists refer to as a 'joint cost' model of strikes: strike frequency has declined because legislation has made industrial action more expensive to unions if certain conditions are not strictly adhered to (mainly through the threat of fines, compensation, sequestration of union assets, and other costs). Interestingly,

---

4   It is important to acknowledge that unions have successfully overcome many of the legal constraints created to restrict industrial action, political funds and the check-off of membership subscriptions (see Brown and Wadhani 1990; Kelly 1988, 1990; Labour Research 1994a). As MacInnes (1990, p.213) observes, rather than leading to an immediate change in union power, legislation probably has had more of an indirect effect upon union behaviour and attitudes. Indeed, Elgar and Simpson (1993) suggest that the law needs to be understood in context, and they identify industrial variations in union responses and employers decisions.

5   Indeed, Gilmour (1992, Chapter 5) argues that the reduction of strikes owes as much to economic and others factors as to changes in the law.

Ingram *et al.* (1993) also found that regional unemployment rates have a positive effect on strike incidence.

Amongst the most serious of new legal restrictions is the requirement that all industrial action must be now be sanctioned by the union's members by means of a secret postal ballot, and then executed within a given, and specified, time period. This tends to detract from collective discussion about a grievance, and makes it difficult for the unions to respond immediately to a complaint. Since the 1993 Trade Union Reform and Employment Rights Act, trade unions have also had to supply the names of all those members who are taking part in any dispute, before the action takes place, and failure to comply with this restriction again invalidates the official status of any dispute. Trade union officials and shop stewards are now potentially liable for the costs of any unofficial strike action, and they are also vulnerable to legal action taken by members of the public who are inconvenienced by strikes. Workers are no longer legally entitled to take strike action over the employment of non-union labour (as in the case of the traditional 'closed shop'), nor are they able to take secondary action in support of workers who are not employed by their own employer. But perhaps of greatest significance is the growing number of incidents where employees have been sacked for going on strike, or taking action short of a strike. By breaking their contracts, workers can be sacked and replaced, thereby losing all entitlement to redundancy payments and grievance procedures.

Referring to the Wapping example,[6] Elgar and Simpson (1993) remark that:

> English law does not recognise our individual right to strike. In the 1980s employers began to appreciate the freedom which this gave them to carry out threats to dismiss workers taking industrial action. Of course this freedom remains limited if the workers concerned are not replaceable. But where, as in the newspaper industry, disputes were over employers' demands for task flexibility linked to the introduction of new technology, awareness of this legal weapon in their armoury reinforced employers' resolve to achieve their goals in full. (p.106)

In short, the room for legitimate industrial action has been considerably circumscribed. Moreover, successive Conservative governments have reinforced this legislative position by taking a firm line in controlling and policing disputes. The large scale, set-piece battles of the 1984–85 coalminers' strike, the Wapping

---

6   The Wapping dispute was a *cause célèbre* of the British labour movement between 1984 and 1986. The dispute was prompted by Rupert Murdoch's decision to close his Fleet Street offices, sack his existing workforce and relocate to new premises in Wapping. There, with the agreement of the electricians' union (EETPU), he elected to employ new, less skilled staff operating new technology on lower wages. Sacked workers from the print unions (NGA and SOGAT 82) picketed the new site for more than a year (often with large numbers of supporters) but they were never reinstated and either remained unemployed or were forced to find work elsewhere.

debacle and the Timex dispute, have all involved state intervention and eventual defeat for those workers concerned. Such losses for the national trade union movement have further dampened down levels of activity more generally, for many workers now assume that defeat is the inevitable result of strike action.

Conservative policy makers have been sharply attuned to the importance of geography in the control of industrial action. And in 'localizing' disputes by outlawing secondary and 'sympathy' action, the government has deprived workers of the possibility of making solidarity coalitions across and between local labour markets whilst remaining within the law. In having their industrial action confined geographically in this way, workers are less able to break down sectional divisions within the labour movement and generalize experiences from one group of workers to another. Indeed, a number of commentators have suggested that the current situation is more likely to promote the 'defence of place' by workers, defending what they have against threats from those outside (see Burawoy 1985; Hudson and Sadler 1986; Herod 1991; Beynon and Hudson 1993). Whereas in the past, strike waves have often been characterized by the translation of experiences and solidarity across space, current economic and political realities have made such possibilities much more difficult. In effect, new highly-centralized legislation has served spatially to 'divide and rule', to geographically fragment and isolate the strategic spaces of collective action.

Understandably, then, some commentators have predicted the 'withering away of the strike' (Bassett 1986). But from the middle of a trough in strike action during the mid 1990s, we would suggest it is unwise to make such prognoses about the future. Union membership and strike incidence have fallen with the defeat of strikes and the onset of recession in the past (during the 1870s, 1890s, and 1920s), only then to resurge once more as economic and political conditions changed. As we have already discussed in Chapters Three and Four, in spite of the general retreat of the unions since the end of the 1970s, trade union density and traditions of collective organization remain uneven across the country, and these contours of trade unionism are almost certain to be reflected in future maps of strike activity.

REGIONS AND STRIKES:
GEOGRAPHIES OF INDUSTRIAL CONFLICT

From the earliest days of the labour movement, commentators have pointed to unevenness in the spatial pattern of industrial action. For example, in his research into strike trends between 1870 and 1880, Bevan (1880, p.44) noted an 'extraordinary prevalence of strikes in Scotland, which...has no industrial population to compare with those [regions] of the same character in England' (see also Figure 5.2). In a similar way, when Daly and Atkinson (1940) looked at the geography of strikes and lock-outs between 1921 and 1936, they found a strong concentration of activity in the northern industrial regions and coal mining areas of the country. Exploring strike incidence in 1931, they commented that:

On the basis of the number of strikes called per thousand of the industrial population in 1931, the workers in the older industrial areas appeared to be nearly four times more prone to strike than the workers in the South East and Midlands. Among the older industrial areas, the workers in the badly distressed areas were more than six times more inclined to strike than the workers in the industrial south. Even within the older industrial areas, there were acute differences in the propensity of workers to strike. The workers in the badly distressed areas were three times more prone to strike than workers in the moderately distressed areas. (p.218)[7]

The uneven geographical incidence of strikes has a long pedigree in Britain. As the development of capital has been profoundly uneven, it is hardly surprising that – as in the case of unionization – industrial action and militancy have also differed across space. As communities grew around the early centres of the industrial revolution, trade unionism and radical politics had more opportunity to take root than was the case in rural and artisanal communities whose people did not have any significant industrial experience.

In his analysis of strike propensity between 1911 and 1945, Knowles (1952) found that South Wales had per capita strike rates five times higher than the national average, whilst the West Riding, Scotland, Cheshire and Lancashire also exceeded national rates (see Table 5.2 and Figure 5.3). Knowles explained this uneven distribution of strikes by reference to the location of those industries which were associated with militancy, such as coal mining and textiles. In such places, strikes were likely to be higher, particularly as the type of communities in which workers lived would also allow the possibility of militancy to spread from one group of employees to another. Just as we discussed in the case of trade union membership in Chapter Four, local 'externalities' can develop when particular cultural norms and traditions are embedded within any community. As Knowles (1952) explained:

> It may be said that regional differences in striking are to a large extent industrial causes in disguise; for example, the unbalanced industrial structure of certain regions makes the effect of economic depression much more acute. But in some of these regions, because people live near their work and near their fellow workers it is easier for them to combine, and for their attitudes to affect their fellows – even in industries other than their own. Nor should the effects of social tradition be ignored. (p.209)

---

7   The industrial south consisted of the South East, Greater London, the West Midlands and the East Midlands. The distressed areas consisted of South Wales, the North East coast, the West Riding and Lancashire and Cheshire. Of these, the first two were classed as badly distressed and the latter two, moderately so.

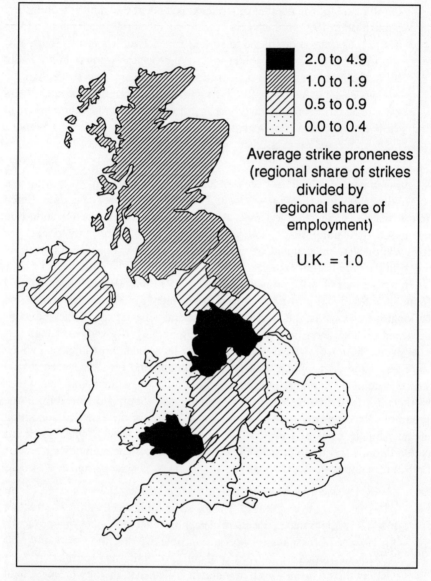

Source: Knowles, 1952

Figure 5.3: Regional strike proneness, 1911–1945

Table 5.2: Regional 'strike proneness' 1911–1945

	Per cent share of industrial population (a)	Per cent share of number of strikers (b)	Strike proneness ratio (a/b)
South Wales	3.6	17.3	4.8
West Riding	7.7	18.2	2.4
Lancs and Cheshire	14.4	28.7	2.0
Scotland	10.2	11.5	1.1
North and Durham	4.3	4.4	1.0
Northern Ireland	2.6	2.1	0.8
North Rural Belt	2.6	1.3	0.5
West Midlands	10.0	4.9	0.5
East Midlands	5.3	2.8	0.5
North and Central Wales	1.4	0.5	0.4
London and South East	30.0	7.7	0.3
Eastern Counties	3.7	0.5	0.1
South West Counties	4.2	0.1	<0.1
All Regions	**100.0**	**100.0**	**1.0**

Source: Knowles (1952, p.197) (These regions are displayed in Figure 5.3).

In order to explore the effect of community and social history in more detail, Knowles then compared the traditions of militancy in two mining regions of the country: South Wales and North East England. These regions had very similar industrial structures at the time, and each contained approximately 18 per cent of the country's mining population. Yet despite these structural similarities, trade union organization and patterns of militancy were very different. In South Wales, industrial relations were characterized by high levels of strikes and political organization, whilst miners in the North East were considerably less prone to striking. In explaining these differences, Knowles used the *Report of the Commission into Industrial Unrest* (1917) which emphasized the concentrated geography of mining communities in South Wales, the high level of industrial accidents there, the rapid immigration of rural workers from depressed regions to South Wales, and the hostility of class relations in the locality. In contrast to the situation in South Wales, miners in the North East were reported to be rather quiescent. During the 1870–75 agitation for nine-hour working days, for example, the North East was the only area not to take part, and in the strike votes of 1912 and 1920, the level of worker support in this region was amongst the lowest in the country (Knowles 1952, p.191). Knowles goes on to quote a report from *The Times* in

1920, summarizing popular perceptions of regional differences between mining communities in that period:

> The Durham miner is a wholly different being from the miner in, say, the South Wales coalfield, to quote a district in which a large majority has favoured a strike. People born and bred in this county are not readily stirred by emotion. They are neither flexible nor reckless; rather they are impatient of change. (quoted in Knowles 1952, p.192)

Whilst acknowledging the dangers of regional stereotyping such as this, Knowles is pointing to the importance of geography beyond industrial structure. He is explicitly illustrating the way in which the industrial, social and political histories of each geographical community can shape the propensity of workers to take industrial action. Industrial structure was only part of the story behind British strike incidence in the early part of this century, and the particularities of community, shared history, trade union traditions and class relations also made a difference to workers' attitudes and ideas. As Shorter and Tilly (1974; see also Tilly and Tilly 1981) have suggested, 'repertoires of collective action' can develop within stable communities of workers over time. And such collective traditions of resistance might then mediate the effects of local industrial structure on strike propensity. For strikes are not simply a matter of industry, they also reflect social and political geography, and both sets of factors play a part in explaining collective action.

More recently, a number of economists have revisited the work of Knowles and investigated regional strike data using multiple regression analysis to try and identify the extra-industrial reasons for strike variation. For example, Bean and Peel (1976), using strike data for 1972, found that regional unemployment rates, female participation in the labour market and wage rate changes were all related to spatial patterns of industrial action. They concluded that:

> In this study we have found *prima facie* support for an explanation of inter-regional differences in patterns of strike activity by industry which is related to a number of economic variables. The extent of regional unemployment appears to be a more important determinant of strike patterns than the rates of unemployment in the industry groups themselves, and differential relative levels of earnings seem to play a bigger part in strike determination than the mere rates of change of earnings. A high number of working days lost by strikes may also be facilitated by the reduced costs to households of strike action where there is a high, female, labour force participation rate. (p.305)

Clifton and Creigh (1977) deployed a similar approach to study spatial strike trends between 1968 and 1973, and they point to a much wider range of factors in explaining geographical disparities in strike proneness. They found that regions with a higher relative strike proneness were likely to be those which had: a higher average plant size; a faster rate of increase of earnings; a higher rate of net outward migration; a higher proportion of employment in the metals and engineering industries; a higher proportion of male employment; higher female activity rates; lower total activity rate; and higher density of population (Clifton and Creigh 1977, p.83).

Numerous influences have thus been identified as determinants of regional differences in strike activity, although the significance of different factors appears to vary over time with changes in the nature of industrial action (see also Smith *et al.* 1977 for analysis of regional strike incidence between 1971 and 1973). Moreover, the degree to which regional patterns of strikes are explained by spatial differences in industrial structure and economic conditions appears to differ internationally. Whilst industrial relations analysts have generally found that local structural factors (including industrial composition, the firm size distribution of employment, relative unemployment and wages) do not offer a complete explanation of British strike geography (see Knowles 1952; Clifton and Creigh 1977; Smith *et al.* 1977), research into strike patterns in the United States suggests that there as much as 85 per cent of the regional variation in strike incidence can be accounted for by the spatial distribution of economic activity (see Ellis 1992). However, regression analyses of this sort are probably not able to provide a general explanation of the spatial pattern of strikes, as each instance of industrial action will have a different set of causes. When strike patterns are so uneven over space and time there is unlikely to be one common set of causes that explain every incidence of activity. Indeed, what is interesting about these studies is that even after various structural, workplace and economic factors influencing regional strike incidence are taken into account, significant unexplained differences in strike activity between regions remain. This also points to the important role that local traditions, union practices and cultural norms may play in determining the geography of industrial action.

To assess the relevance of these ideas to recent strike trends in Britain, particularly before and after 1979, we examined regional industrial disputes data for the period between 1966 and 1993.[8] Annual regional (and sub-regional) strike data exist from 1966 onwards, and for each region these data give the numbers of industrial stoppages, workers involved, and working days lost, all disaggregated by industrial sector. This data series thus allows us to map the spatial pattern of strikes over an extensive period whilst also making a more detailed comparison of

---

8   This data series is known to underestimate the incidence of strike action as the figures are
     submitted voluntarily by employers. Researchers also use press information to collate
     statistics, but it is probable that many small-scale disputes never come to official attention.
     The series excludes all strikes that involve fewer than ten workers and those lasting less than
     one day (unless the equivalent number of days lost exceeds 100). All political strikes (such as
     the national strike to oppose the outlawing of unions at GCHQ during 1984 and action
     taken to support the ambulance workers during 1989) are also discounted, lowering the
     figures. However, the statistics still provide the most detailed indication of trends in industrial
     action that is available (for a more detailed discussion of the data, see Hyman 1989a).

Table 5.3: Average regional strike rates, 1966–1993

	Average annual number of working days lost per thousand employees				Decline in strike rate
	1966–1979		1980–1993		1966–1979 to 1980–1993
	Rate	Rank	Rate	Rank	
South East	263	10	96	8	-167
East Anglia	234	11	75	10	-159
South West	279	9	74	11	-205
West Midlands	685	3	191	7	-494
East Midlands	448	7	265	5	-183
Yorks/Humberside	557	6	675	2	+118
North West	628	5	233	6	-395
North	742	1	651	3	-91
Wales	724	2	704	1	-20
Scotland	647	4	290	4	-357
Northern Ireland	401	8	96	8	-305
United Kingdom	**457**		**250**		**-207**

Source: Department of Employment.
Note: Data for East Anglia is for 1969–1993 (data for 1966–1968 are included in that listed for the South East).

regional strike incidence on an industrial basis.[9] Table 5.3 and Figure 5.4 summarize these regional patterns of strike incidence, as measured by the number of working days lost through industrial disputes per thousand employees, for the two sub-periods 1966–1979 and 1980–1993. This index of strike incidence gives a better indication of the extent and magnitude of industrial conflict than does the number of strikes or the number of workers involved in disputes. And as strike activity is expressed relative to the size of the regional employment base (the number of employees), it also removes the effect of differences in the workforce size of different regions (recall the discussion of union membership numbers versus densities in the previous chapter).

At a national scale, strike activity has fallen from an average annual rate of 457 days lost per thousand employees during 1966 to 1979 to an average annual rate of 250 days lost per thousand employees between 1980 and 1993. This sharp decline in the overall incidence of strikes conceals significant regional differences in strike activity. In each of the two periods there are wide variations amongst the regions. In the 1966–1979 period, average regional strike rates ranged from 234 days per thousand employees in East Anglia, to 742 days in the North. Between

9   Some of these data are also available at the county scale.

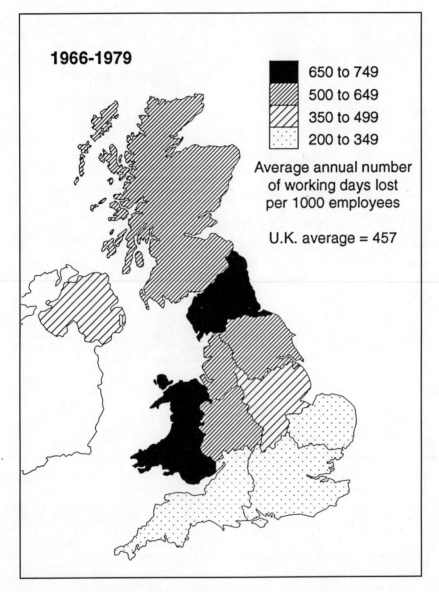

1966-1979

650 to 749
500 to 649
350 to 499
200 to 349

Average annual number
of working days lost
per 1000 employees

U.K. average = 457

Source: Based on Strike Statistics supplied by Department of Employment

Figure 5.4i: The regional incidence of strike activity

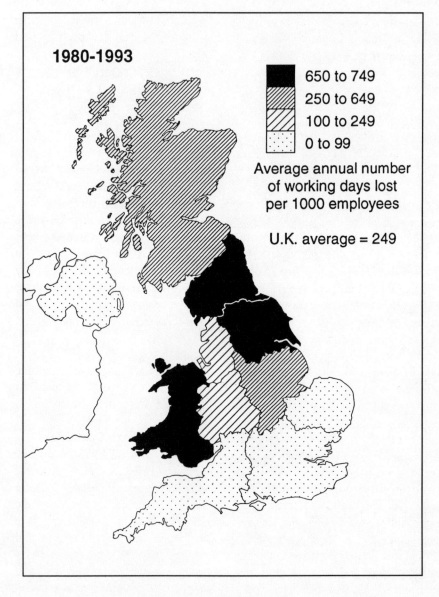

1980-1993

■	650 to 749
▨	250 to 649
▨	100 to 249
⠿	0 to 99

Average annual number
of working days lost
per 1000 employees

U.K. average = 249

Source: Based on Strike Statistics supplied by Department of Employment

Figure 5.4ii: The regional incidence of strike activity

1980–1993, while strike activity declined nationally, the degree of regional strike variation actually increased, ranging from a low of 74 days lost per thousand employees in the South West to a rate of 704 days in Wales. Taking the 1966–1993 period as a whole, there is a clear division between the two highly strike-prone regions of the North and Wales on the one hand, and the three least strike-prone regions of the South East, East Anglia and the South West, on the other. This geographical pattern, perhaps not surprisingly, closely mirrors that found for trade unionism (Chapter Three). But in addition to this, the national decline in strike incidence has itself been constituted by marked regional disparities. Whilst nationally, the average number of working days lost per thousand workers fell by 207 days between 1966 to 1979 and 1980 to 1993, different regions have experienced quite dissimilar relative trends. The West Midlands declined more than twice as much as the national average, falling from the third most strike-prone region in 1966 to 1979 to the seventh in the later period. Scotland and the North West, two other regions which had high rates of strike activity in the 1960s and 1970s, also experienced sharp falls in industrial militancy in the 1980s and early 1990s. In contrast, average strike incidence in Yorkshire-Humberside actually increased between the two periods, and both Wales and the North, as mentioned above, continued to have high rates of strike activity (all three regions were seriously affected by the coal-miners' strike of 1984–1985).

Such spatial differences might be expected on the basis of uneven economic development across the regions, for even if, as Knowles suggested, economic structure is not the only determinant of strike action, it is still likely to be an important factor in shaping the geography of strikes. Strike rates are known to vary between industrial sectors, on average being highest in energy, mining and water, transport, engineering, motor vehicle manufacture, and certain public services, and lowest in electronic engineering, retail and distribution services, banking and other business services, and research and development. Thus, spatial trends in strikes will, to some extent at least, reflect regional variations in the industrial composition of employment. To determine the contribution of these structural factors to regional strike incidence we utilize the same shift-share procedure that we employed in the previous chapter to decompose regional differences in unionization. Unfortunately, however, unlike the data on union representation and recognition, strike data are not available by size of establishment, so that we are unable to incorporate this particular structural dimension into our analysis, which is therefore confined to the role of industrial composition.

Following the methodology deployed in the previous chapter, the expected number of working days lost through industrial action per thousand employees in each region is calculated as the rate that would be expected if each industrial sector in the region had the same strike rate as that sector nationally.[10] That is:

---

10 As in the analysis of unionization in the previous chapter, this method is useful in subdividing regional patterns, but must be interpreted with caution. By using national strike rates for each

$$S^\star{}_r = \sum_i[N_{ir}S_{in}]$$

where the summation is over the relevant industrial sectors (here SIC single digit divisions), and

S_{in} = national strike rate in industry sector i

N_{ir} = the proportion of the region's employees in industry sector i, that is $(E_{ir} / \sum_i E_{ir})$

Then, again following the procedure adopted in Chapter Four, the difference between a region's strike rate and the national rate is equal to the sum of a regional 'structural' effect and a residual 'area' effect:

$$S_r - S_n = (S_r - S^\star{}_r) \quad + \quad (S^\star{}_r - S_n)$$

Regional	Area	Structural
Strike	Effect	Effect
Differential		

where

S_r = actual strike rate in region r

S_n = national overall strike rate

The 'structural' effect indicates how much of a region's strike differential derives from the deviation of its industrial employment structure from the national industrial mix. If regional disparities in strikes were wholly a reflection of the geographical distribution of industry, the expected strike rate in a region would be equal to its actual rate (i.e. no 'area' effects). If all regions had the same industrial structure, each region's expected strike rate would be equal to the national rate, and any regional strike differences would be pure 'area' effects. The 'area' effect captures factors other than industrial composition (according to how the latter is defined), including not only effects such as those stemming from the size, ownership, and other aspects of a region's workplaces, but also other region-specific 'non-economic' characteristics.

---

industrial sector, we are applying data that are already, at least in part, a product of spatially constituted relationships. For example, the fact that mining tends to be relatively strike prone may be related to the particular types of community in which miners live. Geography is constitutive of both parts of the equation: location matters to both industrial and regional strike incidence. As Knowles (1952 p.208) also acknowledged: 'the formal separation of regional "strike proneness" from industrial "strike proneness" is somewhat academic. As has been said, a rigid separation is impossible, but the…figures indicate the kind of distinction which can reasonably be made. As one would expect, regional differences, on analysis, prove much slighter than industrial'. Shorter and Tilly (1974, p.x) make a similar point of clarification stating that 'the effects of region and of industry are not simply additive; neither one reduces to the other; they interact'.

Table 5.4: Structural versus area effects in regional strike rates, all workers and sectors annual averages for 1966–1979 and 1980–1993

	Annual average number of working days lost per thousand employees 1966–1979				Annual average number of working days lost per thousand employees 1980–1993			
	Obs. rate	Reg. diff.	Struct. effect	Area effect	Obs. rate	Reg. diff.	Struct. effect	Area effect
South East	263	-194	-59	-135	96	-154	-60	-94
East Anglia	234	-223	3	-226	75	-175	-66	-109
South West	279	-178	-43	-135	74	-176	-56	-120
East Midlands	448	-9	71	-81	265	15	94	-79
West Midlands	685	228	150	78	191	-59	20	-79
Yorks/Humberside	557	100	40	60	675	425	106	309
North West	628	171	0	171	233	-17	-9	-8
North	742	285	70	215	651	401	109	292
Wales	724	267	51	216	704	454	119	335
Scotland	647	190	-26	216	290	40	8	32
Northern Ireland	401	-56	-107	51	96	-154	-60	-94
United Kingdom	**457**				**250**			

Source: Authors' calculations using Department of Employment data.
Note: Calculations for East Anglia refer to 1969–1979 only (data for this region is included in South East for 1966–1968).

Table 5.4 summarizes the results of this analysis for the two sub-periods 1966–1979 and 1980–1993.[11] Several features are evident. First, in the majority of regions the 'structural' effects are far outweighed by the 'area' effects, the main exceptions being the West Midlands and Northern Ireland in 1966–1979, and the East Midlands and the North West in 1980–1993. Second, the regions of the UK can be categorized into three groups in terms of their 'area' effects. The four southern regions of the South East, East Anglia, the South West and East Midlands

---

11 Knowles (1952 pp.203–209) made a similar calculation, adjusting regional strike data to account for different geographies of industrial structure. He produced an index of 'standardized strike proneness' by amalgamating all the data for the 34-year period (1911 to 1945). In this index, each region would be expected to record a figure of 1.0 if workers in the same industries behaved in the same way, regardless of location. However, the index ranged from 2.3 in South Wales to 0.1 in the South West, and the only other regions greater than 1.0 were the West Riding, Northern Ireland, Lancashire and Cheshire and Scotland. Perhaps of most interest is the fact that regions such as the West and East Midlands, Northumberland and Durham all recorded much lower strike propensity than expected. Obviously, strike incidence in these regions changed considerably in the post-war period. Similar calculations have also been completed for the years between 1971 and 1973 by Smith *et al.* (1977).

have substantial negative 'area' effects in both sub-periods: all recorded far fewer working days lost than expected on the basis of their industrial structures. At the other extreme, are those regions in which strike activity exceeded expected rates – that is, where 'area' effects are strongly positive – over the entire twenty-eight-year period, namely the North, Yorkshire and Humberside, Wales and Scotland. In the middle is a group (the West Midlands, the North West and Northern Ireland) in which 'area' effects were positive in the 1966–1979 sub-period but negative in the 1980–1993 sub-period. The regions at either end of the range of strike incidence have thus been remarkably consistent over the past three decades. Workers living in East Anglia, the South East and the South West have very different strike propensities from those living in the North, Yorkshire and Humberside and Wales. Such spatial variation would suggest that industrial structure alone is insufficient to account for regional differences in strike incidence, and other factors are also important in determining the geography of strikes.

The large 'area' effects highlighted by the above analysis no doubt reflect other facets of regional economic structure, such as firm size, occupational composition, the gender division of labour, workplace characteristics, and so on. Yet while we are unable empirically to assess the role of such factors directly here, other evidence suggests their influence is likely to be relatively minor, and almost certainly insufficient to account for the whole of the large area effects evident in Table 5.4. For one thing, our analysis in the previous chapter suggested that changes in the establishment size structure, gender division, and broad occupational composition of regional employment have contributed little to recent trends in unionization rates across regions. Furthermore, as mentioned above, those industrial relations analysts and economists who have tried to assess how far such factors explain inter-regional, and inter-industry, variations in strike activity in Britain have found their impact to be limited (namely, Knowles 1952; Clifton and Creigh 1977; Smith et al. 1977). One factor in particular that is frequently considered as a causative influence on strike incidence is workplace size, in that large establishments tend to be more strike prone. However, regional differences in the establishment-size composition of employment had become relatively insignificant by the 1980s, especially once differences in industrial composition are allowed for (see Beard 1995).[12] This is not to deny, of course, that these compositional effects may shape industrial conflict, or the role they may have played historically in determining the experiences of workers in strike-prone regions such as the North, Wales and Scotland. However, it is our contention that other cultural and political factors are also important. We would concur with Smith et al. (1977, p.83) who, having found that significant regional variations in strike activity remained unexplained after

---

12 For example, in his comparative study of industrial relations in South Wales and East Anglia, two regions with quite different union traditions, Beard found that the establishment size distributions of the two regions had not only become quite similar by the 1980s but were also of limited value in explaining differences in trade unionism and industrial relations between the two areas.

various structural and economic characteristics had been taken into account, suggested that 'it may be that the wider range of socio-cultural factors not included in this study are responsible'. We consider the role of local socio-cultural context in the remainder of this chapter, but before we do so it is worth commenting on the contemporary geography of strikes in a little more detail.

Despite the marked drop in average strike incidence between 1966 to 1979 and 1980 to 1993, taking the second sub-period as a whole it would seem that significant regional differences in industrial militancy have persisted. However, during the late 1980s, and especially during the deep economic recession of the early 1990s, strike activity declined to extremely low levels, and regional differentials likewise became negligible (see Table 5.5). This raises the question whether the traditional disparities in regional strike proneness and the differing socio-cultural attitudes towards collective militancy that have underpinned them, are now definitely on the wane. It could be that we are witnessing a shift to a new, more evenly distributed geography of strikes, particularly if the bulk of whatever collective action that occurs in the future is primarily limited to nationally-organized public sector unions.

In his exploration of the changing nature of Scottish strikes, Jackson (1988) argues that strike rates there moved closer to those for the UK as a whole during the 1980s. Scotland lost many of the industries where strikes had previously been concentrated, and the communities which depended upon these jobs suffered high unemployment, further undermining strike propensity within the area. In addition

Table 5.5: Regional strike rates in the early 1990s

	Number of working days lost per thousand employees				
	1990	1991	1992	1993	Average rate 1990–93
South East	68	19	33	15	34
East Anglia	32	50	9	4	24
South West	12	6	2	3	6
West Midlands	87	8	16	11	30
East Midlands	21	11	3	2	9
Yorks/Humberside	46	29	25	13	28
North West	298	102	15	5	105
North	70	76	43	20	52
Wales	85	20	11	21	34
Scotland	62	61	27	56	51
Northern Ireland	34	32	15	29	27
United Kingdom	**83**	**34**	**24**	**30**	**43**

Source: Employment Gazette, Department of Employment.
Note: Figures rounded.

to this, Jackson pointed to the effects of changes in the labour force, most particularly to the increase in female and part-time labour, as reasons for this decline in strikes. Women and part-time workers have traditionally been less associated with strong unionization and industrial militancy, and as these groups are becoming increasingly important in the labour market, strikes are likely to continue to decline. A similar point is made by Gilbert (1995a) who also emphasises that the changing complexion of the workforce of the late twentieth century will come to be reflected in the evolution of industrial action in the future. If strikes do take place, they are likely to have a different character to those of the past:

> Any resurgence of industrial conflict in Britain at the end of the twentieth century will require new forms of mobilisation of a workforce which in terms of gender, race, full-time or part-time status, and social geography is far more fractured and differentiated than that of the early post-war years. (p.17)

Whether such new forms of 'mobilization' will emerge is difficult to judge, since much will depend on future economic, employment and political conditions, as well as on the future course of the trade union movement itself. But certainly it would seem premature to declare the 'end of the strike' and the permanent onset of 'labour quiescence'. There is nothing inherent in the supposedly post-Fordist world of production and work that automatically rules out the re-emergence of industrial conflict and strike activity, albeit in different forms and involving different types of worker. And if there is a resurgence of industrial conflict and new types of strike action, and if new forms and fault-lines of worker mobilization do emerge, then new geographies of strikes are also likely to appear. These new geographies may well be connected to the heartlands of trade union tradition which were established in the past, but labour traditions themselves can only evolve by embracing the new in connection with the old (Wills 1995, 1996b). Thus central to the debate over the 'future of the strike' is the issue of whether historical communities of industrial militancy are indeed withering away, and whether – and where – new communities of collective action are likely to develop.

COMMUNITIES OF COLLECTIVE ACTION

The role played by 'community' features at the heart of many explanations of industrial action and collective resistance. From Kerr and Seigel's (1954) work on strike propensity, to analyses of the 1984–85 British coal-miners' strike (Sunley 1990; Griffiths and Johnston 1991; Beynon 1985; Samuel *et al.* 1986), notions of community have been used to explain the existence of collective organization and shared capacities for collective action. As we have seen, industrial structure does not fully account for the regional incidence of strikes, and this may be because the socio-political history of local communities also mediates workers' capacities for industrial action. Regional strike trends are thus sometimes considered to be a reflection of the distribution of particular types, and forms, of 'community'. Strikes can only be sustained when a particular working population has common interests and shared resources which can be directed towards common ends, and such commonality is often the product of the social cohesion, mutual exchange and shared traditions which can develop in particular places. For writers such as Calhoun (1982, 1983, 1987, 1988) or Evans and Boyte (1986), strike propensity is a function of 'community', rather than the result of more abstract notions of class consciousness, cohesiveness or identity. Writers of this school argue that it is only spatially bounded communities which can sustain the social relations upon which collective action depends. Strikes are thus understood as being inherently geographical phenomena, explicitly dependent upon the spatiality of social relations for their very occurrence.

Calhoun suggests that the social organization necessary for collective action will be possible only on a communal basis. In a critique of Marx's distinction between objective class position (class in itself) and class capacity (class for itself), in which the latter arises from experiences of the former, Calhoun argues that collective capacity results from pre-existing communal bonds and traditions. Rather than being due to abstract interests based upon shared class positions, Calhoun argues that it is the 'traditions of community' that form the basis of workers' collective action. Such traditions can, of course, be reactionary or radical. When existing ways of life are threatened by change, socially cohesive communities will tend to react to defend their traditions and resist what is new. When counterpoised to change and development, the conservative traditions associated with small-scale communities can thus become 'radical' and 'radicalizing', in the sense of mobilizing collective action and rebelling in defense of custom.[13] As Calhoun explains, it is the context in which activity is grounded that determines popular responses to economic and political change:

> Traditional communities are important bases of radical mobilization. Community constitutes the pre-existing organization capable of securing the participation of individuals in collective action. Communities provide a social organizational foundation for mobilization, as networks of kinship, friendship, shared crafts, or recreations offer lines of communication and allegiance. People who live in well-integrated communities do not need elaborate formal organization in order to mount a protest. They know, moreover, whom to trust and whom not to. (Calhoun 1983, p.897)

Calhoun associated the resistance of 'reactionary radicals' with a particular historical period, when communities were threatened by industrialization. He argues that the majority of modern workers no longer have the capacity necessary to sustain the sort of collective action needed to take workers beyond reformism. The rise of formal, bureaucratic trade unions as the representatives of workers has,

---

13 This notion of the 'reactionary radical' is also detailed in E.P. Thompson (1991).

he suggests, effectively diluted the scope for radical action.[14] However, Evans and Boyte (1986) have applied these ideas to the American labour movement, and suggest that communal networks have remained important to workers' industrial action in modern capitalist societies. The social relationships that tie people to place in everyday life are those which can also form the bedrock from which collective action is sustained. Evans and Boyte stress that local union infrastructures can function as 'free social spaces' in which workers can create and then re-create collective traditions of organization. The democracy of union locals, they suggest, allows workers to explore ideas, share experiences and support each other, particularly during periods of confrontation. This attention to the geography of everyday life allows Evans and Boyte to suggest that class cannot be separated from other aspects of workers' identities, of which ethnicity, gender and local attachment can all be important in constraining or enabling collective paths to resistance. Community is thus added to more abstract notions of class in explaining collective action:

> It is through the structures of community life, which sustain and reproduce a group's shared memory and culture, that an oppressed people begin to come to self-consciousness. Through their activity in new contexts, groups may acquire public skills, reinforce democratic values, and form new links between sub-communities into larger networks and organisations. And it is through such processes that a powerless people constitutes itself as a force for democratic transformation of the broader social structure and as a school for its own education in a democratic sensibility. (Evans and Boyte 1986, p.201)

Such arguments have been echoed in various accounts of industrial action in the twentieth century. As illustrated by Kerr and Seigel's (1954) geo-social explanation for strike propensity, the cohesiveness of particular working-class communities has often been cited as a major determinant of local strike propensity. For example, Kerr and Seigel argue that where workers live in socially isolated, tight-knit communities, dependent upon one main source of employment, they are more likely to strike. Single-industry towns and villages (epitomized, of course, by mining, steel and textile communities) have come to be associated with strong traditions of collective organization, and Kerr and Seigel suggest that such socially cohesive communities develop their own particular 'codes, myths, heroes and social standards' (p.191). They contrast such locations with 'integrated communities' where traditions of collectivity are diluted through multi-industrial cosmopolitan-ism, a greater distance between home and work, and increased opportunities for cross-class alliances and collaboration. Moreover, Kerr and Seigel note that the

---

14 In this analysis, Calhoun echoes Olson (1965) for whom collective action is only possible in small groups where the free rider problem can be overcome through personal contact (see Gilbert 1992, for further discussion of these themes).

types of jobs on offer in such places might attract workers of a more 'submissive' psychology than those engaged in more unpleasant occupations such as mining, heavy industry or docking, which tend to be geographically concentrated. In combining their understanding of the geographical and psychological predispositions of workers to strike, Kerr and Seigel are able to conclude their analysis of strike incidence in eleven different countries by arguing that:

> (a) industries will be highly strike prone when the workers (i) form a relatively homogeneous group which (ii) is unusually isolated from the general community and which (iii) is capable of cohesion; and (b) industries will be comparatively strike free when their workers (i) are individuals integrated into the larger society, (ii) are members of trade groups which are coerced by government or the market to avoid strikes, or (iii) are so individually isolated that strike action is impossible. (p.195)

Geographical location and the form of community are thus invoked as key factors behind regional differences in industrial action, and although Kerr and Seigel's account is rather crude, this approach has been taken up by others exploring strike incidence in the twentieth century.

For example, in their analysis of strikes in France between 1915 and 1935, Shorter and Tilly (1974) found strikes were concentrated in urban locations. In contrast to the 'isolated mass' hypothesis of Kerr and Seigel, Shorter and Tilly argued that urban centres were ideal environments in which workers could organise, building upon the strengths of past experience. Community relations were still crucial to their understanding of strike patterns as they found that prior collective organization and experience were key determinants of class capacity. As they explained:

> If people strike in a place, it is partly because their fathers and grandfathers also struck, or because they find themselves in a community with firmly rooted conflictual institutions and with collective mentalities of ancient pedigree. If people strike, it is not solely because they are boilermakers or machine assemblers or masons, though the structure of their jobs may limit or shape the exact forms their collective action assumes. It is also because they are en-matrixed in a certain kind of community with certain acquired habits of joint action. (1974, p.238)

Of course, explaining strike action simply as a product of geographical isolation or urban location is a form of spatial fetishism, and thus unacceptable. As Gilbert (1992, p.12) points out in his historical comparison of British mining traditions between 1850 and 1926, collective action has varied between mining communities over time, as a result of their particular social and institutional histories. Community is itself a social construction which changes over space and time, never having a wholly fixed and predictable political manifestation (see Gilbert 1995b; Beynon and Austrin 1994; and the debate between Sunley 1986, and Rees 1985, 1986). Indeed, communities are also fractured by social divisions and exclusions, often not matching up to the image created by social and political scientists. Yet this complexity does not negate the importance of place to collective organization. The story might not be as simple as writers such as Kerr and Seigel suggest, but trade union organization and militancy *are* spatially differentiated: at particular times, some communities have displayed a greater propensity to strike action than others.

Labour historians have pointed to the way in which particular social, political and institutional configurations can generate a 'sense of place' or 'community' that seems to be more conducive to industrial action. In Williams' (1989) writings about the mining communities of South Wales, for example, there is a clear sense that place has made a difference to the political traditions of the region during the twentieth century. Likewise, during the 1984–85 coal-miners strike, there were marked differences in workers' responses to the strike in the Nottinghamshire fields as compared with those in South Wales and Yorkshire (see Sunley 1986, 1990; Rees 1986; Griffiths and Johnston 1991; Samuel *et al.* 1986). The particular social relations of place, and the connections between each location and the world beyond, made a difference to the way people perceived the strike and their role within it. Such geographies of industrial action may not be a transparent reflection of 'community', and they are certainly not consistent over time and space, but the spatial differentiation of collective action remains a legitimate arena of social enquiry.

In a period when industrial action and trade union membership have been in decline, the resilience of collective resources and capacities for industrial action amongst particular groups of workers in particular places has renewed significance for the labour movement. We might legitimately ask how the 300 Timex workers in Dundee were able to conduct their six-month strike during 1991. Or question how the small group of women at Middlebrook Mushrooms in Yorkshire sustained their dispute against a multinational employer during the early 1990s. Similarly, what was it about the bus workers of Chelmsford, Essex, that allowed them to mount a strike against their employer over changes in working hours during 1994, when others in the Badgerline group had already accepted less favourable terms? Even in national disputes, we find spatial differences in workers' responses. Signal workers and bank clerks responded to the call for national strike action in 1994 far more vigorously in some areas than they did elsewhere. Geography remains important to explaining these patterns of industrial action, and this unevenness in collective capacity still has political significance for organized labour as a whole.

Community-based social relationships and traditions must go some way to explaining differences in collective capacity, but community is a notoriously slippery term. It implies social cohesion when there is always division; it also evokes a sense of timeless reproduction when local social relations are constantly being remade, often due to external pressures and events; and 'community' also implies a strength in social relationships which are spatially proximate, when ideas for change and action often also come – indeed increasingly come – from the world beyond any particular place. In short, 'community' is a useful concept but, of itself, it is an insufficient explanation for industrial resistance. Evoking community traditions as an explanation for the geography of strikes effectively elevates place over and above an understanding of the complex nature of the social and political relationships and processes that lie behind strike incidence at any particular time.[15]

MICRO-GEOGRAPHIES OF STRIKES: THE MILITANT OR QUIESCENT WORKPLACE

Geographical strike figures, even at the regional or local level, are often the result of a concentration of industrial action within a number of particularly strike-prone workplaces in the area. When Smith *et al.* (1977) explored sub-regional (county) strike trends in the UK between 1968 and 1973, for example, they found a remarkable concentration of industrial action within a minority of establishments. Even during the strike wave between 1971 and 1973, 95 per cent of manufacturing plants were completely free of stoppages.[16] In any one year, an average of only 2 per cent of manufacturing plants reported any industrial action taking place. Even amongst those establishments which were affected by strikes, a small handful accounted for the vast majority of working days lost. Ten per cent of the strike-active plants were the setting for almost 80 per cent of all working days lost, suggesting that regional and sub-regional trends and differences in industrial action are accounted for by disputes in a very small number of workplaces. Almost all the 61 geographical areas which Smith *et al.* included in their study recorded more than half of the days lost in disputes, in any year, as occurring within only approximately 10 per cent of the strike-affected establishments in an area.

In one sense such findings suggest the need to be cautious in advocating the importance of 'community' in explaining strikes, for even within 'strike-prone' regions and sub-regions, industrial militancy is extremely uneven (see also Black 1987; Bean and Stoney 1986; Church and Stevens 1994). It would appear that it is the state of industrial relations and collective practices found in particular workplaces, at particular times, which has the greatest impact upon the geography of strikes. Strike rates are uneven across particular local areas, and as Bean and Stoney (1986) found in their study of strike patterns in that most archetypal of 'militant' places, Liverpool, over the period between 1974 and 1983, the majority of workplaces were surprisingly strike free. Despite the reputation of Merseyside

---

15 Furthermore, as we shall see in Chapter Seven, some social theorists now argue that contemporary social, economic and cultural trends are leading to the rapid social disintegration of local communities and the traditions associated with them.

16 It is worth noting that the 5 per cent of manufacturing establishments where strikes did occur between 1971 and 1973 employed 30 per cent of the total manufacturing workforce. This suggests, as would be expected, that strikes were concentrated in the larger workplaces (Smith *et al.* 1977, p.54).

as a 'hotbed of industrial unrest' (p.9), strikes were remarkably concentrated and 'two thirds of all working days lost in the period, together with some 40 per cent of all stoppages, came from just three industry groups, with less than 7 per cent of employment between them' (p.13).[17] The workplace militancy and conflict commonly associated with Merseyside thus appeared to be concentrated within a relatively small number of workplaces. Bean and Stoney also point out that it was in these establishments that the effects of recession and anti-union legislation were having the greatest impact and presenting the greatest challenge to Merseyside's long-standing traditions of worker militancy.

This is not to argue, however, that the same subset of workplaces in a region continuously dominates that region's strike record, or that there are fixed and discrete subsets of 'militant' and 'quiescent' workplaces. Obviously, within any sector or geographical area it is likely that individual workplaces will wax and wane in militancy over time. Research into the geography of industrial action in the coal mining industry certainly suggests that workplace activity alters from one period to another (Church *et al.* 1990). In a study of strike trends in coal-mining over the half-century between 1893 and 1940, Church and his co-authors identified Scotland and Wales as consistently exceeding other regions in terms of strike activity. But underlying these patterns, the individual workplaces where strikes were concentrated varied enormously. A pit that suffered poor industrial relations at one particular juncture was not necessarily strike-prone in others:

> The typical strike-prone place, therefore, like the typical strike-prone colliery...has not been strike-prone for year after year. Much more typical is a dramatic upsurge of strike activity in one place which subsides equally rapidly. Fence Houses in Durham exemplifies this pattern particularly clearly. It does not enter the records until 1908; then between December 1908 and January 1913 it experiences 25 disputes; thereafter it disappears from the records until the 1930s with one dispute in October 1935, another in February 1937, another in June 1938. (p.342)

Regional strike trends are thus the result of a complex mosaic of shifting workplace conflict and changes in the politics of workers' militancy. Yet, at the same time, even though in any region the specific incidence of strike activity moves around between workplaces, the fact that particular regions have exhibited persistently high (or low) average strike rates indicates that there are (or have been) regional cultures, 'externalities', or 'community' traditions that make for a higher (or lower) proneness or likelihood of workers to strike in any establishment in those regions. There is a direct, and not unexpected, parallel here with the different regional union cultures that we noted in Chapters Three and Four. As in the case of trade unionism, a multi-scaled approach is needed to understand the geographies of

---

17 The three industries were motor vehicles, shipbuilding, and the port-inland water transport sector.

industrial action. Whilst large scale economic and political trends are clearly significant in shaping the propensities and capacities of workers to engage in industrial action, what happens at a smaller scale is also determined by the nature of local workplace relationships. Strike action depends upon shared traditions and expectations of workers, the responses of management to collective organization and action by employees, and on the scale and availability of union resources to support and sustain workers engaged in industrial stoppages. Geographical location makes a difference to these factors, but both local and non-local influences are involved. Without exploring the complex interrelationships between individual workplaces, local and regional traditions and the national economic-political climate, accounts of worker militancy and quiescence will be incomplete.

CONCLUSIONS

It is clear that strike activity amongst the British workforce has declined far more steeply since 1979 than has unionization. Both have been buffeted by the combined impact of economic and labour market restructuring and a new, more restrictive legislative environment, but unionization seems to have been more resilient to these pressures. There can be little doubt that the high levels of unemployment that have existed since the beginning of the 1980s – averaging over two million – and the insecurity of employment that now characterizes the labour market have exerted a considerable 'disciplinary' effect on the propensity of workers and unions to resort to strike action. Added to this, the series of defeats suffered by several groups of strikers during the 1980s, especially the coal-miners, have also dampened strike activity. The decline of the unions, the trend towards 'strike-free' deals between unions and employers, and the growth of individualism amongst certain segments of the workforce (especially in new growth sectors), have also contributed to the decline in strike incidence, although as we saw in the previous chapter such developments are not as generalized as they are often portrayed. But, almost certainly, the most important factor undermining industrial militancy has been the barrage of employment law since 1980, the cumulative effect of which has been to circumscribe the scope of workers to take industrial action both politically and spatially. Geographically, as the net of national employment legislation has been cast ever wider and has become ever more restrictive, traditional regional and local variations in regulatory practices, industrial cultures and strike propensity have been increasingly 'nationalized', that is, brought under close central Government control.[18]

---

18 Jenkins (1995) uses the term 'nationalization' to describe how under Tory rule since 1979 increasing spheres of British socio-economic life have been brought under central Government control and regulation. The labour market has been no exception. Despite the Conservatives' political rhetoric of 'rolling back the state' and 'freeing up the labour market', employment relations are now more regulated than at any time in post-war history.

A key issue, therefore, is whether as a result of these various pressures and processes we are witnessing the disappearance of the regionally differentiated workplace traditions and cultures that have sustained so much strike action during the last hundred years. Obviously, we cannot know what the future holds for strike activity. Whether the progressive fall in strike incidence since the second half of the 1980s is a permanent feature, or merely a temporary trough, will depend on a host of future economic, social and political factors. It may be that strikes will be replaced by alternative forms of worker dissent and workplace arbitration and conflict resolution.[19] And depending on national political developments, we might see attempts by future governments to extend the embargo on the right to strike that currently applies to certain public employees (GCHQ personnel, the police, the armed forces) into wider spheres of the labour market.[20] But on balance it seems unlikely that industrial conflict has disappeared (Crouch 1990; Regini 1992; Shalev 1992), and it is entirely possible that the historical pattern of long cycles of militancy and quiescence discussed at the beginning of the chapter is not yet exhausted. The question is whether ongoing changes in labour markets, in the organization and management of work, and in the political environment will generate new sources of workplace conflict and new incentives for mass collective action. If the past is any guide to the future, they probably will.

Similarly, it is unlikely that geography will cease to be important in shaping the incidence of industrial action. The map of industrial action has always been spatially uneven, and our data shows that even in the 1980s workers in the North, Yorkshire and Humberside, Wales and Scotland continued to be more strike-prone than their contemporaries in the South East, South West and East Anglia. What is certain is that future industrial action will involve new groups of workers that are less associated with the labour traditions of the past. Historically, the geographies of industrial action have been characterized by a combination of established patterns of strikes with an expansion of activity into newer locations: the old has evolved to meet the changing circumstances of the new, and we may expect future developments in strike activity to repeat this process. As we saw in previous chapters, the map of British trade unionism and tradition remains uneven. Such geographical variations may well prove to be important in shaping the course and development of industrial action in the future. Were industrial conflict to increase significantly, it is likely that spatial variations would widen. The map of industrial conflict and militancy may take on different patterns from those of the past, but

---

19 Such as the spread of 'pendulum arbitration' agreements. While these do not specifically forbid strikes, they oblige both sides – employees and employers – to abide by the arbitrators' verdict, and thereby remove much of the ability of workers to resort to the ultimate expression of rejection, the strike.

20 Given the continuing distancing of the 'new' Labour party in its political relations with and attitudes to the unions, it seems unlikely that any future Labour government would rescind all of the anti-union, anti-strike legislation that the Conservative governments passed in the 1980s and early 1990s.

spatial unevenness is such a long-standing feature of strike activity, being so closely connected to the uneven development of capital and to spatially differentiated patterns of production and traditions of unionization, that it is unlikely to disappear altogether. Indeed, and somewhat ironically, the increasing 'localization' of strike action by the new labour laws may well renew the significance of location and place in shaping the incidence of industrial conflict.

CHAPTER SIX

Decentralization and Local Industrial Politics

INTRODUCTION

The relations between the scope of collective bargaining and trade union organization have long been a topic of industrial relations research. Employers' willingness to engage in collective bargaining on aspects of the employment relationship has rightly been described as one of the key dimensions of the regulatory regime facing the unions. Authors such as Clegg (1976) and Flanders (1970) have argued emphatically that collective bargaining and trade unionism are tied together in a mutually influential relationship. Indeed, Clegg suggests that wide cross-national differences in trade union organization can largely be explained by differences in the structure of collective bargaining from one country to another. While this view has been criticized,[1] one of the implications of this long-standing theme is that the geographical distribution of trade unionism is closely interwoven with the extent and scale of collective bargaining coverage. Despite the simplicity of this basic argument, however, the precise form of this relationship in contemporary capitalist societies is not easily demonstrated as the changing contours of collective bargaining are difficult to trace.

Over the past decade and a half many capitalist states have seen a reconfiguration of the content and structure of their systems of collective bargaining. Most importantly, this reconfiguration is widely seen as a process of *decentralization*, in which the locus of bargaining is shifting away from the national and multi-employer scale to divisional, firm and plant levels. In addition, these reforms have also often involved a degree of *decollectivization* or the disappearance of collective arrangements for setting pay and employment conditions. As we have seen in Chapter One, the proportion of the workforce covered by collective bargaining has fallen in a number of advanced economies, especially in Britain. Most

---

1 Most notably, Hyman has repeatedly argued that the overwhelming emphasis on collective bargaining and job regulation exaggerates the importance of procedural issues and regulatory order at the expense of substantive issues and structural conflicts (see Hyman 1989b).

156

discussions of these changes have adopted a national perspective which treats national economies as single units, and while commentators have been alert to the changing role of scale in collective bargaining, their research has tended to focus on specific industrial sectors or case-studies of individual firms so that the geographical picture of changes in collective bargaining is difficult to piece together. However, we argue here that, in the case of Britain, there has been a significant regional dimension to the reform of collective bargaining.

Those studies which have explicitly considered the effects of decentralization on trade unions have also tended to compare different unions in different economic sectors rather than analyzing geographical and sub-national regional differences. To a certain extent, of course, these are overlapping issues.[2] However, given that decentralization has in many cases been driven by a strategic attempt to make bargaining more responsive to local labour market conditions, it is perhaps surprising that its geographical consequences have not received more attention. Although most statements pertaining to these consequences have been based more on assumption than on detailed research, it is possible to identify two different approaches to understanding the implications of collective bargaining change for trade union geography. In the first, and probably most widely held view, decentralization is closely and reciprocally related to trade union decline. It is suggested that the decentralization and decollectivization of bargaining fragments and weakens the unions' relative power, especially since decentralization is closely associated with the implementation of new human resource management (HRM) techniques which may make union representation in the workplace superfluous. Furthermore, this relative weakening of trade unionism is often argued to facilitate further decentralization, generating a vicious circle of union decline. In contrast, a number of scholars have taken a more circumspect view of decentralization and have argued that its consequences are more ambiguous. In particular, they distinguish between local and central unions and suggest that while the end of national bargaining is disruptive at a national scale, undermining central union organizations, it could well create new opportunities for the resurgence of 'local unionism'. According to this view, one of the reasons for the development of national bargaining structures in the past was precisely to curb the effects of local militancy and wage drift, and in the contemporary drive towards decentralization, governments and employers may be unwittingly rekindling and enhancing local trade union power.

This chapter reviews the debate generated by these two approaches. One of the most significant arguments to emerge is that the consequences of decentralization, and in particular its effects on trade unions, cannot be predicted without

2   Since, in a manner analogous to the discussion of regional differences in unionization and strikes in Chapters Four and Five, the geography of collective bargaining will reflect, in part at least, regional variations in industrial and occupational structure, firm sizes and categories, etc.

reference to the local context in which its occurs. The impact of a shift towards collective bargaining at a smaller scale will depend very much on specific management policies, union capabilities and workplace responses. Our main argument in the second half of the chapter is that it is important to recognize that these factors will vary from place to place. As we argued in Chapter One, industrial relations and industrial politics are spatially embedded in the sense that they are formed by locally varying economic, social and cultural contexts. The outcomes of decentralization will be shaped by the interaction of current institutional change with existing local traditions, norms and practices. We use the example of the British engineering industry to demonstrate this argument and to illustrate the importance of these local contexts. It is clear from this example that the complexity and indeterminacy of the decentralization process imply that it is premature to suggest that unions should respond to current institutional reforms by reorganizing themselves into devolved federations of local unions.

DELIMITING DECENTRALIZATION

Since the late 1980s, commentators have repeatedly argued that the decentralization of collective bargaining is one of the dominant trends in Western European industrial relations. Definitions of decentralization range between a narrow sense, which refers to a shift in the nature of collective agreements away from national and multi-employer levels to enterprise and plant levels, and a broad sense which describes a more general restructuring of the relations between employers and employed and their joint regulation of work. Regini (1992a, p.7) believes that we are witnessing 'a general shift in the centre of gravity of economic and industrial relations systems from the level of macro-economic management to the micro-level of the firm'. Baglioni (1990) likewise suggests that decentralization is one of the more common and visible features of industrial relations in the 1980s and 1990s. Indeed, in his view, the widespread diminution of the role played by central organizations in favour of more localized associations and individual companies is the most important process in the contemporary remodelling of labour relations (see also Turner 1991). Crouch (1993) describes this tendency as part of a shift towards 'disorganized capitalism' which began with the resurgence of localized shopfloor organization and militancy during the 1960s. However, most authors agree that, in contrast to earlier periods, decentralization during the 1980s was driven by the requirements and strategies of employers rather than by union workplace strength (Ferner and Hyman 1992). While decentralization in various forms has been experienced in some Western countries, including Sweden, Italy and the United States, and most strongly in Great Britain (Katz 1993), it is still a very uneven process of change. As the OECD (1994b) recently emphasized, decentralization is by no means universal and in many Western states there have been concurrent moves to both decentralize and centralize particular aspects of collective bargaining and employee relations. Indeed, in the majority of OECD member-states the sectoral level still remains the principal arena for wage determination.

In Britain the restructuring of collective bargaining has been twofold. First, bargaining *coverage,* the proportion of the employed workforce whose pay and conditions are determined by some form of collective agreement, has fallen.[3] While it is estimated that in 1910 only 15 per cent of employees were covered by collective wage agreements, this figure had increased to somewhere around 70 per cent by the 1950s (Milner 1994). The proportion then declined slightly before peaking again in the early 1970s, when in 1973 coverage reached 72 per cent of the employed workforce (87% in public services, 64% in manufacturing, and 47% in private services) (Brown 1993). More recent estimates can be derived from the Workplace Industrial Relations Surveys. These indicate that coverage fell from an average of 71 to 54 per cent between 1984 and 1990. Milner (1994) suggests that if adjustment is made to take account of the WIRS omission of small workplaces, a 1990 figure of 47 per cent is probably a more accurate estimate. After reviewing the declining influence of statutory pay arrangements, he concludes that 'In this context surely the most important finding is that a smaller proportion of Britain's employees are now covered by some form of collective pay setting arrangements than at any time since the Second World War' (p.23).

The second major change is in the *structure* of bargaining. Brown and Walsh (1991) suggest that since the 1950s the number of industry-wide and multi-employer agreements in Britain has been in decline. This, they argue, was a key factor behind the Donovan Commission's finding of a growing divergence between agreed national and multi-employer wage rates and actual earnings. As the 1970s progressed more employers opted out of multi-employer agreements and pay bargaining was assigned to single employers at company, division or establishment level. The WIRS show a continuing decline in the importance of multi-employer bargaining during the 1980s. Indeed, the rate of decline of national bargaining accelerated between 1984 and 1990 (Gregg and Yates 1991). According to Brown and Walsh (1991, p.49) 'At least sixteen major national bargaining groups, covering a total of over a million employees, have been terminated since 1986.' These included engineering, textiles, food retailing, independent television, newspaper distribution, printing, bus and coach industries, retail banking, paint and cement manufacturing and the water industry (see Purcell 1991; Jackson *et al.* 1993). Moreover, this decline in national, multi-employer collective bargaining was accompanied by an increase in the proportion of employees not covered by collective bargaining at all (see Millward *et al.* 1992).

Contrary to expectations, however, while the proportion of manufacturing employees affected by single employer, multi-plant bargaining also fell, the

---

3   In most accounts of this change, the coverage of collective bargaining is used to refer to the proportion of workers whose pay is affected by collective bargaining rather than the stricter definition of those who are party to collective agreements.

proportion of non-manuals whose pay was decided by this type of bargaining actually increased slightly, particularly amongst those in private services. Perhaps more surprising is the fact that *plant-level* bargaining became less influential in all sectors between 1984 and 1990. As Millward *et al.* (1992) concluded from the 1990 WIRS, collective bargaining has not simply been decentralized, and 'rather than leading to more plant-level negotiations, the move away from multi-employer negotiations [has been] accompanied by an increase in negotiating structures at enterprise or company level' (p.355). In Britain, then, the overall decline in collective bargaining has not been accompanied by the universal decentralization of the bargaining process to the individual workplace. While this has occurred in some instances, it has been more common for multi-employer agreements to be replaced by bargaining arrangements at the company level, and many of these have multiple plants and offices under their jurisdiction.

There have been several different explanations and interpretations of the causes and dynamics of decentralization. One explanation is that decentralization is primarily the outcome of a change in corporate and management strategy, involving a devolution of responsibility to smaller units within firms, be they divisions, multi-plant sites or profit-related business centres (Jackson *et al.* 1993). Such change is a type of diversification which increases the autonomy of business units and profit centres and this enhances lower-level managers' responsibility for decision-making on industrial relations matters. This is often argued to be a by-product of a general move to diversify and 'delayer' corporate decision-making and financial management so that it is freed from the dictates and pressures of collective industrial relations considerations (Marginson *et al.* 1988; Purcell and Ahlstrand 1989). Nevertheless, decentralization also reflects a desire by many employers to 'individualize' workplace relationships and to link pay to performance. The aim is relate pay much more to company or unit performance than to national rates of pay decided in multi-employer agreements (Gregg and Yates 1991). According to Brown and Walsh (1991) 'The driving force behind the accelerated decentralisation of pay bargaining in the 1980s has been the desire of employers to gain greater direct control over their unit labour costs' (p.51). Decentralization is therefore likely to have proceeded furthest in companies which produce a heterogeneous range of goods, which are subject to intense competition and which can gain advantage by altering pay-setting arrangements. Yet, even among these firms, the extent of decentralization should not be exaggerated, as many companies with devolved bargaining continue to co-ordinate the setting of wages at higher corporate levels.

Another interpretation of decentralization, which is particularly relevant to the British case, emphasizes the process of economic deregulation which many Western governments have pursued since the 1970s. As we described in Chapter Four, the general aim of these policies has been to remove obstacles and rigidities in the labour market and so to promote greater flexibility. In Britain, the traditional reliance on voluntaristic bargaining has meant that deregulatory policy in the labour market has focused on limiting the powers of trade unions over the labour market, confining the effects of collective bargaining to individual plants and companies and restricting the rights of employees (Deakin and Wilkinson 1991). In addition, the privatization and marketization of public services in conjunction with the introduction of compulsory competitive tendering (CCT) has fragmented and weakened the institutions of collective wage bargaining in the public sector. As Smith and Morton (1993) argue, the fragmentation and decentralization of bargaining has been central to the Conservative governments' policy of union exclusion. Furthermore, it has been suggested that the decentralization of collective bargaining is linked to changes in the nature of the state, whereby a devolution of power and responsibility to lower territorial levels may encourage the decentralization of other political organizations, including unions. According to Friedland and Sanders (1990, p.333) this 'decentralization of the state' will 'reinforce territorial forms of political organization, including the blocs of corporations of unions that are concentrated in certain industries'. However, this view can easily be exaggerated. As we have already noted (see Chapter Five), there has been a gulf of difference between the Conservative governments' rhetoric of decentralizing powers and responsibilities to the local level and the reality of an increasing degree of governmental centralization. In this context, while the British state has sought to promote the localization of collective bargaining, it has simultaneously imposed centralized constraints on public sector wages. Indeed, the 'decentralization' of the state through the marketization and privatization of the public sector has gone hand in hand with increased central control over local state authorities and public employees.

For many commentators, however, the main significance of decentralization is its link to new management techniques, and particularly human resources management (HRM). From this perspective, the restructuring of bargaining and pay determination is part of a more fundamental reworking of employment systems. Decentralization is argued to be a deliberate strategic attempt to increase the identification of employees with the company's goals, to establish a self-regulated, high quality, more flexible and loyal workforce. This involves measures such as the introduction of quality circles and team working as well as individual merit and appraisal schemes (Storey 1989). Moreover, these techniques hinge upon the strategic integration of personnel issues into strategic business plans. Allegedly, in large companies:

> In the UK, as in most of Europe, the preference has been for reducing the disadvantages of unionism by getting collective bargaining linked strongly to firm-specific issues while simultaneously reducing the dependency on collective bargaining as the medium for the management of change, and on trade unions as the main link with the workforce (Purcell 1991, p.37).

While these preferences may have been realized in some prominent cases, more critical studies have described the implementation of human resource management as partial and piecemeal so that its impact to date has been limited (Blyton and Turnbull 1992; Scott 1994). In reality, the achievement of a coherent and comprehensive system of human resource management is also highly problematic and much less straightforward than often supposed (Walsh 1993).

Finally, decentralization is sometimes linked to new, more flexible production and labour systems and the increasing importance of employment in small firms. In this view, company management is now less interested in industrial relations institutions which are designed to deal with aggregate problems, and much more concerned with enhancing the flexibility of work, wages and employment in individual plants, in order to meet the variability and uncertainty of product markets. According to Amoroso 'The new feature of the system is the end of the relative autonomy of the system of industrial relations and its incorporation into the production system...into a new "firm culture", thereby making the firm the centre of the whole system' (1992, p.340). Moreover, several authors have argued that the rise of post-Fordist flexible industrialization means the revival of a regional scale in industrial relations. Perrulli (1993), for example, contends that the region now plays a key role in industrial relations as local external factors have become important to the achievement of co-operative industrial relations. Teague (1993) likewise suggests that a new regional pattern is emerging in European industrial relations. We consider this argument more fully later in this chapter but, again, it is worth noting that while this perspective may be highly relevant to fast-growing industrial districts in continental Europe and the United States, there is a lack of empirical evidence showing its relevance to changes in British industrial relations and wage bargaining structures.

It is evident, then, that the decentralization of industrial relations has been explained in several different ways and has been related to a number of different aspects of contemporary economic and political change. A key question concerns the implications of this decentralization for trade union organization. It is to this issue that we now turn.

TRADE UNIONS AND DECENTRALIZATION

The idea that the decentralization of wage determination profoundly weakens the influence and relative power of trade unions, thereby encouraging membership loss, has been common. Katz (1993) describes this view as part of the 'bargaining power' hypothesis in which decentralization represents an explicit strategy to strengthen management's workplace bargaining position. Indeed, by localizing wage bargaining arrangements it is argued that management can more effectively subject wages to local labour market competition. In this context, some unions are rethinking their strategies. Kassalow (1987), for example, suggests that centrifugal shifts in bargaining necessitate major modifications in union structure and policy. Several authors have pointed out, albeit with some exceptions and qualifications, that cross-national comparisons in union density show that density tends to be higher in countries which have centralized bargaining. Based on this, Western (1995) argues that 'The decentralisation of labor-market institutions and the decline of social democratic parties have limited unions' capacity to coordinate and advance organizing effort at the national level' (p.183). In his view, there are four mechanisms which link the decentralization of bargaining to union decline in the OECD countries. First, centralized bargaining usually extends union wages to unorganized workers, and this defuses employer opposition to unions. By focusing the costs of unionism on the firm, decentralization can increase employer resistance to organization. Second, because the benefits of union membership become more focused at an establishment or company scale, employers can reduce the demand for unions by providing wages and conditions equivalent to collective agreements. Western suggests that this 'avoidance strategy' has been common in the United States. Third, decentralization weakens the influence of central union confederations over macroeconomic policy-making. And, finally, decentralized bargaining weakens the co-ordination between unions in their negotiation initiatives, increases inter-union rivalry, and diverts a greater amount of union resources to jurisdictional disputes.[4] In addition to these processes, decentralization may also weaken trade unionism by breaking down the sense of collective identity and solidarity that national or industry-wide organization and bargaining engender, since:

> a centralised union movement is an institutional embodiment of the norm of collective membership and responsibility. It conveys the idea that, whatever their particular industrial location and job, all workers are part of one unified entity sharing a similar identity and similar interests. (Lange 1984, p.108)

Western concludes that decentralization, together with the decline of social-democratic parties, to which unions are often linked politically, has decisively influenced union decline.

Other commentators, however, have been more circumspect in their analysis of the influence of decentralization on union decline. The House of Commons Employment Committee's (HM Government 1994) report on the future of British trade unionism, for instance, argued that there is no evidence that the decentralization of bargaining in the private sector is linked to the decline of union membership. The Committee suggested that negotiation is merely shifted to lower levels of company structure, and argued instead that the introduction of personalized contracts of employment is far more damaging to unions. In a comparative cross-national study, Visser (1991) insisted that the hypothesis that high union density is ensured by continued multi-employer bargaining fails to explain union decline in countries such as Austria and the Netherlands. Similarly, Storper (1995)

---

4   In addition, one might add that decentralization typically increases the workload of union officials (Industrial Relations Services 1992b) and so leaves less time for recruitment and organization.

has also pointed out that apparently decentralized systems, particularly in Italy, have surprisingly high union densities. He suggests that this is because there are local and regional shared conventions and norms which support unionism in the absence of formal centralized bargaining. The extent of co-ordination between employers and within employers' associations is clearly not synonymous with the degree of centralization (Soskice 1990). The important point is clearly that the decentralization of collective bargaining must be judged in its context and in conjunction with other factors shaping union organization and economic activity.

A similar argument has emerged from studies which emphasize the varied consequences of decentralization. Micro-level approaches to industrial relations research indicate that decentralization can be associated with very different management strategies, not all designed to undermine trade union organization (see Guest 1989). In practice, decentralization is often a contradictory process containing internal tensions which can yield opportunities for new patterns of unionization. Walsh (1993), for example, argues that in Britain decentralization may fail to yield efficiency gains. A recent survey of trade union officers also found that the devolution of pay bargaining to local managers had tended to worsen relations between union officials and managers as the latter were often perceived as incompetent and ill-prepared for bargaining activities (Industrial Relations Services 1992). Furthermore, affected unions can intervene in new management practices and initiatives, shaping the outcome and implementation of change. A case study of the introduction of human resource management by Martinez-Lucio and Weston (1992) for example, found the process to be significantly altered by traditional modes of representation and union negotiation. Finally, and partly as a consequence, decentralization may be much more problematic for central unions and confederations than for locals, for in the former local union officials have much less experience of wage bargaining, workplace negotiation and membership strategies than their counterparts in the latter.

Developing this latter point, Hancke (1993) finds that in Western Europe membership densities in unions without strong locals have declined by as much as a third, whereas those with strong locals have lost relatively few, if any, members. In his view, these membership trends support calls for the development of more local unions. Indeed, several industrial relations analysts have gone so far as to argue that the best response to decentralization is for unions to 'go local' and relocalize themselves. Thus in his review of recent Italian experiences, Locke (1990) suggests that

> The reconstruction of the labour movement along these more horizontal lines
> – as federations of locals firmly embedded in their regional economies – may
> be a viable organisational solution for the entire labour movement. Just as
> the national union was the most appropriate organisational solution in the
> previous era of national markets and large bureaucratic firms, the federation
> of strong locals could be most adept at representing the interests of workers

in this period of market fragmentation and constant industrial change. (pp.372–373)

He believes that such federations of locals are probably the most effective means of representing the interests of workers in an era of fragmentation, decentralization and decollectivization (Locke 1992). Essentially the same view is shared by Kern and Sabel (1992), who in surveying the European industrial relations scene conclude that if they are to survive and prosper, the unions themselves need to decentralize spatially so as to exploit the opportunities that the increasingly locally-specialized character of production offers for revitalizing local labour movements.

Such prescriptive discussions, it should be noted, have been based more on assertion rather than on detailed empirical research. The evidence that is available suggests that union responses to new devolutionary practices have varied both within and between individual unions (Beaumont 1991). Our own interviews with the national research officers of some of the largest unions[5] and of the TUC confirm this finding. As one TUC officer remarked, some unions have been relatively well-equipped to respond to decentralization as they have needed to bargain locally, while in contrast, it is in the nationwide public sector where the shift to local bargaining will have greater impact:

> In the public sector, you've had negotiations only carried out by national union officers, and local representatives having no pay bargaining function whatsoever. They just typically dealt with local grievances. So unions are now having to change their physical organization, to give local representatives the competence to carry out local pay bargaining. (Interview 15 December 1994)

In contrast, an official from the Manufacturing, Science and Finance Union (MSF) acknowledged that the union's membership base in manufacturing had always depended upon local arrangements for negotiating over pay:

> Now in terms of MSF as an organization, we have always been very comfortable with both national and devolved bargaining. We have a lot of experience of devolved bargaining and always have had, because national bargaining was not the case in every industry and sector that we worked with. (Interview 23 November 1994)

While the union is apparently able to cope with changes in the level of bargaining and has 'survived by bargaining where the action is', it is nevertheless opposed to individualized pay and contracts. A research officer of the Transport and General Workers' Union (TGWU) also claimed that 'Although there is clearly a duty for us to increase the level of the service that we have for stewards,…and that is a policy

---

5   Interviews were carried out with Research officers at UNISON, UCATT, TGWU, MSF, BIFU, AEEU and the TUC in November and December 1994.

for the union, it is not such a dramatic shift for us as it has been, or is, for other unions' (Interview, 18 November 1994).

In his analysis of the Transport and General Workers' Union's (TGWU) response to human resource management, Fisher (1995) found that different regions and trade groups in the union had widely different levels of educational activity, organizational ability, political complexion and experience. The unions' internal organizational structures are vitally important when responses to decentralization are considered (Martinez-Lucio and Weston 1992). In those unions which lack appropriate workplace representation there is a need to provide training, guidance and support to local officials whose workload is typically increased by decentralization (Industrial Relations Services 1993a). Before forming UNISON, for example, COHSE and NUPE launched new services for local activists and officers, and NALGO produced a new handbook to guide local representatives in local pay and conditions bargaining within the National Health Service. Local union officers in the public sector are no longer preoccupied with case work but have had to shift to local bargaining (Interview with Unison Research Officer, 6 December 1994). However, improving local organization and activists' negotiating skills does not necessarily imply that unions should be restructured as 'federations of locals'. Indeed, as our case study of engineering later in this chapter will show, there are many reasons for arguing that it is vital for unions to retain their organizational reach at a variety of spatial scales ranging from the local to the national (and beyond).

Even from these few comments, then, it would seem that the assertion that unions need to be reconstructed as 'locals' embedded in regional economies represents a somewhat partial truth which takes inadequate account of the context in which decentralization occurs. Hitherto we have reviewed some accounts which show that this all-important context should be understood as referring to the specific dynamics of different industries and sectors as well as the different historical traditions, industrial relations legacies and constructed priorities of particular unions. In the remainder of this chapter, however, we argue that this context also needs to be understood geographically. There are two sets of reasons why the effects and implications of decentralization should be understood as varying from place to place and region to region. First, as we aim to demonstrate briefly in the next section, the anatomy of decentralization in Britain has shown a marked regional pattern which again suggests that there is a regional dimension to the regulation of labour markets. And second, our case study of engineering unionism is designed to show that, even within a given industrial sector, decentralization will have different consequences in different parts of the country; decentralized bargaining will be shaped by the pre-existing traditions of union organization and the organizational resources bequeathed by the past.

THE ANATOMY OF DECENTRALIZATION REVISITED: THE GEOGRAPHY OF COLLECTIVE BARGAINING

Most accounts of decentralization use change in the structure and level of collective bargaining as a key indicator. In Britain, this indicator has typically been expressed in national aggregate terms. However, it would be wrong to assume that there have been no important differences in collective bargaining across the regions of the country. Tables 6.1 and 6.2 are calculated from the New Earnings Surveys of 1978 and 1985.[6] They show the proportion of employees whose pay was affected by different levels of collective bargaining and those not covered by collective bargaining of any form.

While these tables illustrate that some decline in the degree of collective bargaining coverage had already begun between the late 1970s and mid 1980s, they also show that the process was markedly uneven. In 1978 the coverage of both national-only and that of national plus supplementary bargaining was substantially higher in the Northern regions of England and in Wales and Scotland than elsewhere. The lowest rates were found in London and the South East and, somewhat surprisingly, in the West Midlands. The coverage of national-only agreements remained fairly static up to 1985, while the coverage of national plus supplementary declined in all regions. However, in 1985 the north/south differential was still considerable. The data show that the significant change within the period was not a shift to smaller scales of bargaining but an increase in the proportion of employees not covered by any collective agreement. At the start of the period, regional differences in the lack of collective bargaining agreements were pronounced. Thus, in 1978, nearly 40 per cent of employees in Greater London already had no collective wage agreements compared to only 20 per cent in the North and Wales. Up to 1985, the increase of non-coverage was fairly uniform across the country so that the relative differences between the South East and Wales and the North remained striking.

Tables 6.3 and 6.4 are based on the WIRS of 1984 and 1990.[7] Unfortunately, the results are not directly comparable with the NES figures[8] but they nevertheless show that the changes in collective bargaining in Britain during the 1980s continued to be subject to regional differentiation. Several key trends are apparent. In the first place, despite the marked shift during the 1980s away from collective bargaining, and multi-employer bargaining in particular, a marked geographical

---

6   The NES results are based on a one per cent survey of employees. The survey asks managers and employers to indicate the types of negotiated collective agreements which affect the pay and conditions of the specific employees concerned (see Appendix).

7   The specific WIRS information used here is derived from the question which asks respondents to indicate the level(s) of collective bargaining which normally operate in the establishment.

8   The WIRS and NES results differ because of the different sampling frames and questions used by the two surveys and also because the WIRS does not include workplaces with less than 25 employees.

**Table 6.1: The scope and structure of collective
bargaining in the regions, 1978**

	National agreement with supplementary	National agreement only	District, company, or local agreement	No collective agreement
South East	15.3	36.3	10.7	37.7
Greater London	13.5	37.2	10.2	39.3
Outer South East	17.4	35.4	11.2	36.1
East Anglia	17.7	38.7	10.4	33.1
South West	21.0	42.4	8.0	28.6
West Midlands	16.7	34.7	12.1	29.2
East Midlands	23.6	40.9	8.6	27.0
Yorkshire/Humberside	24.9	40.1	8.7	26.2
North West	23.9	38.0	13.5	24.6
North	25.5	43.4	11.3	20.1
Wales	23.1	46.6	9.9	20.4
Scotland	18.3	44.6	9.7	27.5
Great Britain	**20.3**	**39.2**	**10.6**	**30.0**

Source: Authors' analysis of New Earnings Survey, 1978.
Note: Per cent of employees covered by different types of agreement.

**Table 6.2: The scope and structure of collective
bargaining in the regions, 1985**

	National agreement with supplementary	National agreement only	District, company, or local agreement	No collective agreement
South East	9.3	37.0	9.9	43.9
Greater London	8.8	38.6	9.0	43.6
Outer South East	9.8	35.6	10.6	44.2
East Anglia	12.2	37.2	10.2	39.7
South West	11.7	42.9	10.9	34.5
West Midlands	15.9	36.8	13.1	34.2
East Midlands	15.6	43.3	11.4	32.1
Yorkshire/Humberside	17.0	42.6	9.7	30.6
North West	16.1	38.6	13.6	31.6
North	18.9	44.1	11.1	25.9
Wales	13.7	50.3	9.6	26.3
Scotland	13.1	45.0	9.8	32.2
Great Britain	**13.2**	**40.3**	**10.7**	**35.9**

Source: Authors' analysis of New Earnings Survey, 1985.
Note: Per cent of employees covered by different types of agreement.

Table 6.3: The scope and structure of collective bargaining in the regions, manual workers, 1984 and 1990

	Year	Multi-employer bargaining	Employer bargaining	Plant-level bargaining	None
London	1984	42.8	37.7	18.9	20.8
	1990	21.5	30.1	10.9	43.4
Outer South East	1984	41.2	20.8	17.6	28.2
	1990	30.3	21.4	13.8	44.7
East Anglia	1984	41.6	22.1	19.6	30.4
	1990	24.9	15.9	12.0	50.6
South West	1984	59.2	21.4	13.9	18.6
	1990	22.5	20.7	22.0	39.7
East Midlands	1984	59.6	18.0	42.5	19.1
	1990	24.0	21.8	28.2	33.6
Yorks/Humberside	1984	55.3	35.3	18.7	7.5
	1990	40.0	25.5	20.1	30.0
North West	1984	54.8	25.6	27.3	7.1
	1990	23.0	24.8	27.3	33.9
North	1984	58.8	24.9	22.4	5.8
	1990	43.9	12.6	24.5	29.4
Wales	1984	55.7	32.7	27.2	13.7
	1990	44.7	22.2	30.3	21.5
Scotland	1984	61.4	19.7	14.0	12.8
	1990	39.9	26.4	16.7	29.1
Great Britain	**1984**	**52.6**	**27.0**	**25.8**	**20.1**
	1990	**33.4**	**23.4**	**22.6**	**37.4**

Source: Authors' analysis of WIRS 1984, 1990.
Note: Per cent of manual employees covered by different types of agreement.

division between the more unionized northern regions and the less unionized southern regions of the country has persisted. For manual workers, for example, the coverage of multi-employer agreements in 1990 is lowest in London and the South East and highest in Scotland, Wales and the Northern region. The proportion of manual workers affected by multi-employer agreements in the Northern region was roughly twice the figure for manual employees in London. The decline in collective bargaining coverage has been marked and rapid in most regions. Nevertheless, in 1990 non-coverage was still about 10 per cent greater in London and the South than it was elsewhere. For non-manuals also, it is notable that Scotland the North and Yorkshire and Humberside show much more resistence to the fall in multi-employer bargaining, and in the case of Wales its coverage, as a

Table 6.4: The scope and structure of collective bargaining in the regions, non-manual workers, 1984 and 1990

	Year	Multi-employer bargaining	Employer bargaining	Plant-level bargaining	None
London	1984	41.4	25.1	7.6	35.0
	1990	21.4	23.3	3.9	55.5
Outer South East	1984	46.6	21.8	9.6	28.6
	1990	28.9	23.9	5.2	46.2
East Anglia	1984	44.5	10.5	9.0	40.6
	1990	42.7	22.4	5.3	33.6
South West	1984	50.4	15.0	16.1	28.5
	1990	43.8	26.1	3.9	35.1
East Midlands	1984	50.7	22.5	24.2	24.3
	1990	45.5	23.8	14.9	34.2
West Midlands	1984	60.9	13.4	16.5	14.3
	1990	28.2	19.3	11.5	43.0
Yorks/Humberside	1984	64.5	21.1	15.2	19.3
	1990	50.9	13.9	4.6	34.2
North West	1984	58.7	22.5	11.5	16.2
	1990	27.1	29.5	4.4	41.1
North	1984	69.3	8.8	9.2	14.7
	1990	52.2	16.6	5.8	29.0
Wales	1984	56.4	28.0	8.3	13.3
	1990	59.8	9.5	4.8	28.2
Scotland	1984	60.5	16.6	5.0	19.5
	1990	53.8	23.5	5.3	29.9
Great Britain	**1984**	**54.4**	**21.2**	**13.3**	**27.2**
	1990	**41.0**	**22.5**	**7.1**	**42.8**

Source: Authors' analysis of WIRS 1984, 1990.

Note: Per cent of non-manual employees covered by different types of agreement.

proportion of non-manual employees, actually increased slightly. In addition to this broad differential, it is noticeable that there have been rapid changes in the nature of bargaining in the West Midlands and the North West. The WIRS results indicate that for both manual and non-manual workers in these two regions, and in the East Midlands to a lesser extent, there has been a move away from a bargaining regime characteristic of northern regions towards much more of a 'southern type' with much lower overall coverage. The changes for non-manuals in East Anglia are surprising in that they tend to move against the general trend. For example, the proportion of non-manual employees covered by agreements actually rose by 7 per cent between 1984 and 1990 and the scope of multi-employer agreements here fell only slightly.[9] Finally, while the percentage covered by plant-level negotiation has generally fallen, the change in 'employer level' bargaining has been more variable. This is especially true for non-manuals where it increased in around half of the regions. While we cannot offer a full explanation of these complex changes, and the data do not allow us to take regional changes in industrial structure or establishment size into account,[10] they are consistent with the notion, developed in earlier chapters, that there are 'regional regimes of labour market regulation' or 'spatial sub-systems of industrial relations' in Britain. The geography of collective bargaining closely mirrors that of trade unionism and strike activity, and like these two other facets of industrial relations would seem to be bound up with regional differences in workplace culture and traditions. To provide support for this view, we now examine a leading industry which has experienced decentralization, namely engineering, and we find that regional differences in union capabilities and management attitudes do indeed exist even within sectors.

DECENTRALIZATION IN ENGINEERING AND THE UNION RESPONSE

In addition to these regional differences in the degree and nature of decentralization in wage bargaining, there are important geographies of institutional change which are operating at finer levels within sectors and industries. Our intention is to illustrate some of these geographies through a detailed case study of the British engineering industry.[11] We focus on the strategic production and use of scale by the two main collective actors involved in industrial relations in this sector, namely the Amalgamated Engineering and Electrical Union[12] and the Engineering Employers' Federation. In exploring changes in industrial relations and bargaining in the engineering industry we find that decentralization is not a recent reversal of trends in the industry, nor is it a dramatic shift from one style of wage regulation to another. Moreover, the employers' strategy of decentralization has not forced the union to follow suit.

Decentralization in engineering is not a sudden transformation of collective regulation but is better seen as consisting of two phases. The first is a long-term shift to workplace bargaining, driven by local union strength but occurring within a national collective system. The second, and more recent stage, involves the

---

9   This results corresponds with the findings on union recognition discussed in Chapter Four.

10 Disaggregation by industrial sector or establishment size yielded very small sample sizes for some of the bargaining level categories in certain regions, making any generalizations unreliable.

11 This discussion draws on Martin, Sunley and Wills (1994a).

12 Recall that this union has undergone various changes of name over the years: see note 8 to Chapter Three.

break-up of this national institutional arrangement. The origins of the national negotiation system lay in a policy of procedural containment formulated by the Engineering Employers' Federation (EEF) during the first quarter of this century. As McKinlay and Zeitlin (1989) note, the diversity of the industry at this time generated a constant internal tension between the regional associations of the EEF. However, these associations consented to the creation of a national system of procedure and dispute management which was designed to contain and outflank local pressures from well organized groups of trade unionists. A comprehensive system which allowed national bargaining over wage rates and which elevated all disputes to the national level was imposed by the EEF after the national lockout of 1922 (Zeitlin 1991). This initiative represented the employers' attempt to contain the pressures arising from strong localism amongst engineering trade unionists. Indeed, the historical roots of the Amalgamated Society of Engineers (ASE) lay in quasi-autonomous district societies concentrated in London, the North West, the North East coast and on the Clyde (see Chapter Three). Prior to 1914, the district committees of the union regulated employment terms and often initiated 'trade movements' in which wage claims 'leap-frogged' from area to area (Marsh 1965).

The national system of procedure stayed in place in the engineering industry for over fifty years, operating within all federated firms. Yet one of the major contradictions of the system was that it encouraged an enormous expansion of workplace bargaining. Clegg (1979) argued that an unforseen consequence of the national system was a widening of the scope for shop steward action. The activities of local union officials became focused on procedure, leaving more day-to-day negotiations to shop stewards. Union members were able to secure increased earnings through payment by results and local supplements, and national rates thus became safety nets rather than national standards of pay across the industry. Local workplace bargaining became the primary means of determining pay and conditions despite the provisions of national procedure. According to Marsh and Coker (1963) the number of shop stewards in engineering increased by 50 per cent between 1947 and 1961 reflecting, at least in part, the fact that corporate managers were willing to delegate autonomy to their workplace representatives and to formalize shop steward organization (Tolliday 1985; Jeffreys 1988; Belanger 1987). During this first phase of decentralization, then, national wage rates and negotiations declined in importance as local bargaining took over. By the early 1980s the EEF estimated that only two per cent of its members' employees were paid the nationally negotiated minimum wage rates, although national negotiations continued to set benchmark increases, overtime pay, shift premiums and basic working hours.

Since 1980, however, this national system has disintegrated. The immediate cause of the end of national bargaining was the campaign of the Confederation of Shipbuilding and Engineering Unions (CSEU) to reduce the hours of work. The EEF insisted that any reduction would have to be accompanied by an agreement to increase workplace flexibility and allow the removal of job demarcations. National negotiations reached an impasse in 1989 and in November of that year the EEF announced the end of the 93-year tradition of national bargaining.[13] In effect this formal abandonment of the tradition represented a universal move towards company and enterprise based strategies,[14] and, paradoxically, given the historical extent of workplace level bargaining, this also represents a limited centralization. The EEF's decision was opposed by the AEU, although the other unions that were affected were more ambivalent as the national agreement was seen as a prop to the AEU's dominance of the CSEU (*Financial Times* 1987). The EEF has remained implacably opposed to resuming national talks and according to the EEF Director General, 'the best place for bargaining is in the workplace, and that's where it will stay' (*The Engineer* 1993). The EEF has repeatedly stated that local collective bargaining is now the only legitimate type of bargaining in the industry and its representatives have denied that there is any evidence that this will lead to a resurgence of local wage drift (Evidence to the House of Commons Employment Committee: HM Government 1994).

The abandonment of national bargaining has been reinforced by changes within the employers' federation itself. The EEF now defines its role in terms of political lobbying, legal advice and individual tribunal work, and it has held talks with the Confederation of British Industry about a possible merger. The official focus of the organization has shifted away from bargaining and agreeing procedure with the trade unions towards a role as political lobbyist and adviser to the industry. In 1989 the Federation reformed its membership rules to allow companies to become members without subscribing to national agreements or recognizing a union and such 'nonconforming' membership has expanded rapidly.[15] It is significant that the shift towards nonconforming membership has been particularly marked in the southern half of Britain: in the Southern and East Anglian divisions of the EEF, nonconforming membership now accounts for over 40 per cent of total membership, whereas in the North West (the Southern Lancashire division) it accounts for only just over 20 per cent.

The decline of national bargaining *per se* has not dictated the scale of the engineering union's strategic response. Indeed, the AEU's immediate response to

---

13 At the time of writing a similar sequence of events may possibly be occurring in the German engineering industry where the employers' federation has threatened to dissolve itself and pull out of collective bargaining. The point of contention is the refusal of the engineering union, IG Metall, to accept more flexible working patterns when a 35 hour week is introduced (*Financial Times*, 28 July 1995, p.2).

14 According to one AEEU District Secretary, 'What we are finding is that the policies are determined nationally, the conditions are being set nationally and then the personnel managers are sent down to negotiate with the full-time officials at each establishment' (Interview 25 May 1993).

15 This increase is in part because of the drop in conforming member firms either through closure or withdrawal from the Federation.

the EEF's withdrawal from central talks with the CSEU in 1989 was a national campaign (see Richardson and Rubin 1993). The AEU introduced a national strike levy to fund strikes at selected prominent companies such as Lucas Industries, Smiths Industries, British Aerospace and Rolls Royce. By 1991, this 'least out, most effect' campaign had achieved a 37-hour week at the majority of EEF-affiliated companies. Hours were more commonly reduced in federated firms, but again local union activity varied across the country.[16] According to an AEEU national officer, 'Some local officials were very assiduous and will have systematically gone round every firm in their district and will have negotiated a shorter working week deal. Others I suspect are still struggling to get to 38 hours, and are still not getting anywhere' (Interview, 16 June 1993). Perhaps the most significant impact of the formal cessation of national agreements, however, has been on new recognition rates. At a local level the union has been less successful in recruiting new members in unrecognized workplaces. Union recognition is now a matter for company decision and an increasing number of firms are resisting recognition. All the district officials of the AEEU interviewed in our research cited examples of local firms where, despite having a majority of the workforce in union membership, the union was not able to win recognition. Without recourse to legal arbitration, industrial action was repeatedly described as the only way to gain recognition. Partly as a result of this difficulty, the AEEU is losing members through job cuts and closures but is not compensating for these losses with new recruits in unrecognized workplaces (Figures 6.1 and 6.2).

In response to decline, the union's organizational structure is being recast. The long-term decline in the importance of local branches has continued. More and more of the administrative functions of the branch, such as paying benefits and keeping membership records, are being centralized at AEEU headquarters in London. There has been a reduction in the number of branches: in the late 1970s there were over 2600 but there are now only about 1200. Furthermore, the districts and district offices of the union have been restructured. By 1994 the AEEU had reduced the number of its full-time officials from 220 to 140. Only one of the ten district secretaries that we interviewed had not been asked to take on an extra district or an enlarged district during the last few years. District offices have been closed and the officials grouped into regional offices. In our south-eastern case study area, for example,[17] the four officers covering the area stretching from

---

16 By April 1991 the CESU estimated that 37 hours had been achieved in 1660 companies although the EEF estimate was much lower (Richardson and Rubin 1993).

17 Recall this is one of the two case-study regions (the other being in north-western England) in which we conducted our own establishment-based surveys, and in which detailed interviews of engineering establishments and AEEU and EEF officials were also carried out (see Chapter One and Appendix). We utilize the results from this survey of engineering establishments below.

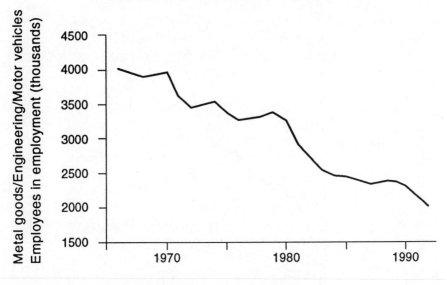

Source: Employment Gazette (Employees in Employment Series)

Figure 6.1: Employment in the UK engineering sector 1966–1992

Milton Keynes, Bury St Edmunds, and Bedford to North London are now all located in Luton. Traditionally, the route to the post of district secretary has been a 'journey' from shop steward to district committee member, so that district officials have had a profound knowledge of the local area. It was often the case that district officials had been convenors at one of the largest workplaces in the locality. As districts are amalgamated this relationship is being undermined. It is now likely that district officials will not be based within the area which they serve, and may not even be elected by the members they have come to represent. In addition, the composition of district committees has changed. Whereas many committees were formerly subject to vigorous and hard-fought elections, all the district secretaries interviewed reported a reduced interest in standing for committee positions and these posts are increasingly occupied by retired or unemployed members.

Furthermore, the role of the district committee has been subject to critical review and it appears that this tier of the institutional structure of the union is being dismantled. In the view of one AEEU official:

> I don't think the district as such will disappear as a concept in the union, but what will disappear I suspect is the district committee. The focus of the full-time officials' work will cease to be the district and will shift to objectives that are perhaps set centrally or set by executive members of the executive council. It'll move much more in that direction. (Interview, 16 June 1993)

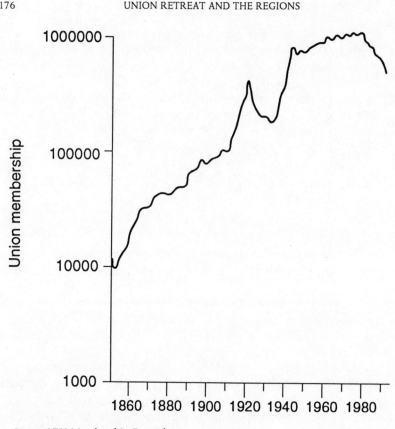

Source: AEU Membership Records

Figure 6.2: Membership of the A.E.U. 1851–1992

In 1990, a parallel industrial structure was created within the union. This new structure of national industrial conferences may eventually replace district committees as a means of formulating union policy (see Figure 6.3). Local workforce representatives from seven industrial groups meet annually in each division to elect delegates and pass motions to be sent to the national meeting for their industry:

> What we're starting to develop is something that has been very strongly resisted in this union for many years: an industrial structure of the kind you find in many other unions. This year [1993] we will have held seven industrial conferences. They all elect delegates to the national policy conference, and although it's not stated constitutionally, they are effectively setting policy for these industries. Rule doesn't state that, but it's effectively what they're doing. We've got them in nuclear, steel, electricity supply, chemicals, energy, aerospace, civil air transport and motor vehicle building… This has been running since 1990, and our rules say that by 1995 we should have fifteen of these conferences. (Interview, 16 June 1993)

In terms of strategy and structure, the union is becoming more centralized and industrial relations in engineering now consist of a complex set of centripetal and centrifugal forces. The union's response to the employers' formal decentralization has been to apply a nationally-focused strategy and to centralize its activities along the lines of industrial structure. But not only is geography implicated in these strategic shifts, the consequences for trade unionism are also unfolding differently in different places.

THE ROLE OF LOCAL CONTEXT: ENGINEERING IN THE NORTH WEST AND THE SOUTH-EAST COMPARED

In the final section of this chapter, our focus moves away from the formal decentralization imposed by the engineering employers and onto the local institutional contexts and regimes in which changes in workplace industrial relations in the industry actually occur. In our view, the effects and consequences of efforts to decentralize collective bargaining cannot be properly understood without an appreciation of the locally varied nature of industrial politics in the industry. In order to illustrate the diversity of these local institutional settings and to examine their historical construction, we compare industrial relations in our two case-study regions of Lancashire and Manchester in the 'north west' region, and the counties of Hertfordshire, Bedfordshire and Cambridgeshire in the 'south east' (Figure 6.4; see Appendix for details). The results of our interviews with over 90 engineering establishments in these areas display a remarkable spatial differentiation in trade union organization. In spite of the fact that there is no significant difference in size structure or activity types of the establishments sampled in each area, the north west has almost twice the recognition rate of that found in the south east, and 30 per cent more establishments in the former area reported union members amongst their workforce than did those in the latter (Figure 6.5). It is in the small and medium sized companies, those employing between 25 and 499 workers, where the spatial variation in recognition is most significant (see Figure 6.6). Whilst 81 per cent of companies with 100 to 499 employees in the north west recognize unions, only 38 per cent of the corresponding firms in the south east have recognition agreements. All companies with more than 1000 employees, regardless of area, were found to recognize unions. As recognition is one of the fundamental determinants of union presence, this difference among small and medium companies is central to the current and potential strength of unionism in these districts.

These spatial variations, to an important degree, are reflections of the different histories of the engineering industry and union in each area. The industry in the south east is largely a product of the post-war era. Of the 26 establishments interviewed in the south east, 42 per cent had been in existence for less than 25 years, and of these, only one was unionized. In the north west, in contrast, only 16 per cent of the establishments visited were of this age, although again only one

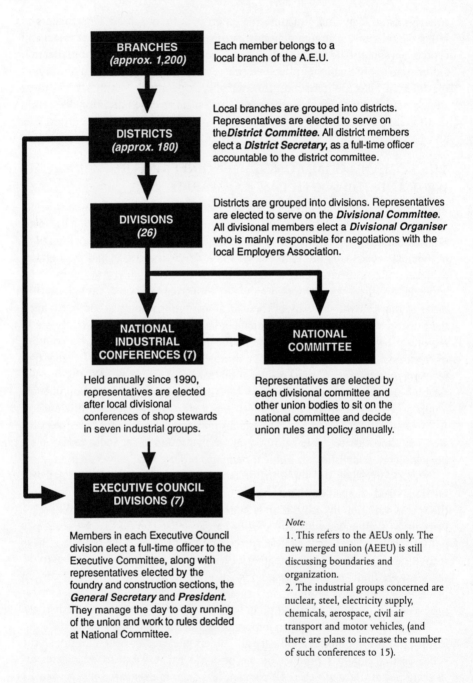

Source: AEU Records

Figure 6.3: The geographical and organizational structure of the AEU

was unionized. The spatial expansion of unionism into the areas of 'new' industry in the South and Midlands in the postwar period was associated with a distinctive type of organization (see Chapter Three). Marsh and Coker (1963) found that the number of AEU shop stewards per full-time local official in the Midlands region was twice the national average. Likewise, McCarthy (1966) found that the extent of shop steward involvement in branch activity[18] was much higher in the South and London branch of the union. In contrast, stewards played a proportionately smaller role in the North, Wales and Scotland because of the greater involvement of rank and file. This has important implications as it suggests that the union in the south would be more vulnerable to the workplace reforms that occurred from the 1970s onwards. While deindustrialization and the decline of craft skills undermined the union's strength in the older centres of heavy engineering, its dependence on shop stewards in the newer sectors of light engineering meant that its presence was fragile and liable to be weakened by a shift from piecework to the more direct administration of production (for example, see Tolliday and Zeitlin 1986).

Nevertheless, the union experienced considerable membership growth during the 1970s and the changes tended to be greatest in the southern areas of post-war industry (see Figure 6.7). In the districts we have included in this research, it was the areas of Bedford, Luton, Letchworth and Cambridge which saw membership growth in excess of 20 per cent between 1970 and 1979, whilst more established areas of industry such as Preston, Blackburn and Manchester, were already registering the effect of employment decline. These trends conform with data for the seven Executive Council areas, which show growth being greatest in the East Midlands and East Anglia (Figure 6.8). In many of these areas rapid membership growth was taking place under conditions of full employment when the demand for engineering workers was high.

Consequently, dissatisfied workers could move between firms within the region rather than using the local union machinery to fight for improvements. Many of the union activists who organized these areas in the South East have since been made redundant and the younger workers have been used to good conditions of employment. One union official in the South East stated that the union's present problems stem from the successes of the 1960s and 1970s as good conditions and perks became expected as norms amongst younger workers rather than being seen as the results of union activism. A representative from EEF South offered a similar view on traditions:

> It all relates to the culture, tradition and expectations within the industry. In the south…going back to the early 1970s, employers recruited people from outside engineering, typically people with the traditions of trade union membership, and so not bringing with them the bank balance of benefits

---

18 McCarthy used the number of stewards in each branch, their presence on branch committees and whether stewards were branch officials as indicators of involvement in branch life.

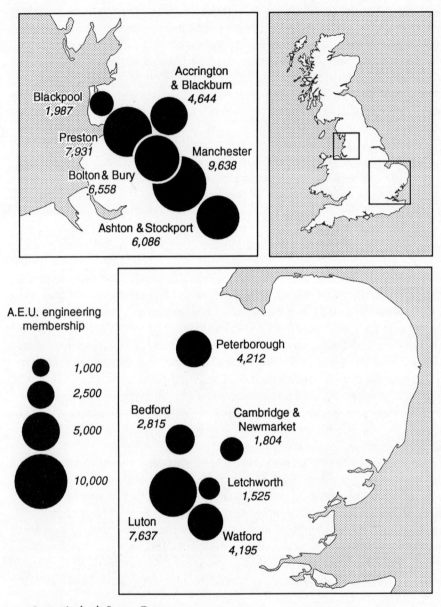

Source: Author's Survey Data

Figure 6.4: AEU districts surveyed: membership in 1992

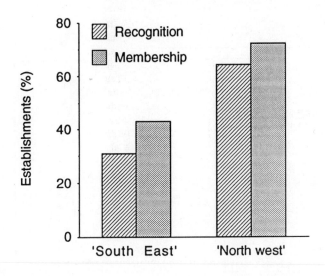

Source: Author's Survey Data

Figure 6.5: AEU union recognition and membership: Engineering establishments in the 'South East' and 'North West'

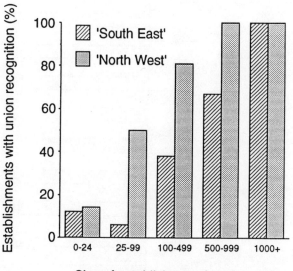

Source: Author's Survey Data

Figure 6.6: AEU union recognition by size of establishment engineering establishments in the 'South East' and 'North West'

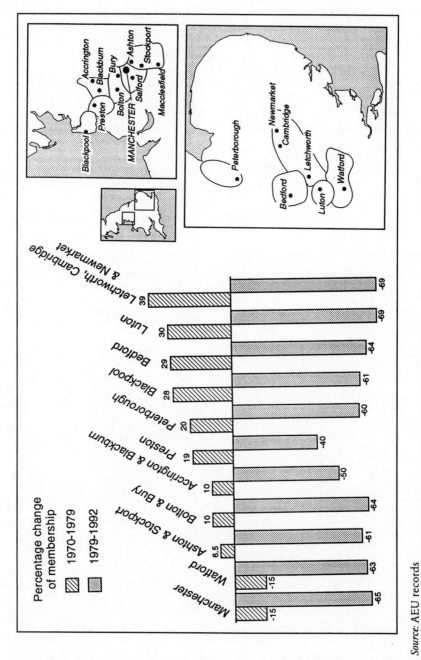

Source: AEU records

Figure 6.7: Percentage change in AEU membership (engineering section only) 1970–1979 and 1979–1992: selected districts

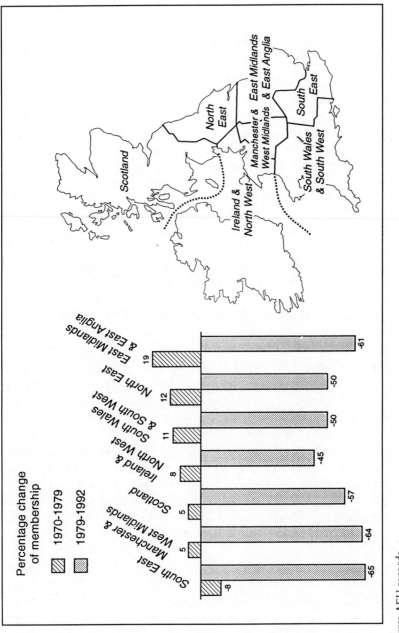

Source: AEU records

Figure 6.8: Percentage change in AEU membership (engineering section only) 1970–1979 and 1979–1992; Executive Council divisions

built up over the years within the trade union...So, if there was a trend towards lesser union density in trade union membership within a workforce in that type of scenario, what typically would happen is that those people with no particular traditional allegiance would simply stop their membership... Often, it's not been possible for the union to field credible representatives, and that illustrates the process of decay which takes place. (Interview with representative from EEF South, 1993)

Since 1979 no geographical area in the union has escaped a massive decline in membership, although the districts which have 'lost least' are the heartlands of Preston and Blackburn. Furthermore, it has been firms in the southern area where workers have been least able to maintain union organization. Although almost all the unionized establishments surveyed have seen redundancies since 1980, redundancies have not always undermined union density among the employees who remain. Five companies in the north west reported 100 per cent union density, and two others as having a density in excess of 95 per cent. There were no cases of this level of density in the South East, and redundancies coupled with the deteriorating economic climate have had a more serious effect on union organization there. For example, one company in Stevenage which has lost more than 400 manufacturing jobs since 1989 reported that only 10 per cent of its remaining 150 production workers were in the union. The one shop steward no longer bargains in the plant, and merely passes information from management to the shop-floor and vice versa. The five stewards and convenor who had kept the union functioning previously were made redundant in 1989, and since then there has been no one with sufficient interest to take up this work. The resource pool of potential stewards among the membership is weak and without a union representative present in the workplace the recognition agreement becomes meaningless to the workforce. In three other south eastern establishments each employing about 80 shop-floor workers the managers interviewed claimed that it was lack of interest among the membership, rather than deliberate management policy, which had brought their recognition agreements to an end.[19] The personnel manager at a Cambridge electronics factory, with about 500 manual workers, about half of whom belonged to trade unions, also expressed his anxiety that the union stewards were so inactive, and the members so uninterested, that the value of the union as a means of communication was in danger of vanishing. In both regions this trend to derecognition was more common among white-collar engineering staff than manual workers.

Figures showing the incidence of industrial relations conferences held between the EEF and trade unions illustrate that the process of 'deinstitutionalization' has gone further in southern regions. There are regional differences in the propensity

---

19 The only case of threatened shop-floor derecognition where membership was still considerable was reported in the North Hertfordshire and Cambridge district of the AEEU when, in May 1993, two local companies announced their intention to end union agreements.

of shop stewards, and possibly managers as well, to use procedure to address workplace grievances (Table 6.5 and Figure 6.9). In the north west the average incidence of meetings at conforming member companies between 1981 and 1992 was twice that of the EEF South and considerably greater than that of firms in the Mid-Anglian district. In the north west, industrial relations remain more closely tied into an institutional framework. Stewards there will often register a failure to agree over pay or any dispute, simply as a matter of course, and then follow procedure to its conclusion. A good example is a company in Manchester which has shrunk in size from 1000 to 150 employees since 1981. This firm holds an annual conference on pay even though the workforce reduction has meant a move from two full-time union officials on site to five stewards and one working convenor. The present convenor is the son-in-law of the previous convenor and the union traditions of the factory appear to have been handed down so that they shape the present. A neighbouring company with 100 per cent AEU membership amongst its 70 shopfloor employees is similar. In the words of the Managing Director, by using procedure the four stewards 'always like to push it all the way, even if it's used in a half-hearted spirit' (Interview, 3 June 1993). Another Manchester company, employing 200 production workers, reported that it always expects some kind of industrial action to be taken once the procedure on pay is exhausted. The firm still recognizes ten stewards and one convenor and the union has maintained 100 per cent density in the factory. The local stewards still work to make their presence felt by using procedure when they have particular grievances although strike action is obviously much harder in the present climate.

The results of our survey also found that a greater proportion of firms in the north west were willing to describe their pay-setting procedures as involving collective bargaining. In contrast, in the South East a majority of establishments stated that their wages were 'management determined' with no negotiation. In the North West also, several of the management representatives interviewed had a favourable view of the use of procedure and the role of stewards. The managing director of a Manchester firm praised the six CSEU stewards, who represent 200 shopfloor employees, and described the discipline and control ensured by the mutual adherence to procedures. For an internal regulation to be effective it needs to be agreed and bound by procedure, and he believed that this was impossible without the independent structure of union organization in the plant. He regularly called in local full-time officials to help to resolve problems. The persistence of procedural conference work was seen by the representative of the South Lancashire EEF as evidence that industrial relations in the area were still 'traditional'. He attributed changes in the content of negotiations and members' attitudes primarily to the difficult recent economic climate rather than to a fundamental reworking of industrial relations. 'In this area there is very little change in the role of the AEEU...the difference is tempered more by the change in economic climate than by anything else' (Interview, 24 March 1993). Together with a number of

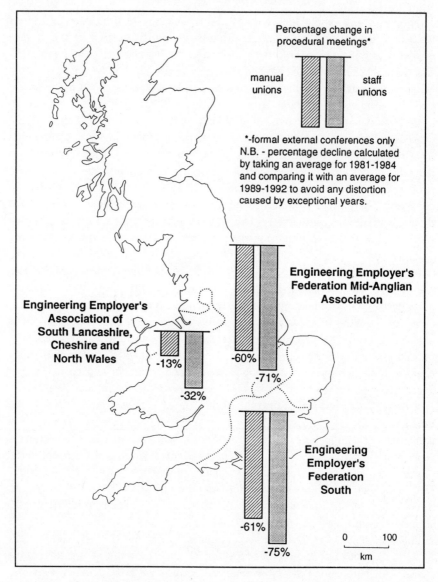

Figure 6.9: Changes in EEF procedural industrial relations meetings in selected associations,
   1981–1992.

Sources: Data supplied by the Engineering Employers' Association of South Lancashire,
   Cheshire and North Wales

**Table 6.5: The incidence of procedural industrial relations
conferences in engineering companies belonging
to the Engineering Employers' Federation**

Year	'South' All	'South' Manuals	'Mid-Anglian' All	'Mid-Anglian' Manuals	'South Lancs' All	'South Lancs' Manuals
1981	1.0	0.6	1.2	0.9	2.0	1.4
1982	0.9	0.6	1.1	0.8	1.7	1.1
1983	0.6	0.5	1.0	0.8	1.5	1.0
1984	0.7	0.5	0.8	0.6	1.5	1.1
1985	0.7	0.4	0.9	0.7	1.3	0.9
1986	0.6	0.4	0.9	0.7	1.4	1.0
1987	0.7	0.4	0.95	0.7	1.3	1.2
1988	0.6	0.45	0.9	0.7	1.4	1.0
1989	0.6	0.4	0.6	0.5	1.3	1.1
1990	0.6	0.4	0.7	0.5	1.3	1.0
1991	0.6	0.45	0.8	0.7	1.3	1.0
1992	0.6	0.5	0.8	0.6	1.1	0.9
1981–92	**0.68**	**0.47**	**0.89**	**0.69**	**1.43**	**1.06**

Source: Records held by EEF South, Mid-Anglian EEF, and South Lancs, Chester and North Wales EEF.

Notes: (i) Incidence calculated as the average annual number of procedural meetings (informal and external) per company (in companies with conforming membership of the EEF). All is for staff and manuals rather than manuals only.

(ii) The 'Southern' and Mid-Anglian Divisions of the EEF cover our Southern case study area, while that of 'South Lancashire' covers the North West case study area.

personnel officers interviewed in the area, he believed that the local union had appointed more 'realistic' and 'business-minded' officials in recent years.

In contrast, in the South East there was more evidence of radical change. Several of the medium-sized companies have established representative bodies which perform many of the traditional functions of a union, without the need for any outside 'interference' from a union organization. One company with 100 shop-floor employees in Welwyn Garden City, Hertfordshire, had had a joint consultative committee in place for 16 years. Representatives are elected to sit on this monthly committee to discuss pay and conditions with the management. A larger American-owned company in St Neots, Bedfordshire, had a similar system for its 300 employees, called the Plant Consultative Committee. The personnel manager there valued the absence of 'outside interference' in this approach and argued that 'if more companies set up a committee like we have, then unions wouldn't be needed anymore' (Interview, 12 January 1993). There was a ballot at the factory for AUEW recognition during 1982, and although other subsidiaries of the company are unionized, it resisted this unionization attempt. A component producer interviewed in Huntingdon had also created a non-union consultative body as a means of reducing trade union influence amongst its 275 workers. Negotiations at this factory are now conducted through a Joint Consultative Committee rather than with union stewards and union density on the shopfloor has fallen to about 10 per cent. The one similar case identified in the North West is a family-owned company in Blackburn which has expanded by 50 per cent during the last five years. It has a non-union committee for wage negotiation. However, it had a check-off agreement with the Manufacturing Science and Finance Union for its skilled patternmakers and the personnel manager expected to recognize a union as the firm increased in size.

Both managers and workforces appear to have been profoundly influenced by the historical trajectories of their respective areas. In the North West, trade unionism remains more firmly established in the local fabric where it has had longer to mature and prove its worth. We are not suggesting that this can be explained by overdrawn stereotypes of 'militant northerners' and 'individualist southerners'. In the southern area, for example, both of the survey establishments employing more than 2,000 workers had over 95 per cent union density on the shopfloor and full complements of shop stewards. However, crucially, the pool of current and potential union activists in the small and medium-sized companies in the south east is numerically weaker. There are fewer workers with the historical experience and current motivation which would lead them to actively support union organization. Both the workplace consequences of decentralization and the union's ability to respond in different areas are shaped by the legacies of antecedent labour relations. Hence it appears likely that the recent decentralization and weakening of the industry's institutions will lead to a widening of differences in the social relations of employment between the two areas.

CONCLUSIONS

This chapter has been constructed around two main geographical themes. First, the consequences of the decentralization of wage determination and negotiation systems is a complex process which is having different outcomes in different areas within Britain. This is partly because it appears to have been pursued to a different extent within different regional regimes of labour regulation and partly because, in itself, decentralization does not rigidly determine management policies towards labour, and these may continue to reflect the historical legacies imparted by the course of labour relations in the past. Second, the variety of these local outcomes means that it is unwise to suggest that unions should also decentralize and focus their activities solely or mainly through local organizational units ('locals'). There is no doubt that employers in engineering have been pushing for a more decentralized system of industrial relations. But the response of the union, the AEEU, has been in the opposite direction, namely to centralize its activities and to begin to reconfigure its organizational structure along national-industrial lines rather than on the basis of local districts. Its current shift to national industrial conferences can be seen, in part, as an attempt to counter the decentralization strategies of employers by linking and uniting its members across different areas on a sectoral basis. Whether such sector-based alliances provide a more effective organizational structure for union strategy than do regionally-based alliances remains, however, an open question. But, certainly, the union's recent merger with the electricians' union, EETPU, to form the AEEU, has enabled it to extend and consolidate this reorientation along national–industrial rather than geographical district lines.

Indeed, such mergers have become increasingly common in Britain in recent years (an issue we take up in the final chapter). By uniting the members of different unions, mergers can produce strong locals where previously membership and influence were divided between separate, possibly rival, unions. However, the opportunities for forming new strong 'locals' will not be the same everywhere, but will depend upon local circumstances and resources. Strong locals are more likely to emerge precisely in those areas in which the unions are already firmly embedded in the local economy and already enjoy high rates of representation and recognition (which in the case of engineering means the northern regions). Securing that presence and recognition in areas in which the unions have traditionally been weaker (such as the southern areas of Britain) is a very different proposition. Rather than seeking a common general strategy across different regions of membership, the unions may well have to develop different strategies for different localities.

Some of the advocates of decentralization as a union strategy tend to ignore that decentralization is only one, albeit important, dimension of the new regulatory environment faced by unions. Other dimensions of this environment, such as the structure of firms and the tendency for greater co-ordination between firms, show a tendency to integration and centralization. How to theorize this dual process is a key issue in economic-geographical research (Amin and Thrift 1992). The organizational challenge of this conjoint process of integration and decentralization is one of combining local flexibility and adaptability with a wider pooling and sharing of resources. The same is true for unions. They will have to establish various forms of networks which encourage local activity and flexibility and facilitate an exchange of information, personnel and financial resources (Martinez-Lucio and Weston 1993, 1994). But this does not mean that the national union is anachronistic. Networking between different local branches is likely to be more successful the more it can receive support from the resources of the national union. Even if the shift away from national negotiations towards local deals and company bargaining continues, the national union still has a key role to play in fostering and assisting recruitment and bargaining strategies within its local memberships. As we argued in Chapter Two, changes in the geography of regulation are unlikely to be simply mirrored by spatial patterns of representation.

CHAPTER SEVEN

Mapping Union Futures
Representation and Organization
in a Detraditionalized Economy

INTRODUCTION

It is no exaggeration to suggest that Britain, like other advanced industrialized countries, is going through a workplace revolution which involves a decisive transformation of its industrial relations system. Not since the 1920s has the union movement faced such a critical juncture in its history. But the contemporary crisis of British trade unionism is different from that earlier climacteric: history, by definition, never repeats itself exactly. For while the decline of the 1920s to early 1930s was just as dramatic as that of the 1980s to early 1990s – in both cases trade union membership declined by more than 4 million – the underlying trajectory of industrial, economic and political development in the earlier crisis was nevertheless consistent with, indeed conducive to, the renewed expansion of mass labour organization in the workplace.[1] In contrast, the current structural and organizational changes in the socio-economy all seem to point to a new developmental trajectory that is intrinsically far less accommodating of unions and collective industrial relations, and the task confronting the union movement with respect to maintaining, let alone reviving, its membership and workplace influence would appear to be considerably more difficult than it was in the inter-war period.

Yet, as we argue later in this chapter, at the same time that the unions have declined the need for effective worker representation and protection has actually increased. The key issue is that while the re-awakening of trade unionism as a central influence in the British labour market may be necessary, it is by no means inevitable (Monks, 1994). For the union movement faces a whole range of problems in seeking to revive their memberships and workplace influence. One major challenge is how best to secure its presence among those groups of workers

---

1   Namely, the rise of large-scale Fordist mass production and new manufacturing industries, the increasing importance of the Labour Party, and the progressive shift towards an interventionist, welfare state.

in the new growth sectors of the economy, especially services and new technol-ogy-orientated activities. These sectors tend to be structured around smaller establishments, new forms of employment and higher concentrations of women, professional and young workers, all features which traditional union structures have found it difficult to accommodate. A second challenge is the need to adapt organizational forms and practices to the new flexible, participatory, culturally based models of production that are emerging. These new models of industrial organization, often involving the subcontracting of activities and the networking of production relations, are intensifying the relationship of some workers with their firms while distancing others both contractually and physically. The unions will have to respond anew in their own structures and services to the potentially complex levels of representation that these developments entail. Thirdly, the unions will also have to respond to the transformation of social identities in the labour market, not only as witnessed by the increasing diversity of employment status within firms but also the more amorphous changes in personal identities within contemporary society. Changes in social, political and cultural values, the shifting focus of education, and the development of new employer strategies which seek to promote exclusivist and individualist enterprise-based identities, mean that the unions will have to find ways of renewing individuals' sense of belonging to the larger group.

Probably the most difficult obstacle to their future, however, is the legislative environment. The present legal framework constitutes a considerable barrier to unionization as there are are now few legal channels open to individuals seeking to unionize their place of employment. The unions will need to campaign for a new, more equitable legal terrain, and in so doing must grasp the logic of evolving European Union employment law and argue for its integration into an emerging system of positive legal rights based on the accepted conventions and fair standards of workplace behaviour laid down by the International Labour Office. For example, the European Union's Works Council Directive is seen by many trade unionists as an important means of reasserting trade union rights and repre-sentation in Britain: according to the General Secretary of the GMB union 'works councils are changing the face of the UK's industrial relations by giving employees a seat at the table (*Guardian* 1995; see also TUC 1995). Of course, much will depend on the development of EU employment and social law and on the stance of future British governments towards it.[2] However, as Taylor (1994) argues, the EU route provides the British unions with the minimum but necessary means to protect and renew their activities.

---

2   Thus far, of course, the Conservative governments have adopted a consistently negative attitude to what they regard as the strongly pro-worker bias of EU legislation and directives. For example the government has opposed the Social Chapter of the Maastricht Treaty, the idea of a basic minimum wage, and the new directive on work councils.

How far and in what specific ways the unions will succeed in responding to these challenges remains to be seen. Our aim in this chapter is not to advocate any particular strategy or manifesto for securing this regeneration and restructuring of British trade unionism. Rather, following the analysis of the preceding chapters, we focus on the ways that geography is implicated in the future of the union movement as it struggles to maintain and revive its workplace role. We begin by outlining the three main scenarios for the future geography of the unions, and in this context raise the question as to whether and how much longer the historic labourist traditions of the northern industrial regions of Britain can continue to survive. This leads us on to examine in some detail whether in fact trade unionism is caught up in a more widespread process of 'detraditionalization' of socio-economic life, and what the consequences might be for the landscape of organized labour. Finally, we conclude by tracing the geographical implications of what seems to be the dominant structural strategy of British unions to the problem of rekindling their organizational and political strength, namely merging to form 'super unions'.

MAPPING FUTURE UNION LANDSCAPES: THREE SCENARIOS

Our research has repeatedly encountered three main perspectives on the implications of the current crisis for the future of organized labour. The first is perhaps the most obvious and suggests that this crisis signals the collapse and disappearance of trade unionism at all spatial scales. There are two versions of this prognosis. One argues that the decollectivization of labour and the deregulation of local labour markets are irreversibly undermining the structural foundations of trade unionism: the institutions that mediate labour market relations are being eroded and, as a consequence, their operation is moving closer to the 'free-market' model espoused by neo-liberal theorists and politicians. The second version envisages a progressive replacement of unionism by new, more individualized forms of regulation in the workplace. More specifically, advocates of this view focus on the introduction and spread of human resource management (HRM) techniques by employers, and argue that these new techniques are taking the place of local union representation and collective modes of worker negotiation and bargaining. Both of these versions, then, suggest that the thrust of current trends entails a radical crisis of representation for trade unions, a crisis that geographically will involve the decline of trade union traditions in the places where the unions have historically been firmly implanted and the shrinkage of the union map towards a landscape of non-unionism.[3]

The second scenario suggests that although in general terms the new legislative and regulatory environment confronting the unions has weakened their overall political power and influence in the economy, the actual responses of employers

---

3   This is essentially the scenario that Davis (1986) envisages for the US union movement.

and employees have varied markedly at the local and regional scales, and in many areas changes in labour regulation have been much more 'sticky' and resistant. This interpretation recognizes that in many local areas the presence of unions has been supported by more informal traditions, norms and expectations. In these labour markets, industrial relations have remained firmly incorporated into local social contexts and regional cultural legacies. This view suggests that despite the changed regulatory climate that now surrounds the unions, the uneven geography of unionization will continue because of the 'persistence' in particular areas of local social traditions and norms and their interactive effects with spatially differentiated economic change. Indeed this perspective might well lead to the conclusion that regional differences in trade unionism in Britain could actually widen as the weakest areas of organization collapse while the stronger or more embedded areas survive as the unions in the latter succeed in translating organization to new sectors and places of production.

The third scenario is the most optimistic from a union point of view, as it posits that the profound national change in economic structure and regulation provides a new opportunity for unionism to reassert its vitality at regional and local scales. As we have seen, most of those who advocate this position have drawn on the experience of trade unionism in Western Europe outside Britain. It is argued that in many European countries, local and regional unionism is undergoing, or has the potential to undergo, a revival and is filling the vacuum left by national decollectivization. Most of these accounts suggest that there has been a reconsolidation of the region as an economic and political unit, and that the resurgence of regional economic growth has been built upon the basis of new forms of regional regulation. In most cases, this regional regulation is seen as collaborative and therefore amenable or favourable to local trade unionism and new representational structures. In one sense this scenario echoes the argument advanced by those who believe that, in time, the trade unions in Britain will organize the new sectors and new regions of employment growth. In general such a view depends on the idea that some form of consensus formation and conflict resolution between capital and labour is necessary for successful economic accumulation.[4] Hence if this function is not fulfilled at a national scale then, it is argued, it will shift to smaller, more localized economic spaces. Spatially, this scenario would seem to predict a Massey–Painter style flattening of the union map, inasmuch that the old core areas of trade unionism are envisaged as declining further while the country's leading areas of economic expansion, where union presence has hitherto been limited, experience new membership growth.

---

4   Of course, the idea that unions might actually be beneficial for economic growth and that unionized firms might be more productive than non-unionized ones, flies in the face of neoclassical and neo-liberal wisdom. However, there is convincing empirical work to support this view (see, for example, Freeman and Medoff 1984).

Evaluating which of these prognoses is most likely to capture the future course of the geography of British trade unionism is an enormously difficult task. Predicting the future prospects and trajectory of any aspect of trade unionism is obviously a hazardous exercise: the only certain things about socio-economic predictions is that they are doomed to error and tell us as much if not more about the conceptual and political orientation of their authors than about the likely course of events. Moreover, each of the scenarios sketched above contains some elements of truth with respect to the current restructuring of trade unionism. Having said this, our research suggests that at the moment the second of the three would seem to be the most probable outcome.

As we have argued throughout the book, the landscape of organized labour has been intimately bound up with the process of uneven regional development in two ways. Inevitably, from its origins onwards, the geography of trade unionism has been closely moulded by the shifting spatial patterns of capital accumulation, industry and employment. But equally important has been the influence exerted by the uneven regional development of the socio-political traditions, customs and practices which frame workers' and employers' attitudes and behaviour towards collective organization within the workplace. Those traditions are linked to differences in industry and work, to be sure, but they also have had specifically local and regional 'emergent' effects. As we have seen, trade unionism had its main origins in the industrial 'heartland' regions of the country – Wales, the Northern region, Scotland, the North West and West Midlands – where the bulk of the nineteenth and early twentieth-century industrial working classes were concentrated. In contrast, the early development of labourist traditions in the southern part of the country (the South East, East Anglia, and the South West) was much weaker. Although rooted in their respective regional economic histories, over time these different regionally based labourist traditions became endogenously socialized and institutionalized, and thereby proved to be remarkably persistent. As part of the local socio-institutional embeddedness of workplace industrial relations, these traditions helped to impart a high degree of relative stability in the regional patterns of unionization, industrial militancy and collective bargaining over the course of the twentieth century.

Our analyses suggest that these different regional workplace traditions and cultures have been of key importance in mediating the process of union decline that has taken place since 1979. Although the union movement has experienced retreat in every part of the country, in its historic 'heartland' regions – where it might have been expected to have retreated most – it has shown a surprising degree of relative resilience. After more than a decade and a half of continuous decline, trade unionism still remains significantly more prominent in the northern regions of Britain than in the south of the country. Yet, in accord with the first scenario outlined above, the question must be raised as to whether and how much longer the historic labourist traditions and workplace cultures of the northern industrial regions can survive. If the decline and legislative suffocation of the unions continues, the social reproduction of the regional traditions and cultural norms that help to support trade unionism will itself be weakened and undermined: the 'collective memory' by which traditions are reproduced and reinvented will rapidly fade and decline. Traditions need to be continuously reproduced to maintain their influence, and if union cultures are not sufficiently embodied in day-to-day labour practices on a wide enough scale, they will, of course, eventually atrophy.[5] Furthermore, this threat may itself be compounded by what some see as a fundamental process currently affecting the cultural and institutional bases of society more generally. For if we are to believe leading social theorists, the decline of trade unionism and collective forms of industrial relations is emblematic of a wider systemic process of 'detraditionalization'.

THE DETRADITIONALIZATION OF INDUSTRIAL RELATIONS?

These theorists argue that Western industrial societies like Britain have entered a new phase of modernization – what they call 'reflexive' modernization – in which 'detraditionalization' is a central structural tendency affecting every sphere of socio-economic life, from the individual to the family to the industrial enterprise to the state (Beck 1994; Giddens 1994a, b; Lash 1994). 'Detraditionalization' they stress, does not mean a move to a society in which traditions cease to exist altogether; indeed 'in many respects there are impulses, or pressures, towards the sustaining or the recovery of traditions' (Giddens 1994b, p.83). Rather, 'post-tra-ditional' society is one in which tradition changes its status: 'traditions have to explain themselves, to become open to interrogation' (Giddens 1994b, p.5). Traditions are no longer simply inherited and reinvented from the past, but are now subject to reflexive deconstruction and reassessment in a world where the de-contextualization, de-centering and 'space-time distanciation' of social rela-tions are unravelling the collectivistic and communitarian values and norms that characterized industrial society.[6]

By virtue of its own inherent dynamic, modern industrialism, it is argued, is 'refracting' back upon and undercutting the very basic social, economic, political and cultural formations that it created. The increasing uncertainty, competitiveness, 'informationization', flexibilization and globalization of socio-economic activity are promoting the rapid dissolution of the social structures, class identities and local contexts that both sustained and were sustained by the traditions and institutions of industrial capitalism. These traditions and institutions have now become the focus of critical interrogation and abandonment in the face of the

---

5   Several social and cultural theorists have emphasized that traditions need to be constantly reinvented if they are to survive (see, for example, Shils 1984; Tilly and Jerome 1992).

6   For these writers the concepts of 'reflexive modernization' and 'post-traditional society' are intended to break the protacted and rather sterile debate about modernity versus postmodernity that has preoccupied social science in recent years.

increased autonomy and fluidity of the new information-based economy (see also Block 1990). Social actors, from individuals to institutions, are being forced into a world of intensified social and institutional reflexivity, where decisions have to be taken on the basis of a more or less continuous filtering of information about the conditions of activity as a means of regularly re-ordering and redefining what that activity is. In this emerging age of high reflexivity, the argument continues, there is no longer a 'fixed landscape' of tradition, custom and institutions structuring economic and social relations. The appropriation and exploitation of individual 'expertise' in all its many forms is freeing individuals from the guidance and force of tradition, and conferring greater autonomy to the individual in the process. In Giddens' view, the intensified social reflexivity of our times is the key influence on a diversity of changes that otherwise seem to have little in common. Thus he argues that the reason for the growth of flexible production and bottom-up decision-making in the economy is due not so much to technological change – as is often claimed – but to the fact that a universe of high reflexivity leads to greater autonomy of action, which the enterprise must recognize and draw upon (Giddens 1994b, p.7).

On the face of it, this detraditionalization thesis would seem to have profound implications for the unions. As we have repeatedly noted, to a significant extent the traditions of trade unionism and labourism are place specific, embedded in local socio-political contexts. However, in Giddens' view it is precisely the 'evacuation' of local contexts of action – the 'disembedding' of activities – that is a key feature of detraditionalization. If this is right, then the unions may be faced not just with the problem of finding ways to attract new support in the growth sectors and regions of the country, especially the southern regions where unionism has always been less developed, but also with the detraditionalization of their historical heartlands of organizational strength. If the detraditionalization theory is correct, local labour markets and communities in these heartland areas could be increasingly 'emptied' of the embedded collective social values and political cultures on which historically their high rates of union representation have depended.

However, the concept of detraditionalization needs to be applied with caution. The idea of a sweeping movement towards the break-up and dissolution of traditions and their associated institutions is clearly over-generalized. While the process described by theorists such as Beck, Giddens and Lash may be apparent amongst certain segments of British society, it is by no means the universal process they imply. The concept of reflexive modernization appears to have most relevance to professional service sector workers and skilled employees in technology inten-sive activities. Indeed, the emphasis on the increasing significance of expertise and autonomy is redolent of the stress which post-industrial theorists placed on technocratic knowledge as a key economic resource (Bell 1973; see also Block 1990). Moreover, the counterposition of a past structured by tradition and a present saturated by social reflexivity has to be understood as a graduated shift of emphasis rather than any abrupt and all-embracing societal transition.[7] Nevertheless, in directing our attention to the trend towards increasing social diversity and fragmentation, the notion of detraditionalization certainly highlights the problematic nature of 'tradition' for the unions.

According to proponents of the reflexive modernization thesis, one of the key aspects of the contemporary disembedding of tradition is that of 'individualization'. For example, Lash (1994) argues that the new 'reflexivity' reaches down though economic production ('reflexive accumulation') to the 'reflexive regulation' of the labour process and employment relations. In this context he believes that individuated and autonomous forms of workplace regulation are replacing the collective, communal and institutional forms of the past. This accent on individualization finds a direct parallel with those commentators who believe the unions are being marginalized by a rising tide of 'individualism' in society. Thus in the words of a former Employment Secretary:

> We have seen a cultural shift in this country. People have become more individualistic. They are less inclined to belong to mass organizations like trade unions. They do not identify with such bodies. The union members of the future will be motivated by pragmatic considerations when joining a union, not by some spurious notion of class solidarity... Unions clearly need to sell themselves to individuals more effectively. The sales pitch will need to focus more and more on the value of membership to each individual. (Hunt 1994)

Likewise, the Institute of Personnel Management (IPM) has argued that:

> A growing emphasis on individual responsibility within the workplace has been reinforced by increasing home ownership which has limited the propensity of trade union members to make economic sacrifices in pursuit of collective aims... These changes may indeed reflect a more profound move away from collective representation, security and action within society; a move which for good or ill throws more responsibility on individuals and their families for their own welfare. (IPM 1993b, p.390)

Yet, while it is true that societal values have become more atomistic and individualistic, it is misleading, or at least simplistic, to contrast a 'new individualism' with an 'old collectivism'. As Taylor (1994) argues, the concept of worker individualism is not in fact new to trade unions. The unions have always been concerned with improving and protecting the conditions of their individual members. The form of collectivism employed by unions has invariably been what Goldthorpe *et al.*

---

7   Like most of the other 'transition' models that have been proposed in recent years in the attempt to grasp the nature and direction of contemporary socio-economic change, the 'reflexive modernization – detraditionalization' thesis tends to commit the error of *pars pro toto*, of mistaking the part for the whole, as well as ignoring the strong element of continuity in both the formative structures and the daily routines of socio-economic life.

(1969) term 'instrumental', a means by which individual workers can best persuade employers to improve their terms and conditions of employment:

> Neither as way to greater worker participation in the affairs of the enterprise nor as a political force is unionism greatly valued. Rather, one would say, the significance that unionism has for workers is largely confined to issues arising from their employment which are economic in nature and which are local in their origins and scope (p.26).

Trade unions have always been collective vehicles for individual aspirations. They exist to protect, by collective action where needed, the individual rights of their members. The fact that working conditions and wages are negotiated collectively does not make them any less individual rights. Indeed, it can be argued that because of the imbalance in workplace power relations, most individual benefits and rights can only be achieved through collective organization.

Not only is the neo-liberal distinction between collectivism and individualism misplaced, equally the implications of increasing reflexive individualism do not simply conform with the populist and right-wing emphasis on the individual as sovereign consumer. Such a view depends upon 'individualism' being construed as the resurgence of the self-seeking, maximizing behaviour of the market-place, and this, it is argued, makes unions largely obsolete. In this conception, if collective institutions such as unions are to survive at all, they must embrace the spirit of market individualism unreservedly. Some industrial relations analysts appear to adopt a similar view. Thus according to Bassett and Cave (1993):

> The trend towards individualised employee relations is the most substantial and significant workplace development of the past decade... Individualism is the key element in modern employee relations. It is the heart of modern trade unionism. Unions need to try to determine what individual employees want, to examine their current products to find out whether they meet that need – and if they do not, to re-engineer themselves to provide new products which will appeal more strongly to the individual employee market (p.27).

For adherents of the reflexive modernization argument, however, this view of individualism (as the free-acting, rational and self-centred consumer of goods and services, including union 'products') is a mistaken interpretation of what should more appropriately be conceived of as the expansion of social reflexivity, of individual autonomy. Moreover, they stress that individual autonomy does not logically necessitate the disintegration of collective cohesion or collective interests: individual autonomy still implies interdependence and reciprocity, and is not, therefore, inconsistent with social solidarity.

One of the problems of applying the notion of detraditionalization to the question of union decline, however, is that it seems to blur the numerous tensions which exist between the concepts of individual autonomy and individual reflexivity. Whilst it may well be that individual autonomy and reflexivity are increasing for certain social groups, it is clear that numerous changes in the socio-economy are in fact restricting and undermining the individual autonomy of many others. In the labour market, in particular, many of the changes that are taking place would seem to be acting *against* individual worker autonomy. For the large numbers of unemployed workers that have become a structural feature of British society, the lack of a job and a meagre existence on dwindling social benefits would hardly seem to add up to a life of increased autonomy, reflexivity and flexibility. In fact, growing job insecurity and uncertainty are now prominent trends of the contemporary labour market, not only for unskilled workers but also increasingly for many skilled and even professional workers, and for these groups, too, notions of greater individual autonomy, independence and choice have a rather hollow ring. Furthermore, the widespread expansion of part-time and temporary work may well have given employers more flexibility in their use of labour inputs, but for many of the employees involved it has meant an erosion of their workplace rights and a decline in their relative pay (see, for example, Allen and Henry 1996). Many celebratory accounts of employment flexibility have failed to consider the increased insecurity and risk that it implies for many workers (Pollert 1988). Indeed, one of the most disturbing aspects of the flexibilization and deregulation of the British labour market has been the marked widening of the earnings distribution since 1979, and particularly the rapid deterioration in the relative position of the low paid (see, for example, Jenkins 1994; Goodman and Webb 1994; Robinson 1994; Martin 1995).[8] Although shifts in the demand for and supply of different types of labour have been partly responsible for this growth in pay inequality, several authors also point to the role of institutional factors: the decline in trade unionism, the decentralization and 'flexibilization' of wage determination, the reduction in the scope of minimum wage protection, and the controls on public sector pay (Robinson 1994). Geographically, these trends towards greater labour market flexibility have led to a significant widening of regional wage differentials (see Martin 1995).

There can be no doubt, therefore, that in Britain (as in many other advanced economies) labour market inequalities have become much more pronounced, and employment more polarized, casualized and segmented. Given current trends in government employment policy and in the decline of the unions, there seems little prospect that this fragmentation of the labour market into privileged and marginalized sectors will be reversed. These developments actually erode rather than enhance individual autonomy as they effectively deny many employees the basis of opportunity for any real participation in decision-making and 'reflexive'

---

8   Since the early 1980s, the earnings distribution has widened faster in the UK than in any other OECD country (OECD 1994).

evaluation of their employment conditions.[9] Many employees have little choice but to submit to the increasingly common 'take or leave it' attitude of their employers. This return to an 'individualized' and 'flexible' labour market with features akin to those of the nineteenth century ought to make the unions more in demand than they have been since the First World War. As one union has observed, 'these developments have made trade unions more necessary than ever...to ensure that fairness and equity are done and seen to be done in the workplace (USDAW 1994, p.75). Even the Institute of Personnel Management (IPM), in general a pro-employer body, has expressed concern at the consequences of the new 'flexible' labour market for workers:

> While encouraging flexibility in matching the needs of organisations with those of their employees and prospective employees, we must stand out against abuse. The creation of a permanently causalised industrial peasantry, with little protection and no stake in the future, cannot be in the interests of organisations or society. (Armstrong 1993)

Thus, potentially, the trend towards a fragmented labour market and mosaic economy presents trade unions with far more opportunities for organization than many contemporary commentators and academic theorists acknowledge. And it does so precisely because, in the context of growing social and workplace inequalities, individual reflexivity appears likely to generate a heightened sense of social injustice and dissatisfaction. In our view, the opportunity offered to trade unions is to exploit some of these central tensions and contradictions between a labour market which is creating marked inequalities in the degree and nature of 'individual autonomy' and a society which rhetorically emphasizes individualism and choice.

Within this context, and perhaps in contrast to what the detraditionalization approach might lead us to expect, social attitudes do not appear to be moving sharply against unions. Although in his analysis of the British Social Attitudes Surveys of 1985 and 1989 Millward (1990) found that the proportion of respondents who agreed that employees need strong unions declined between these years (from 45% to 41% respectively), other surveys suggest that public support for and belief in trade unions has held up well. In 1979, the MORI survey found that some 80 per cent of respondents thought the unions had 'too much power'. But by 1994, only 26 per cent felt this to be true. Moreover, 82 per cent of those surveyed in 1994 felt that unions were 'essential to protect workers' interests'. Likewise, the NOP poll commissioned by the TUC in 1993 found that 79 per cent of people surveyed believed trade unions were 'necessary to protect peoples' interests at work', and by 1994 this proportion had increased to 89 per

---

9   It is significant in this context that the TUC has recently launched a confidential 'phone-in' scheme for members in the regions appealing to them to notify it of cases of exploitation at work and to expose bad employers.

cent. Other surveys have produced similar results. Thus using Gallop Opinion Poll data, Marsh (1990) concluded that there was a rise in the popularity of trade unions during the second and third terms of Mrs Thatcher's Conservative government. He suggests that this continued acceptance of the unions was probably due, in part, to the fact that the excesses of union power had been curbed. This rise in public support for the unions may well also reflect a growing awareness of the need for trade unions in a labour market characterized by increasing polarization and insecurity (see Labour Research 1994; Taylor 1994). In parallel with these various findings, our own survey of establishments in our two case-study regions in the southeast and northwest of Britain suggests that employers do not seem to have become noticeably more resistant to trade unionism in the workplace. The majority of employers reported no change in their attitudes, and within unionized workplaces a significant proportion of managers stated that their attitudes towards unions have, if anything, become more favourable (see Table 7.1). Perhaps most importantly, thus far there appears to be no major trend towards disaffection with

Table 7.1: Management attitudes towards union organization in the workplace, unionized and non-unionized establishments, two regions compared

| | Per cent of Establishments | | | |
| | 'South East' | | 'North West' | |
	Non-Union	Union	Non-Union	Union
Unions are obstructive and should be resisted	19	2	13	1
Unions hinder attempts to change working practices	13	12	11	10
No fixed position on unions in this establishment	64	44	70	34
Unions improve some aspects of working relationships	4	36	6	49
Unions definitely beneficial to working relationships	0	5	0	6
Changes in attitudes during last five years				
More favourable	4	20	2	22
Less favourable	6	13	6	11
No change in attitude	89	66	92	67
No of Establishments	**159**	**63**	**108**	**90**

Source: Authors' own survey (see Appendix).
Notes: 1. Percentages may not add to 100 due to rounding.
          2. Date of survey: 1992–93.

unions by employers in the traditionally more unionized north-western region of the country.

All this is not meant to imply that, as institutional actors, the unions do not need to become more interrogative of their aims and strategies, or that they can to continue to rely on the force of inherited tradition. Clearly, clinging onto and attempting to reassert old collective traditions around the margins of a more individualistic and flexible marketplace is not a viable option. The unions must identify members' needs more accurately and cater for them more effectively, especially for those groups which have been marginalised in the past, such as women, and temporary and part-time workers. In addition, they need to develop and codify collective identities which are consistent with the shifting individual identities of the persons they seek to organize and represent. Certainly there is scope for enlarging the range of services that unions offer to their members, and some unions have begun to move in this direction. Thus the leader of the MSF has talked of 'the need to see our members as our customers' and his counterpart at the TGWU has suggested that unions should become 'a "one-stop shop" for advice and action on the range of issues which impact on the well-being of the worker at work and at home', while UNISON will offer its members 'free financial advice tailored to individuals in personalized packages'. However, while this new 'consumer-orientation' is a necessary condition for the revival of the unions, it is not a sufficient one. For the majority of union members themselves still see the primary role of unions as pursuing traditional collective priorities such as campaigning for better wages, better working conditions, better health and safety at work, equal opportunities in the workplace, and so on (Whitston and Waddington 1994; Bradley 1994).

It would seem, therefore, that the unions would be unwise to abandon traditional collective campaigning issues altogether in favour of the individualist consumer policies advocated by Bassett and Cave (1993). Rather they should aim to combine both consumer-orientated policies and traditional collective concerns, thereby appealing to the pluralistic needs of the increasingly diverse worker groups within the membership as well to the more activist core. But Taylor (1994) goes further and suggests that in searching for guidance and inspiration the unions should also try to recover and build upon their own rich historical traditions of the nineteenth century, when they were much more than voluntary institutions involved in collective bargaining over pay, working conditions and employment security. They were also more than just friendly societies, providing their members with a range of insurance benefits in times of difficulty. For they acted as important organizational expressions of worker citizenship in a wider sense, articulating and campaigning for a range of democratic rights and principles. Taylor argues Britain's trade unions need to look to that neglected tradition of free-thinking libertarianism, and 'reassert themselves by bringing workplace civil rights to the forefront of their public policy agenda for continued survival and future advance' (p.228).

In effect, Taylor seems to be arguing for the sort of 'recovery of traditions' that Giddens suggests is one of the impulses triggered by 'detraditionalization'.

REPRESENTATION, ORGANIZATIONAL STRUCTURE AND GEOGRAPHY

The future of the unions will not just depend on expanding the services they provide, on developing their capacity to represent increasingly diverse groups of workers, or on re-evaluating workplace trade union identities and traditions. They will also have to forge new organizational structures. Union structures provide the framework for the representation of workers and the codification of their interests and identities. It is through such structures that workers' identities and interests are translated into union activity, policy and strategy. Furthermore, as we saw in Chapters One and Two, the nature of the relationship between a union and its members is mediated by the institutional and organizational spaces of the union. The geographical structure of the unions around local, district, regional and national organizational bodies, and the nature of the interaction between these layers, shape the way in which workplace identities are both formed and reflected over time. As economies, worker identities and cultures change, so too must union organizational and representational structures. In other words, new representational requirements from workers may necessitate new geographical structures in trade union organization.

From his review of union developments in five leading OECD economies (the United States, the United Kingdom, Japan, France and Canada), Murray (1994) identifies four main trajectories of trade union representational form: *micro-corporatism*, entailing 'strategic alliances' between a local union, usually plant- or site-based, and the employer; *associational unionism*, in which unions offer various user-services without the necessity of union membership (essentially the model advanced by Bassett and Cave, referred to above); *community unionism*, in which representational structures are organized on a spatially decentralized basis, along local and regional community lines (as discussed in Chapter Six); and *general or social unionism*, involving the formation by merger and amalgamation of new nationwide multi-industry conglomerates. Each of these models represents an attempt by the unions to come to terms with the historical limits of the pre-existing organizational forms of collective worker representation. No single model is likely to prove dominant, and different countries may well end up with different models. In Britain's case, although examples of experiments with micro-corporatist, associational and community unionism can be found, thus far the most common organizational response to the crisis of the unions has been the fourth route to structural reform, that is, union merger and what some see as a new movement towards the formation of 'super unions'.

There has been a steady process of union merger and amalgamation throughout the past century of union history. But according to Waddington (1988, 1995) merger activity has tended to be more intense during periods of economic slump and union decline. This suggests that merger activity tends to be a defensive reaction, a strategy intended to reconsolidate a contracting membership. Since the early 1980s the merger movement has accelerated. In 1979 there were 453 unions; by 1993 the number had fallen to 254, with the 10 largest unions accounting for 5.86 million (67%) of the total union membership of 8.7 million in that year.[10] For example, COHSE, NUPE and NALGO have combined to form the super union UNISON; the MSF has been created through the merger of the Association of Scientific Technical and Managerial Staffs (ASTMS) and the Technical Adminis- trative and Supervisory Staff union (TASS); the AEU and EETPU have joined forces as the AEEU; the Boilermakers' Society amalgamated with the General Municipal Workers to form the GMB, which subsequently subsumed APEX the white-collar union, the Greater London Staff Association, and the Tailor and Garment Workers' Union; the National Communications Union (NCU) and the Union of Communi- cation Workers (UCW) have amalgamated to form the Communication Workers Union (CWU); and recently there have been merger discussions between the GMB and the TGWU. These unions have sought to project their merger activities as a sign of dynamism and strength rather than as defensive moves. Merger is argued to confer several advantages: for example the pooling of membership bases, the consolidation of financial resources, the strengthening of bargaining power, and the elimination of duplicated effort in overlapping or complementary spheres of membership recruitment and representation. Above all, it brings 'economies of scale' to the unions involved: specialization can be combined with size so that more efficient services and products can be offered to members. As Herod (1991) has argued, the geographical scale at which unions and employers have political influence is itself a powerful weapon in determining the outcome of organizational initiatives.

Perhaps less obviously, mergers change the contours of the trade union map. The geographical structure of a new combined union will of course depend on the respective regional and local structures of the individual unions that merge. It will involve a complex intermingling of each union's local traditions, workplace cultures, organizational histories and representational forms. In this sense, just as merger is easier if the combining unions have complementary membership pools and if they share similar organizational and representational structures, so too will it be easier if those unions have similar or at least closely overlapping geographies. Mergers may thus function to reconsolidate union membership and workplace influence around new organizational structures, prompting the unions involved to re-evaluate their traditional practices and policies.

---

10 The top ten unions, in terms of membership, were: UNISON (1.465 million), TGWU (0.949 million), AEEU (0.835 million), GMB (0.809 million), MSF (0.516 million), Royal College of Nursing of the UK (0.303 million), USDAW (0.299 million), Graphical Paper and Media Union (0.250 million), National Union of Teachers (NUT) (0.232 million) and National Association of School Masters and Union of Women Teachers (0.207 million).

Yet, mergers themselves do not guarantee the revival of union memberships and fortunes.[11] The danger with the 'super' or 'mega' unions strategy is that the structure of organization becomes too monolithic, too cumbersome, and bureaucratic, disconnecting the aims of the union from the experiences and concerns of their members at the local grass-roots level. As the CBI stated in its evidence to the House of Commons Employment Select Committee on the future of the unions, 'some employers do sense a potential conflict between the growth of large general unions and the continuing need for them to get closer to their members in the workplace' (HM Government 1994, p.323). Likewise the Civil and Public Service Association expressed the concern that the distinctive sense of identity, based on jobs and industries, characteristic of smaller unions would be lost (p.52). The General Secretary of the GMB, however, believes the role of small unions to be a limited one, in that:

> there is a case for the maintenance of small unions if they are to operate in one area of occupation or in one locality. If they are to provide a national service across a range of specialist skills, then they really need to be big... The trick is to ensure that as you grow big you operate as a cluster of unions, rather than one great monolith. (Edmonds 1994, p.171)

As a consequence, the GMB and TGWU, like the AEEU we discussed in Chapter Six, have created industrial sections and trade groups to represent the different sectional interests within the membership body.

Indeed, although the rationalization of the British trade union movement into a small number of large multi-sector national unions might well allow those super unions to combine and consolidate different membership geographies and to extend their spatial coverage accordingly, the cost might well be a weakening of sensivity to local variations in representational and organizational traditions and concerns, and even a decline in the role and relative significance of local and community-based layers of union structure. A large union needs to be attentive to the varying conditions and circumstances of its many local memberships if it is to retain their allegiance and support. At a time when the thrust of change in work organization and industrial relations is towards localization and decentralization, the trend towards ever larger national unions may thus contain the seeds of future difficulties for union representation and organization.

Our research suggests that trade union organization needs to unite the concerns of members at very local scales with the political task of campaigning at the national (and even international) level. Local trade unionism can play a very significant role in influencing, regulating and co-ordinating local labour markets, and in improving the quality of labour through promoting and participating in

---

11 Mergers produce a smaller number of larger unions but do not necessarily promote subsequent 'organic' growth in membership. The problem is akin to that found in the corporate sector, where the quick route to company growth via takeovers, acquisitions and mergers tends to rearrange the ownership of the nation's capital stock rather than increase it.

training and retraining schemes (Mahnkopf 1992; Streeck 1992; Rutherford 1995). There is growing evidence that a high level of institutionalized co-ordination and co-operation between firms and between employers and the employed is vital to successful competitive economic growth, both nationally and locally.[12] The danger is that as trade unions become increasingly occupied with 'vertical' strategies of centralization and merger, they will miss the opportunity to strengthen horizontal (that is geographically based) forms of organization. Instead, there is a strong case for arguing that unions would benefit from adopting representational strategies which make more use of the local dynamics and networks of political, economic and community affairs.

We are not arguing here that the unions should simply 'downsize' or decentralize. It is much too simplistic to suggest that organization and representation should be focused at any one scale of socio-economic life. Strategies at different spatial scales should not be seen as alternatives. As we argued in Chapter Six, neither general 'super unionism' nor locally decentralized 'community unionism' are likely to be successful on their own. Rather they should be seen as complementary, each strengthening the other. Indeed, one of the strongest organizational resources which the unions possess is their ability to create and integrate social spaces for organization at a variety of spatial scales. We would argue that the rediscovery and strategic deployment of geography should be a key component of the unions' structural and representational reforms. If Britain is to avoid the 'shrinking perimeter of unionism' that Davis (1986) describes in the United States, the unions need to attend to the geographical particularities they have inherited from the past alongside those that are certain to characterize the future.

---

12 What this implies is that the strength of regional economic performance can not be simply equated with the degree of union penetration *per se* in a local or regional economy. It is rather the *type or role* which unions play in these economies that is important for regional growth.

Appendix

Several different data sets have been utilized in this study. Table A.1 lists the main sources. As mentioned in Chapter One, there are no regularly published data on regional union membership, and we used six different sources as the basis for our various analyses. The three Workplace Industrial Relations Surveys (WIRS), undertaken in 1980, 1984 and 1990, provide the only comprehensive workplace-based data sets. These national surveys, each based on detailed questionnaire returns for a sample of about 2000 workplaces, have been used in numerous studies of the changing nature of British industrial relations since the end of the 1970s. The basic questionnaires, sampling methods and general interpretations of the findings of WIRS are fully documented elsewhere (see Daniel and Millward 1983; Millward and Stevens 1986; Millward *et al.* 1992). The surveys also permit a regionally disaggregated analysis of the trends in unionism and industrial relations over the 1980–90 period, although only a few studies have thus far examined this dimension of the data (for example, Beaumont and Harris 1988a, 1988b; Church and Stevens 1994; Martin, Sunley and Wills 1994e).

The WIRS are not without problems or limitations, however. In particular, workplaces of less than 25 employees are excluded, and given that union membership and recognition rates are significantly lower in establishments in this size band, the WIRS estimates tend to overstate the degree of unionization. This problem is compounded by the oversampling of larger establishments, in which unionization and recognition rates tend to be high. At the same time, certain sectors of employment are omitted, most notably agriculture, fishing and forestry, and coal mining. In addition, there are some significant differences in the questions and definitions used between the three surveys. Moreover, the 1990 WIRS, in contrast to its earlier counterparts, does not contain locational identifiers below the level of the British standard regions, so that the latter are the only areas for which consistent geographical trends across all three surveys can be analyzed. Even so, the relatively small sample sizes for the regions restrict the degree of region-specific industrial, occupational or workplace-size disaggregation that can be carried out. A number of problems were encountered in processing the raw data files. Not only was there a lengthy delay in the official release of the full data files (with regional identifiers) for the 1990 WIRS, which in turn delayed our own analyses, but accessing information on a regional basis proved to be a time-consuming and not altogether straightforward process.

The second major source of regional data on trade unionism is that contained in the Labour Force Surveys (LFS). The annual LFS is based on a sample survey of around 60,000 households across the country, and since 1989 has contained questions on trade union membership. These data can be grouped on a standard regional basis, and like the WIRS allow a certain degree of industrial disaggregation by individual region. Being household- rather than workplace-based, the LFS data are not directly comparable with

Table A.1: Main sources of data used in the study

Data Source	Period
A. Trade Unionism and Industrial Relations	
1. Workplace Industrial Relations Surveys (WIRS)	1980, 1984 and 1990
2. Labour Force Surveys (LFS)	Annual, 1989 to 1994
3. Individual Union Records (from Unions)	1979–1991
4. Survey of Establishments in North West and South East England	1992–1993
5. Interviews with Engineering Establishments drawn from above Survey	1992–1993
6. Interviews with AEU District Secretaries and National Officials in North West and South East England	1992–1993
7. Interviews with Head Office and Regional Representatives of the Engineering Employers' Federation	1992–1993
8. Interviews with Union and TUC Officials at Head Offices and in North West and South East England	1994
B. Employment and Work Force	
9. Regional Estimates from Census of Employment and Regional Employment Series (Department of Employment)	Various
10. Local Authority Employment Estimates (NOMIS)	Annual 1981–1991
C. Strike Activity	
11. Number of Strikes and Working Days Lost, Industrial Stoppages Series (Department of Employment)	1966–1993
D. Collective Bargaining	
12. Collective Agreement Coverage, by Region (New Earnings Survey)	1978 and 1985
13. Levels of Collective Bargaining (from WIRS)	1984 and 1990

the WIRS estimates, and give a slightly different picture of the extent of unionization from that provided by WIRS. In particular, unlike WIRS the LFS covers employees from firms with fewer than 25 workers, so that the LFS estimates of union density tend to be lower than those calculated from WIRS. However, given that the last WIRS was in 1990 (and the next one is not planned until 1997, so that direct access is unlikely to be possible until 1998), the LFS series are at present the only source of data which permit an analysis of broad regional trends in unionization into the 1990s.

These two sets of secondary data were supplemented by our own estimates of regional membership for a number of individual unions. Twenty unions were approached initially, and while some declined to allow us access to their archival records, and others had incomplete data series, ten unions provided consistent and usable regional data on their memberships: namely, the AEEU, BIFU, FBU, GMB, ISTC, NALGO, NUPE, TGWU,

UCATT, and USDAW. Annual regional membership figures were obtained for these unions for the period 1979 to 1991 (and are described in detail in Chapter Three). The wave of merger activity that involved some of these unions in the early 1990s effectively dictated the end-year for this data set. Geographical analysis of these union series was complicated by the fact that each union is organized on a different geographical basis, with different regional divisions. This precluded any combination of the regional data for our ten unions, and each union had to be analyzed separately. It also meant that standard regional employment data could not be used to calculate regional densities for the unions, and instead local authority level employment estimates (obtained from NOMIS) had to be used to construct regional employment figures (potential member-ships) on an individual union-by-union basis (excluding the AEEU and GMB), as described in Chapter Three. This method, although liable to inaccuracies, enabled us to calculate for the first time regional union densities for individual unions (see Martin, Sunley and Wills 1993).

In addition to these sources, we also generated our own micro-level data from a postal questionnaire survey of trade unionism and industrial relations practices in a sample of establishments in two case study areas: Lancashire and Greater Manchester in the north west of England, and Bedfordshire, Hertfordshire and Cambridgeshire in the south east. A randomly selected address list of establishments from the Dun and Bradstreet business directory was used for this survey. Completed returns were received from 455 individual establishments (workplaces): 244 from the south-eastern area and 211 from the north-western region. Of these returns, 20 per cent (91) were from engineering establishments of various kinds (49 in the south-eastern counties and 42 in the north-western ones), and the extent of spatial variations in trade unionism amongst these particular workplaces between the two areas prompted us to explore this subset in more depth. Semi-structured interviews of up to two hours were thus conducted with industrial relations or personnel managers in 45 of these engineering establishments. These data were supplemented with information on trade union practices and attitudes in each area from semi-structured interviews with eleven district secretaries from the AEEU, and data on procedural conferences in the engineering industry in our two case study regions were derived from interviews with representatives of the Engineering Employers' Federation (EEF) in its South Lancashire–Cheshire–North Wales, Southern, and Mid-Anglian divisions. For a summary of the findings from these various interviews see Martin, Sunley and Wills (1994a).

To investigate the geographical dimensions of union organizational structure and strategy more generally, semi-structured interviews were also conducted with both head office and regional officials of the ten individual unions referred to above. The emphasis here was on officials' views and interpretations of the challenge to and changes in their specific union, with particular attention being directed to their perceptions of the regional and local impact of contemporary change.

The employment data used at various points in the book derive from two main sources. The local authority level data used to compute the regional potential memberships for the sample unions (excluding the AEEU and GMB) were from the 1981 and 1991 Census of Employment (obtained from NOMIS). The series used in the discussion of regional employment recomposition in Chapter Four and regional strike rates in Chapter Five relate to the Department of Employment's regular (quarterly and annual) estimates published in the *Employment Gazette* (now *Labour Market Trends*).

The data on regional strikes were taken from the Department of Employment's series on industrial stoppages. These data are annual and extend back on a relatively consistent regional basis to 1966. Two measures are collected, namely the number of strikes and the number of working days lost in industrial disputes. We used the latter, converted to a rate per thousand employees in employment to remove the effect of differences in employment size between regions. These regional series are also disaggregated on an industrial basis (SIC first digit orders).

Two main sources were used for information on the geography of collective bargaining. The first is from the New Earnings Survey (NES). This is an annual survey of the wages, hours and types of collective wage agreement in Great Britain, based on a one per cent sample of employees in employment. In 1978 and 1985, the surveys contained additional questions on the degree of collective agreement coverage, by different levels of bargaining (national, national with supplement, district-company-local, and no agreement) and cover all establishment sizes and all industrial sectors, for both manual and non-manual employees separately. Both regional and county-level results can be obtained for these two years. Unfortunately this valuable survey has not been repeated since. The second source used was the information on collective wage agreements in the 1984 and 1990 WIRS. These provide different estimates from those in the NES. Not only are the levels of collective agreement classified differently (multi-employer, employer, plant-level and none), but unlike the NES surveys the WIRS data exclude establishments with fewer than 25 employees, in which collective agreements are less common. This, together with the differences in sample size, probably explains the higher estimates of overall collective bargaining coverage in the regions given by the 1985 NES compared to the 1984 WIRS (Chapter Six).

Bibliography

Aglietta, M. (1979) *A Theory of Capitalist Regulation: The US Experience*. London: New Left Books.

Allen, J. (1988) 'Fragmented firms, disorganized labour.' In J. Allen and D. Massey (eds) *Restructuring Britain: The Economy in Question*. London: Sage.

Allen, J. and Henry, N. (1996) 'Ulrich Beck's risk society at work: labour and employment in the contract service industries.' *Transcations of the Institute of British Geographers*, Forthcoming.

Allen, J. and Massey, D. (eds) (1988) *Restructuring Britain: The Economy in Question*. London: Sage.

Amin, A. (ed) (1994) *Post-Fordism: A Reader*. Oxford: Blackwell.

Amin, A. and Thrift, N. (1992) 'Neo-Marshallian nodes in global networks.' *International Journal of Urban and Regional Research 16*, 571–587.

Amoroso, B. (1992) 'Industrial relations in Europe in the 1990s: New business strategies and the challenge to organized labour.' *International Journal of Human Resource Management 3*, 331–345.

Armstrong, G. (1993) Speech to Annual Conference of the Institute of Personnel Management, Harrogate.

Armstrong, H. and Taylor, J. (1985) *Regional Economics and Policy*. Oxford: Philip Allen.

Atkinson, J. (1985) *Flexibility, Uncertainty and Manpower Management*. Institute of Manpower Studies Report 89. Brighton: IMS.

Atkinson, J. and Gregory, D. (1986) 'A flexible future; Britain's dual labour force.' *Marxism Today*. April, 12–17.

Atkinson, J. and Meager, N. (1986) *Changing Work Patterns: How Companies Achieve Flexibility to Meet New Needs*. London: NEDO.

Baglioni, C. (1990) 'Industrial relations in Europe in the 1980s.' In C. Baglioni and C. Crouch (eds) *European Industrial Relations: The Challenge of Flexibility*. London: Sage.

Bain, G.S. and Price, R. (1980) *Profiles of Union Growth*. Oxford: Blackwell.

Barnes, T. and Sheppard, E. (1992) 'Is there a place for the rational actor? A geographical critique of the rational choice paradigm.' *Economic Geography 68*, 1–21.

Barnett, J. (1982) *Inside the Treasury*. London: Andre Deutsch.

Bassett, P.D. (1986) *Strike Free: New Industrial Relations in Britain*. London: Macmillan.

Bassett, P. and Cave, A. (1993) *All For One: The Future of the Union*. London: Fabian Society.

Batstone, E. (1988) *The Reform of Workplace Industrial Relations: Theory, Myth and Evidence*. Oxford: Clarendon.

Bean, R. and Peel, D.A. (1976) 'A cross sectional analysis of regional strike activity in Britain.' *Journal of Regional Studies 10*, 3, 299–305.

Bean, R. and Stoney, P. (1986) 'Strikes on Merseyside, A regional analysis.' *Industrial Relations Journal 17*, 1, 9–23.

Beard, J. (1995) 'The geography of private sector trade unionism: a regional comparison.' *Area 27*, 3, 218–227.

Beaumont, P.D. (1987) *The Decline of Trade Union Organisation*. London: Croom Helm.

Beaumont, P.D. (1990) *Change in Industrial Relations*. London: Routledge.

Beaumont, P.D. (1991) 'Trade unions and human resource management.' *Industrial Relations Journal 22*, 300–308.

Beaumont, P.D. (1995) *The Future of Employment Relations.* London: Sage.

Beaumont, P.D. and Harris, R. (1988a) 'Subsystems of industrial relations: The spatial dimension in Britain.' *British Journal of Industrial Relations 26*, 397–407.

Beaumont, P.D. and Harris, R. (1988b) 'The North–South divide in Britain: The case of trade union recognition.' Paper presented at the EMRY Labour Economics Study Group, University College of Swansea, 28–30 March.

Beaumont, P.D. and Harris, R. (1991) 'Trade union recognition and employment contract, Britain 1980–84.' *British Journal of Industrial Relations 29*, 49–58.

Beck, U. (1994) 'The reinvention of politics: Towards a theory of reflexive modernisation.' In U. Beck, A. Giddens and S. Lash (1994) *Reflexive Modernisation; Politics, Tradition and Aesthetics in the Modern Social Order.* Cambridge: Polity Press.

Belanger, J. (1987) 'Job control after reform: A case study in British engineering.' *Industrial Relations Journal 18*, 50–62.

Bell, D. (1973) *The Coming of Post-Industrial Society.* New York: Basic Books.

Berger, S., Hirschmann, A. and Maier, C. (1981) *Organizing Interests in Western Europe: Pluralism, Corporatism and the Transformation of Politics.* Cambridge: Cambridge University Press.

Berman, E., Bound, J. and Griliches, Z. (1994) 'Changes in the demand for skilled labour within US manufacturing: Evidence from the Annual Survey of Manufactures.' *Quarterly Journal of Economics 109*, 367–97.

Bevan, G.P. (1880) 'The strikes of the last ten years.' *Journal of the Statistical Society 43*, 35–54.

Beynon, H. (ed) (1985) *Digging Deeper: Issues in the Miners' Strike.* London: Verso.

Beynon, H. and Austrin, T. (1994) *Masters and Servants: Class and Patronage in the Making of a Labour Organisation.* London: River Oram Press.

Beynon, H. and Hudson, R. (1993) 'Place and space in contemporary Europe: Some lessons and reflections.' *Antipode 25*, 3, 177–190.

Black, B. (1987) 'Collaboration or conflict? Strike activity in Northern Ireland.' *Industrial Relations Journal 18*, 1, 14–24.

Blanchflower, D. and Freeman, R. (1990) *Going Different Ways: Unionism in the United States and Other Advanced Countries.* Discussion Paper No. 5, Centre for Economic Performance, London School of Economics.

Block, F. (1990) *Post-Industrial Possibilities.* Berkeley: University of California Press.

Blyton, P. and Turnbull, P. (eds) (1992) *Reassessing Human Resource Management.* London: Sage.

Booth, A. (1984) *Individual Trade Union Membership in the UK. Evidence from the National Training Survey.* Discussion Paper 61. London: ESRC.

Booth, A. (1985) 'The free-rider problem and a social custom model of trade union membership.' *Quarterly Journal of Economics 100*, 253–61.

Booth, A. (1989) *What do Unions do Now?* Discussion Papers in Economics, No. 8903. Brunel University.

Boyer, R. (1988) *The Search for Labour Market Flexibility: The European Economies in Transition.* Oxford: Clarendon Press.

Boyer, R. (1990) *The Regulation School: A Critical Introduction.* New York: Columbia University Press.

Boyer, R. (1993) 'Labour institutions and economic growth: A survey and a "regulationist" perspective.' *Labour: Review of Labour Economics and Industrial Relations 7*, 1, 25–72.

Bradley, H. (1994) 'Divided we fall.' *Employee Relations 16*, 2, 41–52.

Brown, W. (1993) 'The contraction of collective bargaining in Britain.' *British Journal of Industrial Relations 31*, 189– 200.

Brown, W. and Wadhwani, S. (1990) 'The economic effects of industrial relations legislation since 1979.' *National Institute Economic Review 131*, February, 57–70.

Brown, W. and Walsh, J. (1991) 'Pay determination in Britain in the 1980s: The anatomy of decentralisation.' *Oxford Review of Economic Policy 7*, 44–59.

Brunetta, R. and Dell'Aringa, C. (eds) (1990) *Labour Relations and Economic Performance.* London: Macmillan.

Burawoy, M. (1985) *The Politics of Production.* London: Verso.

Cadbury, A. (1985) *The 1980s: A Watershed in British Industrial Relations.* IMS, 4th Hitachi Lecture, UNCRIR.

Calhoun, C.J. (1982) *The Question of Class Struggle: Social Foundations of Popular Radicalism During the Industrial Revolution.* Oxford: Blackwell.

Calhoun, C.J. (1983) 'The radicalism of tradition: Community strength or venerable disguise and borrowed language.' *American Journal of Sociology 88*, 5, 886–914.

Calhoun, C.J. (1987) 'Class, space and industrial revolution.' In N.J. Thrift and P. Williams (eds) *Class and Space: The Making of Urban Society.* London: Routledge and Kegan Paul.

Calhoun, C.J. (1988) 'The radicalisation of tradition and the question of class struggle.' In M. Taylor (ed) *Rationality and Revolution.* Cambridge: Cambridge University Press.

Carruth, A. and Disney, R. (1988) 'Where have two million trade union members gone?' *Economica 55*, 41–61.

Casey, C. (1995) *Work, Self and Society: After Industrialism.* London: Routledge.

Casson, M. (1983) *Economics of Unemployment: An Historical Perspective.* Oxford: Martin Robertson.

Charlesworth, A., Gilbert, D., Southall, H. and Wrigley, C. (1996) *An Atlas of Industrial Protest in Britain 1750–1990.* London: Macmillan.

Chisholm, M.D.I. and Oeppen, J. (1973) *The Changing Pattern of Employment: Regional Specialisation and Industrial Localisation in Britain.* London: Croom Helm.

Church, A. and Stevens, M. (1994) 'Unionisation and the urban–rural shift.' *Transactions of the Institute of British Geographers, NS, 19*, 111–118.

Church, R., Outram, Q. and Smith, D.M. (1990) 'British coal mining strikes 1893–1940: Dimensions, distribution and persistence.' *British Journal of Industrial Relations 28*, 3, 329–349.

Clark, G.L. (1989) *Unions and Communities Under Seige: American Communities and the Crisis of Organized Labour.* Cambridge: Cambridge University Press.

Clark, G. (1992) '"Real regulation": The administrative state.' *Environment and Planning A, 24*, 615–27.

Clark, G. and Johnston, K. (1987) 'The geography of US union elections 3: The context and structure of union electoral performance.' *Environment and Planning A, 19*, 289–311.

Clegg, H. (1976) *Trade Unionism under Collective Bargaining: A Theory based on Comparisons of Six Countries.* Oxford: Basil Blackwell.

Clegg, H. (1979) *The Changing System of Industrial Relations in Great Britain.* Oxford: Basil Blackwell.

Clifton, R.F. and Creigh, S.W. (1977) 'Regional strike proneness: A research note.' *Journal of Regional Studies 11*, 2, 79–86.

Coates, D. (1989) *The Crisis of Labour: Industrial Relations and the State in Contemporary Britain.* Oxford: Phillip Allan.

Cole, J. (1994) 'There's no substitute for class.' *New Statesman and Society*, February 18, 8.

Commission of Inquiry Into Industrial Unrest (1917) *Report*, Cmnd. 8698. London: HMSO.

Confederation of British Industry (CBI) (1994) Written Evidence Submitted to House of Commons Select Committee on *The Future of the Trade Unions.* London: HMSO.

Cooke, P. (1985) 'Class practices as regional markers: A contribution to labour geography.' In D. Gregory and J. Urry (eds) *Social Relations and Spatial Structures.* London: Macmillan.

Cowling, K. and Sugden, R. (1994) *Beyond Capitalism: Towards a New World Economic Order.* London: Pinter.

Cregan, C. and Johnston, K. (1990) 'An industrial relations approach to the free rider problem: Young people and trade union membership in the UK.' *British Journal of Industrial Relations 28*, 84–104.

Cronin, J.E. (1979) *Industrial Conflict in Modern Britain.* London: Croom Helm.

Crouch, C. (1986) 'The future prospects for trade unions in Western Europe.' *Political Quarterly 57*, 5–17.

Crouch, C. (1993) *Industrial Relations and European State Traditions.* Oxford: Oxford University Press.

Crouch, C. and Pizzorno, A (1978) *The Resurgence of Class Conflict in Western Europe since 1968,* 2 vols. London: Macmillan.

Daly, M. and Atkinson, E. (1940) 'A regional analysis of strikes 1921–1936.' *Sociological Review 32*, 216–223.

Daniel, W.W. and Millward, N. (1983) *Workplace Industrial Relations in Britain.* London: Heinemann.

Daniels, P. (1986) 'Producer services and the post-industrial space economy.' In R.L. Martin and R. Rowthorn (eds) (1986) *The Geography of De-industrialisation.* London: Macmillan.

Darlington, R. (1994) *The Dynamics of Workplace Unionism.* London: Mansell.

Davies, R.J. (1979) 'Economic activity, incomes policy and strikes.' *British Journal of Industrial Relations 17*, 2, 205–23.

Davis, M. (1986) *Prisoners of the American Dream: Politics and Economy in the History of the US Working Class.* London: Verso.

Deakin, S. (1992) 'Labour law and industrial relations.' In J. Michie (ed) *The Economic Legacy, 1979–92.* London: Academic Press.

Deakin, S. and Wilkinson, F. (1991) 'Labour law, social security and economic inequality.' *Cambridge Journal of Economics 15*, 125–48.

Disney, R. (1990) 'Explanations of the decline in trade union density in Britain: An appraisal.' *British Journal of Industrial Relations 28*, 168–177.

Disney, R., Gosling, A. and Machin, S. (1993) *British Trade Unions in Decline; What has Happened to Trade Union Recognition in British Establishments?* Paper presented to the Employment Research Unit Conference, University of Wales, Cardiff, September.

Dunford, M. and Perrons, D. (1983) *The Arena of Capital.* London: Macmillan.

Dunford, M. and Perrons, D. (1986) 'The restructuring of the post-war British space economy.' In R.L. Martin and R.E. Rowthorn (eds) *The Geography of De-industrialisation.* London: Macmillan.

Durcan, J., McCarthy, W.E.J. and Redman, G.P. (1983) *Strikes in Post-War Britain.* London: Allen and Unwin.

Eder, K. (1993) *The New Politics of Class: Social Movements and Cultural Dynamics in Advanced Societies.* London: Sage.

Edmonds, J. (1994) Oral evidence to the House of Commons Select Committee on *The Future of the Trade Unions* (volume 2), 170–173.

Edwards, P.K. (1995) 'Strikes and industrial conflict. In P.K. Edwards (ed) *Industrial Relations: Theory and practice in Britain.* Oxford: Blackwell, 434–460.

Edwards, R. (1986) 'Unions in crisis and beyond: Introduction.' In R. Edwards, P. Garonna and F. Todtling (eds) *Unions in Crisis: Perspectives from Six Countries.* London: Auburn House.

Elgar, J. and Simpson, B. (1993) 'The impact of the law on industrial disputes in the 1980s.' In D. Metcalf and S. Milner (eds) *New Perspectives on Industrial Disputes.* London: Routledge.

Elger, T. (1991) 'Task flexibility and the intensification of labour in UK manufacturing.' In A. Pollert (ed) *Farewell to Flexibility?* Oxford: Blackwell.

Ellis, M. (1992) 'The determinants of regional differences in strike rates in the U.S., 1971–77.' *Annals, Association of American Geographers 82*, 48–63.

Engels, F. (1958) *The Condition of the Working Classes in England.* Oxford: Basil Blackwell.

Engineer (1993) News Section, 8 July, p.7

Evans, S.M. and Boyte, H.C. (1986) *Free Spaces: The Sources of Democratic Change in America.* New York: Harper and Row.

Farnham, D. and Pimlott, J. (1990) *Understanding Industrial Relations.* London: Cassell.

Feinstein, C. (1988) 'Economic growth since 1870: Britain's performance in international perspective.' *Oxford Review of Economic Policy 4,* 1, 1–13.

Ferner, A. and Hyman, R. (eds) (1992) *Industrial Relations in the New Europe.* Oxford: Basil Blackwell.

Financial Times (1987) 'The collapse of negotiations in engineering.' 5 November, p.5.

Fisher, J. (1995) 'The trade union response to HRM in the UK: The case of the TGWU.' *Human Resource Management Journal 5,* 7–23.

Flanders, A. (1970) *Management and Unions: The Theory and Reform of Industrial Relations.* London: Faber and Faber.

Fosh, P. (1993) 'Membership participation in workplace unionism: The possibility of union renewal.' *British Journal of Industrial Relations 31,* 577–592.

Fosh, P. and Heery, P. (eds) (1990) *Trade Unions and their Members: Studies in Union Democracy and Organisation.* London: Macmillan.

Fothergill, S. and Gudgin, G. (1982) *Unequal Growth: Urban and Regional Employment Change in the UK.* London: Heineman.

Fothergill, S., Gudgin, G., Kitson, M. and Monk, S. (1986) 'The de-industrialisation of the city.' In R.L. Martin and R.E. Rowthorn (eds) *The Geography of De-industrialisation.* London: Macmillan.

Freeman, R. (1990) 'On the divergence in unionism among developed countries.' In R. Brunetta and C. Dell'Aringa (eds) *Labour Relations and Economic Performance.* London: Macmillan.

Freeman, R. and Medoff, J. (1984) *What Do Unions Do?* New York: Basic Books.

Freeman, R. and Pelletier, J. (1990) 'The impact of industrial relations legislation on British union density.' *British Journal of Industrial Relations 28,* 141–164.

Friedland, R. and Sanders, J. (1990) 'Private and social wage expansion within the advanced economies.' In S. Zukin and P. DiMaggio (eds) *Structures of Capital: The Social Organization of the Economy.* Cambridge: Cambridge University Press.

Friedman, A.L. (1977) *Industry and Labour: Class Struggle at Work and Monopoly Capitalism.* London: Macmillan.

Gallie, D. (1983) *Social Inequality and Class Radicalism in France and Britain.* Cambridge: Cambridge University Press.

Gallie, D. (1990) *Trade Union Allegiance and Decline in British Urban Labour Markets.* ESRC Social Change and Economic Life Initiative Working Paper, 9. Swindon: ESRC.

Gamble, A. (1988) *The Free Economy and Strong State.* London: Macmillan.

Gamble, A. (1990) *Britain in Decline,* Third Edition. London: Macmillan.

Gardner, N. (1987) *Decade of Discontent: The Changing British Economy Since 1973.* Oxford: Blackwell.

Garrahan, P. and Stewart, P. (1989) *Post-Fordism, Japanisation and the Local Economy.* Paper presented to CSE Conference, Sheffield Polytechnic.

Garrahan, P. and Stewart, P. (1991) *The Nissan Enigma.* London: Cassell.

Garrahan, P. and Stewart, P. (1992) 'Management control and a new regime of subordination: Post-Fordism and the local economy.' In N. Gilbert, R. Burrows and A. Pollert (eds) (1992) *Fordism and Flexibility: Divisions and Change.* London: Macmillan.

Geroski, P.A., Hamlin, A.P. and Knoght, K.G. (1982) 'Wages, strikes and market structure.' *Economic Journal 101,* 1438–1451.

Gertler, M. (1992) 'Flexibility revisited: Districts, nation-states and the forces of production.' *Transactions of the Institute of British Geographers, NS 17,* 259–45.

Giddens, A. (1984) *The Constitution of Society.* Cambridge: Polity Press.

Giddens, A. (1994a) 'Living in a post-traditional society.' In U. Beck, A. Giddens and S. Lash. *Reflexive Modernisation; Politics, Tradition and Aesthetics in the Modern Social Order*. Cambridge: Polity Press.

Giddens, A. (1994b) *Beyond Right and Left: The Future of Radical Politics*. Cambridge: Polity Press.

Gilbert, D. (1992) *Class, Community and Collective Action: Social Change in two British Coalfields 1850–1926*. Cambridge: Cambridge University Press.

Gilbert, D. (1995a) 'Strikes in post-war Britain.' Forthcoming in C. Wrigley (ed) *A History of British Industrial Relations 1939–1979: Industrial Relations in a Declining Economy*. London: Edward Elgar.

Gilbert, D. (1995b) 'Imagined communities and mining communities.' *Labour History Review 66*, 2, 47–55.

Gilbert, N., Burrows, R. and Pollert, A. (eds) (1992) *Fordism and Flexibility: Divisions and Change*. London: Macmillan.

Gilmour, I. (1992) *Dancing with Dogma: Britain under Thatcherism*. London: Simon and Schuster.

Glyn, A. and Harrison, J. (1980) *The British Economic Disaster*. London: Pluto Press.

Glyn, A., Hughes, A., Lipietz, A. and Singh, A. (1990) 'The rise and fall of the Golden Age.' In S. Marglin and J. Schor (eds) *The Golden Age of Capitalism: Re-interpreting the Post-War Experience*. Oxford: Clarendon.

Goldthorpe, J. (ed) (1984) *Order and Conflict in Contemporary Capitalism*. Oxford: Clarendon.

Goldthorpe, J., Lockwood, D., Bechhofer, F. and Platt, J. (1969) *The Affluent Worker*. Cambridge: Cambridge University Press.

Goodman, A. and Webb, S. (1994) *For Richer, For Poorer: The UK Income Distribution*. London: Institute for Fiscal Studies.

Grant, D. (1994) 'New style agreements at Japanese transplants in the UK: The implications for trade union decline.' *Employee Relations 16*, 2, 65–83.

Green, F. (1989) *The Restructuring of the UK Economy*. London: Harvester Press.

Green, F. (1992) 'Recent trends in British trade union density: How much of a composition effect?' *British Journal of Industrial Relations 30*, 445–457.

Gregg, P. and Yates, A. (1991) 'Changes in wage-setting arrangements and trade union presence in the 1980s.' *British Journal of Industrial Relations 29*, 361–76.

Griffiths, M.J. and Johnston, R.J. (1991) 'What's in a place? An approach to the concept of place as illustrated by the National Union of Mineworkers' Strike, 1984–1985. *Antipode 23*, 2, 185–213.

Guest, D. (1989) 'Human resource management: Its implications for industrial relations and trade unions.' In J. Storey (ed) *New Perspectives on Human Resource Management*. London: Routledge.

Guest, D. and Rosenthal, P. (1992) *Industrial Relations in Greenfield Sites*. Paper presented to the Centre of Economic Performance, March. London School of Economics.

Hall, P. (1991) 'Structural transformations in the regions of the United Kingdom.' In L. Rodwin and H. Sazanami (eds) *Industrial Change and Regional Economic Transformation*. London: Harper Collins.

Hakim, C. (1990) 'Core and periphery in employer's workforce strategies.' *Work, Employment and Society 4*, 2, 82–99.

Hancke, B. (1993) 'Trade union membership in Europe, 1960–1990: Rediscovering local unions.' *British Journal of Industrial Relations 31*, 4, 593–614.

Hanson, S. and Pratt, G. (1992) 'Dynamic dependencies: A geographic investigation of local labour markets.' *Economic Geography 68*, 373–405.

Harvey, D. (1989) *The Condition of Postmodernity*. Oxford: Blackwell.

Hayek, F. (1984) *Unemployment and the Unions*. London: Institute of Economic Affairs.

Herod, A. (1991) 'Local political practice in response to a manufacturing plant closure: How geography complicates class analysis.' *Antipode 23*, 4, 385–402.

Herod, A. (1992) 'The production of scale in United States labour relations.' *Area 23*, 82–88.

Hirst, P. and Zeitlin, J. (1991) 'Flexible specialisation versus Post-Fordism: Theory, evidence and policy implications.' *Economy and Society 20*, 1, 1–156.

HM Government (1983) *Regional Industrial Development.* Department of Industry, Cmnd 9111. London: HMSO.

HM Government (1992) *People, Jobs and Opportunity.* Department of Employment. Cmnd 1810. London: HMSO.

HM Government (1994) *The Future of the Trade Unions,* House of Commons Select Committee on Employment, Third Report: Volume 1 (Report) and Volume 2 (Minutes of Evidence), Session 1993–94, HC 676–1 and HC676–2, London: HMSO.

Hobsbawm, E. (1964) *Labouring Men.* London: Weidenfeld and Nicholson.

Hoover, E. (1937) *Location Theory and the Shoe and Leather Industries.* Cambridge, Mass.: Harvard University Press.

Hoover, E. (1948) *The Location of Economic Activity.* New York: McGraw Hill.

Hudson, P. (1992) *The Industrial Revolution.* London: Edward Arnold.

Hudson, R. (1989) 'Labour-market changes and new forms of work in old industrial regions: Maybe flexibility for some but not flexible accumulation.' *Environment and Planning D: Society and Space 7*, 5–30.

Hudson, R. and Sadler, D. (1986) 'Contesting works closure in Western Europe's old industrial regions: Defending place or betraying class?' In A. Scott and M. Storper (eds) *Production, Work, Territory.* University of California Press.

Hunt, D. (1994) *Speech to the Industrial Society.* March, London.

Hunter, L.C. and McInnes, J. (1991) *Employer's Labour Use Strategies: Case Studies.* Employment Department Research Paper 87. London.

Hyman, R. (1975) *Industrial Relations: A Marxist Introduction.* London: Macmillan.

Hyman, R. (1988) 'Flexible specialisation: Miracle or myth?' In R. Hyman and W. Streek (eds) *New Technology and Industrial Relations.* Oxford: Blackwell.

Hyman, R. (1989a) *Strikes.* London: Macmillan. (Originally published 1972: Fontana).

Hyman, R. (1989b) *The Political Economy of Industrial Relations: Theory and Practice in a Cold Climate.* London: Macmillan.

Hyman, R. (1992) 'Trade unions and the disaggregation of the working class.' In M. Regini (ed) *The Future of Labour Movements.* London: Sage.

Hyman, R. and Streeck, W. (eds) (1988) *New Technology and Industrial Relations.* Oxford: Basil Blackwell.

Industrial Relations Services (1992) 'The changing role of trade union officers 1: The devolution of pay bargaining.' *Employment Trends 526*, 5–12.

Industrial Relations Services (1993a) 'The changing role of trade union officers 2: Collective bargaining and working practices.' *Employment Trends 527*, 3–11.

Industrial Relations Services (1993b) 'Single union deals.' *Employment Trends 528*, 3–15.

Industrial Relations Services (1995a) 'Spotlight on electronics.' *Employment Trends 578*, 4–11.

Industrial Relations Services (1995b) 'Lean suppliers to lean producers, 1: Changes in working practices.' *Employment Trends 583*, 3–9.

Industrial Relations Services (1995c) 'Lean suppliers to lean producers, 2: Employment relations strategies.' *Employment Trends 584*, 11–16.

Industrial Relations Services (1995d) 'Decentralisation in theory and in practice: A review of issues.' *Employment Trends 595*, 11–16.

Ingram, P., Metcalf, D. and Wadsworth, J. (1993) 'Strike incidence and duration in British manufacturing.' *Industrial and Labor Relations Review 46*, 704–717.

Institute of Personnel Management (1994) Written evidence submitted to House of Commons Select Committee on *The Future of the Trade Unions,* London: HMSO.

Jackson, M.P. (1987) *Strikes: Industrial Conflict in Britain, the USA and Australia.* London: Wheatsheaf.

Jackson, M.P. (1988) 'Strikes in Scotland.' *Industrial Relations Journal 19*, 2, 106–116.

Jackson, M.P., Leopold, J. and Tuck, K. (1993) *Decentralisation of Collective Bargaining: An Analysis of Recent Experience in the UK.* Basingstoke: St Martin's Press, Macmillan.

Jacobi, O., Jessop, B., Kanstendiek, H. and Regini, M. (eds) (1984) *Technological Change, Rationalisation and Industrial Relations.* London: Croom Helm.

Jacoby, S.M. (ed) (1995) *Workers of Nations: Industrial Relations in a Global Economy.* Oxford: Oxford University Press.

Jeffreys, J. (1945) *The Story of the Engineers, 1800–1945.* London: Lawrence and Wishart.

Jeffreys, S. (1988) 'The changing face of conflict and shopfloor organisation at Longbridge.' In M. Terry and P. Edward (eds) *Shopfloor Politics and Job Controls: The Postwar Engineering Industry.* Oxford: Basil Blackwell.

Jenkins, S. (1994) *Winners and Losers: A Portrait of the UK Income Distribution during the 1980s.* Department of Economics, Swansea University.

Jenkins, S. (1995) *Accountable to None: The Tory Nationalisation of Britain.* London: Hamish Hamilton.

Jessop, B. (1992) 'Fordism and Post-Fordism: Critique and reformulation.' In M. Storper and A.J. Scott (eds) *Pathways to Industrialisation and Regional Development.* London: Routledge.

Jonas, A. (1996) 'Local labour control regimes; Uneven development and the social regulation of production.' *Regional Studies 30*, (forthcoming).

Jones, B. and Rose, M. (1986) 'Redividing labour: Factory politics and work reorganisation in the current industrial transition.' In K. Purcell, S. Wood, A. Waton and S. Allen (eds) *The Changing Experience of Employment: Restructuring and Recession.* London: Macmillan.

Joseph, K. (1979) *Solving the Union Problem is the Key to Britain's Recovery.* London: Conservative Party Central Office.

Kassalow, E. (1987) 'Trade unions and industrial relations: Toward the twenty-first century.' *Bulletin of Comparative Labour Relations 16, (Special Issue on Unions and Industrial Relations: Recent Trends and Prospects)*, 1–26.

Katz, H. (1991) 'Policy debates over work reorganisation in North American unions.' In R. Hyman and W. Streeck (eds) *New Technology and Industrial Relations.* Oxford: Blackwell.

Katz, H. (1993) 'The decentralisation of collective bargaining: A literature review and comparative analysis.' *Industrial and Labor Relations Review 47*, 3–22.

Keeble, D.E. (1992) 'High technology industry and the restructuring of the UK space economy.' In R.L. Martin and P. Townroe (eds) *Regional Development in the 1990s: The British Isles in Transition.* London: Jessica Kingsley Publishers.

Kelly, J. (1988) *Trade Unions and Socialist Politics.* London: Verso.

Kelly, J. (1990) 'British trade unionism 1979–1989: Changes, continuity and contradictions.' *Work, Employment and Society* (Special Issue), May, 29–65.

Kelly, J. and Heery, E. (1994) *Working for the Union: British Trade Union Officers.* Cambridge: Cambridge University Press.

Kern, H. and Sabel, C. (1992) 'Trade unions and decentralized production: A sketch of strategic problems in the German labour movement.' In M. Regini (ed) *The Future of Labour Movements.* London: Sage.

Kerr, C., Dunlop, J., Harbinson, F. and Meyers, C. (1962) *Industrialism and Industrial Man: The Problems of Labor and Management in Economic Growth.* London: Heinemann.

Kerr, C. and Siegel, A. (1954) 'The inter-industry propensity to strike: An international comparison.' In A. Kornhauser, R. Dubin and A.M. Ross (eds) *Industrial Conflict.* New York: McGraw Hill.

Kessler, S. and Bayliss, F. (1992) *Contemporary British Industrial Relations.* London: Macmillan.

Kilpatrick, A. and Lawson, T. (1980) 'On the nature of industrial decline in the UK.' *Cambridge Journal of Economics 4*, 85–102.

Knowles, K.G.J.C. (1952) *Strikes: A Study of Industrial Conflict.* Oxford: Basil Blackwell.

Kochan, T. (1980) *Collective Bargaining and Industrial Relations.* Homewood: Richard Irwin.

Korpi, W. and Shalev, M. (1980) 'Strikes, power and politics in the Western nations, 1900–1976.' *Political Power and Social Theory 1*, 301–334.

Kotz, D., McDonough, T. and Reich, M. (eds) (1994) *Social Structures of Accumulation: The Political Economy of Growth and Crisis.* Cambridge: Cambridge University Press.

Labour Research (1993) 'The Tories' union-ballot mania.' *Labour Research 82*, 2, 14–16.

Labour Research (1994a) 'Signing up – A hard slog.' *Labour Research 83*, 9, 11–13.

Labour Research (1994b) 'Unions popular as work more insecure.' *Labour Research 2.*

Lane, T. (1972) 'The unions: Caught on the ebb tide.' *Marxism Today.* September, 6–13.

Lane, T. (1974) *The Union Makes Us Strong: The British Working Class, Trade Unionism and Politics.* London: Arrow Books.

Lange, P. (1984) 'Unions, workers and wage regulation: The rational bases of consent.' In J. Goldthorpe (ed) *Order and Conflict in Contemporary Capitalism.* Oxford: Clarendon.

Lange, P., Ross, G. and Vannicelli, M. (1982) *Unions, Change and Crisis: French and Italian Union Strategy and the Political Economy, 1945–1980.* London: Allen and Unwin.

Langton, J. and Morris, R.J. (1986) *Atlas of Industrialising Britain.* London: Methuen.

Lash, S. (1984) *The Militant Worker: Class and Radicalism in France and America.* London: Heinemann Educational Books.

Lash, S. (1994) 'Reflexivity and its doubles: Structures, aesthetics and community.' In U. Beck, A. Giddens and S. Lash (1994) *Reflexive Modernisation; Politics, Tradition and Aesthetics in the Modern Social Order.* Cambridge: Polity Press.

Lash, S. and Bagguley, P. (1988) 'Labour relations and disorganised capitalism: A five nation comparison.' *Society and Space 6*, 263–280.

Lash, S. and Urry, J. (1987) *The End of Organised Capitalism.* Oxford: Blackwell.

Lash, S. and Urry, J. (1994) *Economies of Signs and Space.* London: Sage.

Leadbeater, C. and Lloyd, J. (1987) *In Search of Work.* Harmondsworth: Penguin.

Leborgne, D. and Lipietz, A. (1988) 'New technologies, new modes of regulation: Some spatial implications.' *Environment and Planning D: Society and Space 6*, 263–280.

Lee, C.H. (1979) *British Regional Employment Statistics, 1841–1971.* London: McGraw Hill.

Lewis, R. (1990) 'Strike free deals and pendulum arbitration.' *British Journal of Industrial Relations 28*, 1, 32–56.

Locke, R. (1990) 'The resurgence of the local union: Industrial restructuring and industrial relations in Italy.' *Politics and Society 18*, 327–79.

Locke, R. (1992) 'The demise of the national union in Italy: Lessons for comparative industrial relations theory.' *Industrial and Labor Relations Review 45*, 229–249.

Longstreth, F. (1988) 'From corporatism to dualism? Thatcherism and the climacteric of the British trade unionism in the 1980s.' *Political Studies 36*, 413–432.

Lösch, A (1954) *The Economics of Location.* New Haven: Yale University Press.

MacInnes, J. (1987) *Thatcherism at Work.* Milton Keynes: Open University Press.

MacInnes, J. (1990) 'The future of this great movement of ours.' In P. Fosh and E. Heery (eds) *Trade Unions and Their Members.* London: Macmillan.

McBride, S. (1986) 'Mrs Thatcher and the post-war consensus: The case of trade union policy.' *Parliamentary Affairs 39*, 330–340.

McCarthy, W. (1966) *The Role of Shop Stewards in British Industrial Relations.* Royal Commission on Trade Unions and Employers' Associations, Research paper No. 1. London: HMSO.

McConnell, S. and Takla, L. (1990) 'Mrs Thatcher's trade union legislation: has it reduced strikes?' *Discussion Paper 374,* Centre for Labour Economics. London: LSE.

McGregor, A. and Sproull, A. (1991) *Employer Labour Use Strategies: Analysis of a National Survey,* Research Paper 83. Sheffield: Department of Employment.

Machin, S. (1994) 'Changes in the relative demand for skills in the UK labour market.' In A. Booth and D. Snower (eds) *The Skills Gap and Economic Activity.*

McIlroy, J. (1988) *Trade Unions in Britain Today.* Manchester: Manchester University Press.

McKinlay, A. and Zeitlin, J. (1989) 'The meanings of managerial prerogative: Industrial relations and the organisation of work in British engineering, 1880–1939.' *Business History 39*, 32–47.

McLoughlin, I. and Gourlay, S. (1994) *Enterprise Without Unions: Industrial Relations in the Non-Union Firm.* London: Open University Press.

Maheu, L. (1995) (ed) *Social Movements and Social Class.* London: Sage.

Mahnkopf, B. (1992) 'The "skill-oriented" strategies of German trade unions: Their impact on efficiency and equity objectives.' *British Journal of Industrial Relations 30*, 61–81.

Marginson, P., Edwards, P., Martin, R., Purcell, J. and Sisson, K. (1988) *Beyond the Workplace: Managing Industrial Relations in the Multi-Establishment Enterprise.* Oxford: Basil Blackwell.

Marsh, A. (1965) *Industrial Relations in Engineering.* London: Pergamon Press.

Marsh, A. and Coker, E. (1963) 'Shop steward organisation in the engineering industry.' *British Journal of Industrial Relations 1*, 170–190.

Marsh, D. (1990) Public opinion, trade unoins and Mrs Thatcher. *British Journal of Industrial Relations 28*, 1, 57–65.

Marsh, D. (1992) *The New Politics of British Trade Unionism: Union Power and the Thatcher Legacy.* London: Macmillan.

Marshall, M. (1987) *Long Waves of Regional Development.* London: Macmillan.

Martin, R.L. (ed) (1981) *Regional Unemployment and Wage Inflation.* London: Pion.

Martin, R.L. (1986a) 'Getting the labour market into geographical perspective.' *Environment and Planning, A, 18*, 569–572.

Martin, R.L. (1986b) 'Thatcherism and Britain's industrial landscape.' In R.L. Martin and R. Rowthorn (eds) *The Geography of De-industrialisation.* London: Macmillan.

Martin, R.L. (1988a) 'Industrial capitalism in transition: The contemporary reorganistion of the British space economy.' Chapter 10 in D. Massey and J. Allen (eds) *Uneven Redevelopment.* London: Hodder and Stoughton.

Martin, R.L. (1988b) 'The political economy of Britain's North-South divide.' *Transactions of the British Institute of Geographers, New Series 13*, 389–418.

Martin, R.L. (1989a) 'The new economics of economic and political restructuring.' In L. Albrechts, F. Moulaert, P. Roberts and E. Swyngedouw (eds) *Regional Planning at the Cross-Roads: European Perspectives.* London: Jessica Kingsley Publishers.

Martin, R.L. (1989b) 'The reorganisation of regional theory: Alternative perspectives on the changing capitalist space economy.' *Geoforum 20*, 2, 187–201.

Martin, R.L. (1994) 'Economic theory and human geography.' In D. Gregory, R.L. Martin and G.E. Smith (eds) *Human Geography: Society, Space and Social Science.* London: Macmillan.

Martin, R.L. (1995) 'Income and poverty inequalities across regional Britain: The North-South divide lingers on.' Chapter 2 In C. Philo (ed) *Off The Map: The Social Geography of Poverty in the UK.* London: CPAG.

Martin, R.L. and Rowthorn. R. (eds) (1986) *The Geography of De-industrialisation.* London: Macmillan.

Martin, R.L., Sunley, P. and Wills, J. (1993) 'The geography of trade union decline: Spatial dispersal or regional resilience?' *Transactions of the Institute of British Geographers, NS, 18*, 1, 36–62.

Martin, R.L., Sunley, P. and Wills, J. (1994a) 'The decentralisation of industrial relations? New institutional spaces and the role of local context in British engineering.' *Transactions of the Institute of British Geographers, NS, 19*, 4, 457–481.

Martin, R.L., Sunley, P. and Wills, J. (1994b) 'Unions and the politics of de-industrialisation.' *Antipode 26*, 1, 59–76.

Martin, R.L., Sunley, P. and Wills, J. (1994c) 'Local industrial politics: Spatial subsystems in British engineering.' *Employee Relations 16*, 2, 84–99.

Martin, R.L., Sunley, P. and Wills, J. (1994d) 'Labouring differences: Method, measurement and purpose in geographical research on trade unions.' *Transactions of the Institute of British Geographers, NS, 19,* 1, 102–110.

Martin, R.L., Sunley, P. and Wills, J. (1994e) *The Shrinking Landscape of Organised Labour: Union Retreat in the British Regions.* Paper presented at the 90th Annual Conference of the Association of American Geographers, San Francisco, March–April.

Martin, R.L. and Townroe, P. (eds) (1992) *Regional Development in the 1990s: The British Isles in Transition.* London: Jessica Kingsley Publishers.

Martinez-Lucio, M. and Noon, M. (1994) 'Organisational change and the tensions of decentralisation: The case of Royal Mail.' *Human Resource Management Journal 5,* 65–78.

Martinez-Lucio, M. and Weston, S. (1992) 'The politics and complexity of trade union responses to new management practices.' *Human Resources Management Journal 2,* 77–91.

Martinez-Lucio, M. and Weston, S. (1993) *Trades Unions and Networking in the Context of Organisational Change: Reconsidering the Dynamics of Decentralisation in Industrial Relations.* Paper presented at the Employment Research Unit Conference, 'Unions on the Brink: The Future of the Trade Union Movement', University of Wales Cardiff, September.

Mason, B. and B.P. (1993) 'The determinants of trade union membership in Britain: A survey of the literature.' *Industrial and Labor Relations Review 46,* 332–351.

Mason, C. (1992) 'New firm formation and growth.' In R.L. Martin and P. Townroe (eds) *Regional Development in the 1990s: The British Isles in Transition.* London: Jessica Kingsley.

Massey, D. (1979) 'In what sense a regional problem?' *Regional Studies 13,* 233–243.

Massey, D. (1984) *Spatial Divisions of Labour.* London: Macmillan (New Edition: 1995).

Massey, D. (1991) 'The political place of locality studies.' *Environment and Planning D: Society and Space 23,* 267–281.

Massey, D. (1994) 'The geography of trade unions: Some issues.' *Transactions of the Institute of British Geographers, New Series 19,* 95–98.

Massey, D. and Miles, N. (1984) 'Mapping out the unions.' *Marxism Today,* May, 19–22.

Massey, D. and Painter, J. (1989) 'The changing geography of trade unions.' In J. Mohan (ed) *The Political Geography of Contemporary Britain.* London: Macmillan.

Mayhew, K. (1979) 'Economists and strikes.' *Oxford Bulletin of Economics and Statistics 41,* 1, 1–19.

Metcalf, D. (1991) 'British unions: Dissolution or resurgence?' *Oxford Review of Economic Policy 1,* 18–32.

Metcalf, D. (1994) 'The transformation of British industrial relations? Institutions, conduct and outcomes, 1980–1990.' In R. Barrell (ed) *The UK Labour Market: Comparative Aspects and Institutional Developments.* Cambridge: Cambridge University Press.

Miller, B. (1992) 'Collective action and rational choice: Place, community and the limits to individual self-interest.' *Economic Geography 68,* 22–42.

Millward, N. (1990) 'The state of the unions.' In R. Jowell, S. Witherspoon, L. Brook and B. Taylor (eds) *British Social Attitudes.* Aldershot: Gower.

Millward, N. (1994) *The New Industrial Relations?* London: Policy Studies Institute.

Millward, N., Smart, D., Stevens, M. and Hawes, W.R. (1992) *Workplace Industrial Relations in Transition.* Aldershot: Dartmouth Publishing.

Millward, N. and Stevens, M. (1986) *British Workplace Industrial Relations, 1980–84.* Aldershot: Gower.

Milne, S. (1994) 'Unions count the cost of legal challenges.' *Guardian,* May 24.

Milner, S. (1994) *Charting the Coverage of Collective Pay-Setting Institutions: 1895 –1990.* Discussion Paper No. 215. London: LSE Centre for Economic Performance.

Minford. P. (1985) *Unemployment: Cause and Cure.* Oxford: Basil Blackwell.

Minford, P. and Stoney, P. (1991) 'Regional policy and market forces.' In A. Bowen and K. Mayhew (eds) *Reducing Regional Inequalities.* London: Kogan Page.

Mingione, E. (1991) *Fragmented Societies: A Sociology of Economic Life Beyond the Market.* Oxford: Blackwell.

Monks, J. (1993) 'A trade union view of WIRS 3. *British Journal of Industrial Relations 31,* 2, 228.

Monks, J. (1994) 'Introduction.' In R. Taylor *The Future of the Trade Unions.* London: Andre Deutsch.

Morgan, K. and Sayer, A. (1988) *Microcircuits of Capital: 'Sunrise' Industry and Uneven Development.* Cambridge: Polity Press.

Mulhearn, C. (1984) *Urban Employment Decline and Labour Movement Response: The Impact of Technology.* mimeo. London: Department of Town Planning, South Bank Polytechnic.

Murray, G. (1994) 'Structure and identity: The impact of union structure in comparative perspective.' *Employee Relations 16,* 2, 24–40.

Murray, R. (1989) 'Fordism and Post-Fordism.' In S. Hall and M. Jaques (eds) *New Times: The Changing Face of Politics in the 1990s.* London: Lawrence and Wishart.

Nickell, S. and Bell, B. (1995) 'The collapse in demand for the unskilled and unemployment across the OECD.' *Oxford Review of Economic Policy 11,* 1, 40–62.

Nielsen, K. (1991) 'Towards a flexible future – Theories and politics.' In B. Jessop, H. Kastendick, K. Nielsen, and O. Pedersen (eds) *The Politics of Flexibility: Restructuring State and Industry in Britain, Germany and Scandinavia.* London: Edward Elgar.

North, D.C. (1990) *Institutions, Institutional Change and Economic Performance.* Cambridge: Cambridge University Press.

OECD (1994a) *The OECD Jobs Study* (Vols 1 and 2). Paris: Organisation for Economic Cooperation and Development.

OECD (1994b) 'Collective bargaining: Levels and coverage.' *Employment Outlook,* July. Paris: Organisation for Economic Cooperation and Development.

Offe, C. (1985) *Disorganised Capitalism: Contemporary Transformations of Work and Politics.* Cambridge: Polity Press.

Oliver, N. and Wilkinson, B. (1988) *The Japanisation of British Industry.* Oxford: Blackwell.

Olson, M. (1965) *The Logic of Collective Action.* Cambridge, MA: Harvard University Press.

Overbeek, H. (1989) *Global Capitalism and Britain's Decline.* London: Unwin Hyman.

Painter, J. (1991) 'The geography of trade union responses to local government privatisation.' *Transactions of the Institute of British Geographers, NS, 16,* 214–226.

Painter, J. (1994) 'Trade union geography: Alternative frameworks for analysis.' *Transactions of the Institute of British Geographers, New Series, 19,* 99–101.

Peck, J. (1992) 'Labour and agglomeration: Control and flexibility in local labour markets.' *Economic Geography 68,* 4, 325–347.

Peck, J. (1994) 'Regulating labour: The social regulation and reproduction of labour markets.' In N. Thrift and A. Amin (eds) *Globalization, Institutions and Regional Development in Europe.* Oxford: Oxford University Press.

Peck, J. and Tickell, A. (1992) 'Local modes of social regulation? Regulation theory, Thatcherism and uneven development.' *Geoforum 23,* 347–63.

Pelling, G. (1992) 'A History of British Trade Unionism (Fifth Edition). London: Macmillan.

Pencavel, J.H. (1970) 'An investigation into industrial strikes activity in Britain.' *Economica 37,* 239–55.

Penn, R. (1992) 'Flexibility in Britain during the 1980s: Recent Empirical evidence.' In N. Gilbert, R. Burrows and A. Pollert (eds) (1992) *Fordism and Flexibility: Divisions and Change.* London: Macmillan.

Penn, R. and Scattergood, H. (1990) *The Experience of Trade Unions in Rochdale during the 1980s: Evidence from the Social change and Economic Life Initiative.* Working Paper 63. University of Lancaster.

Perulli, P. (1993) 'Towards a regionalisation of industrial relations.' *International Journal of Urban and Regional Research 17,* 98–113.

Phelps-Brown, H. (1959) *The Growth of British Industrial Relations.* London: Macmillan.

Phelps-Brown, H. (1990) 'The counter-revolution of our time.' *Industrial Relations 21,* 1–15.

Piore, M. and Sabel, C. (1984) *The Second Industrial Divide.* New York: Basic Books.

Pollard, S. (1981) *Peaceful Conquest: The Industrialisation of Europe, 1760–1970.* Oxford: Oxford University Press.

Pollard, S. (1982) *The Wasting of the British Economy.* London: Croom Helm.

Pollert, A. (1988) 'Dismantling flexibility.' *Capital and Class 34,* 42–75.

Pollert, A. (ed) (1991) *Farewell to Flexibility?* Oxford: Blackwell.

Poole, M. (1986) *Industrial Relations: Origins and Patterns of National Diversity.* London: Routledge.

Price, R. and Bain, G. (1983) 'Union growth in Britain: Retrospect and prospect.' *British Journal of Industrial Relations 21,* 46–66.

Purcell, J. (1991) 'The rediscovery of management prerogative: The management of labour relations in the 1980s.' *Oxford Review of Economic Policy 7,* 33–43.

Purcell, J. (1993) 'The end of institutional industrial relations.' *Political Quarterly 64,* 6–23.

Purcell, J. and Ahlstrand, B. (1989) 'Corporate strategy and the management of employee relations in the multi-divisional company.' *British Journal of Industrial Relations 27,* 396–415.

Reed, M. (1992) *Experts, Professions and Organisations in Late Modernity.* Paper presented at the Employment Research Unit Annual Conference on 'The Challenge of Change: Theory and Practice of Organisational Transformations'. University of Wales, Cardiff, September.

Rees, G. (1985) 'Regional restructuring, class change and political action: Preliminary comments on the 1984–1985 miners' strike in South Wales.' *Environment and Planning D: Society and Space 3,* 389–406.

Rees, G. (1986) 'Coal culture and the 1984–1985 miners' strike: A reply to Sunley.' *Environment and Planning D: Society and Space 4,* 469–476.

Regini, M. (1992a) 'Introduction: The past and future of social studies of labour movements.' In M. Regini (ed) *The Future of Labour Movements.* London: Sage.

Regini, M. (ed) (1992b) *The Future of Labour Movements.* London: Sage.

Richardson, R. and Rubin, M. (1993) 'The shorter working week in engineering: Surrender without sacrifice?' In D. Metcalf and S. Milner (eds) *New Perspectives on Industrial Disputes.* London: Routledge.

Rico, L. (1987) 'The new industrial relations: British electricians' new style agreements.' *Industrial and Labor Relations Review 41,* 63–78.

Robinson, P. (1994) *Is There an Explanation for Rising Pay Inequality in the UK?* Centre for Economic Performance, Discussion Paper 206. London: London School of Economics.

Rowthorn, R.E. (1986) 'Deindustrialisation in Britain.' In R.L. Martin and R. Rowthorn (eds) *The Geography of De-industrialisation.* London: Macmillan.

Rubery, J. (1986) 'Trade unions in the 1980s: The case of the United Kingdom.' In R. Edwards, P. Garonna and F. Todtling (eds) *Unions in Crisis: Perspectives from Six Countries.* London: Auburn House.

Rubery, J. (1989) 'Labour market flexibility in Britain.' In F. Green (ed) *The Restructuring of the UK Economy.* London: Harvester Wheatsheaf.

Rubery, J. (1992) 'Productive systems, international integration and the single European market.' In A. Castro, P. Mehaut, and J. Rubery (eds) *International Integration and Labour Market Organisation.* London: Academic Press.

Rubery, J. and Wilkinson, F. (1994) 'Introduction.' In J. Rubery and F. Wilkinson (eds) *Employment Strategy and the Labour Market.* Oxford: Oxford University Press.

Rutherford, T. (1991) 'Industrial restructuring, local labour markets and social change: The transformation of South Wales.' *Contemporary Wales 4,* 9–44.

Rutherford, T. (1995) *The Emergence of a Strategic Union Training Policy? The Canadian Autoworkers and the United Steel Workers of America.* Paper presented at the 91st Annual Conference of the Association of American Geographers, Chicago, March 1995.

Samuel, R. (1986) 'Introduction.' In R. Samuel, B. Bloomfield and G. Bonas (eds) *The Enemy Within: Pit Villages and the Miners' Strike of 1984–5.* London: Routledge and Kegan Paul.

Samuel, R., Bloomfield, B. and Bonas, G. (1986) (eds) *The Enemy Within: Pit Villages and the Miners' Strike of 1984–5.* London: Routledge and Kegan Paul.

Sayer, A. (1985) 'Industry and space: A sympathetic critique of radical research.' *Environment and Planning D: Society and Space 3,* 3–29.

Sayer, A. (1989) 'Post-Fordism in question.' *International Journal of Urban and Regional Research 13,* 666–695.

Sayer, A. and Walker, R. (1992) *The New Social Economy: Reworking the Division of Labour.* Oxford: Blackwell.

Scott, A. (1994) *Willing Slaves? British Workers under Human Resource Management.* Cambridge: Cambridge University Press.

Scott, A.J. and Storper, M. (eds) (1992) *Pathways to Industrialization and Regional Development.* London: Routledge.

Screpanti, E. (1987) 'Long cycles in strike activity: An empirical investigation.' *British Journal of Industrial Relations 25,* 1, 101–124.

Shalev, M. (1980) 'Trade unionism and economic analysis.' *Journal of Labour Research 1,* 133–174.

Shalev, M. (1983) 'Strikes and the crisis: Industrial conflict and unemployment in the Western nations.' *Economic and Industrial Democracy 4,* 417–460.

Shalev, M. (1992) 'The resurgence of labour quiesence.' In M. Regini (ed) *The Future of Labour Movements.* London: Sage.

Shils, E. (1984) *Tradition.* Chicago: University of Chicago Press.

Shorey, J. (1976) 'An inter-industry analysis of strike frequency.' *Economica 43,* 349–365.

Shorey, J. (1977) 'Time series analysis of strike frequency.' *British Journal of Industrial Relations 15,* 63–75.

Shorter, E. and Tilly, C. (1974) *Strikes in France 1830–1968.* Cambridge: Cambridge University Press.

Smith, C.T.B., Clifton, R., Makeham, P., Creigh, S.W. and Burn, R.V. (1977) *Strikes in Britain.* Department of Employment (Manpower Paper No.15). London: HMSO.

Smith, P., Fosh, P., Martin, R., Morris, H. and Undy, R. (1993) 'Ballots and union government in the 1980s.' *British Journal of Industrial Relations 31,* 365–382.

Smith, P. and Morton, G. (1993) 'Union exclusion and the decollectivization of industrial relations in contemporary Britain.' *British Journal of Industrial Relations 31,* 97–114.

Smith, P. and Morton, G. (1994) 'Union exclusion – Next steps.' *Industrial Relations Journal 25,* 3–14.

Soskice, D. (1990) 'Wage determination: The changing role of institutions in advanced industrial countries.' *Oxford Review of Economic Policy 6,* 36–61.

Southall, H. (1988) 'Towards a geography of unionisation: The spatial organisation and distribution of the early British trade unions.' *Transactions of the Institute of British Geographers, New Series 13,* 467–483.

Storey, J. (ed) (1989) *New Perspectives on Human Resource Management.* London: Routledge.

Storper, M. (1995) 'Boundaries, compartments and markets: Paradoxes of industrial relations in growth pole regions of France, Italy and the United States.' In S.M. Jacoby (ed) (1995) *Workers of Nations: Industrial Relations in a Global Economy.* Oxford: Oxford University Press.

Storper, M. and Walker, R. (1984) 'The spatial division of labour: Labour and the location of industries.' In L. Sawers and W. Tabb (eds) *Sunbelt/Snowbelt: Urban Development and Regional Restructuring.* Oxford; Oxford University Press.

Storper, M. and Walker, R. (1989) *The Capitalist Imperative: Territory, Technology and Industrial Growth.* Oxford: Basil Blackwell.

Streeck, W. (1992) *Social Institutions and Economic Performance: Studies of Industrial Relations in Advanced Capitalist Economies.* London: Sage.

Sunley, P. (1986) 'Regional restructuring, class change and political action: A comment.' *Environment and Planning D: Society and Space 4*, 465–468.

Sunley, P. (1990) 'Striking parallels: A comparison of the geographies of the 1926 and 1984–1985 coalmining disputes.' *Environment and Planning D: Society and Space 8*, 35–52.

Taylor, R. (1994) *The Future of the Trade Unions.* London: Andre Deutsch.

Teague, P. (1993) 'Coordination or decentralisation? EC social policy and industrial relations.' In J. Lodge (ed) *The European Community and the Challenge of the Future.* London: Pinter.

Thelen, K. (1994) 'Beyond corporatism.' *Comparative Politics*, October, 107–24.

Thirlwall, A. (1982) 'Deindustrialisation in the UK.' *Lloyds Bank Review*, April, 22–37.

Thompson, E.P. (1991) *Customs in Common.* London: Merlin.

Thrift, N. and Williams, P. (eds) (1987) *Class and Space: The Making of Urban Society.* London: Routledge and Kegan Paul.

Tilly, C. and Jerome, N. (1992) 'Tradition and the working class.' *International Labor and Working Class History 42*, 1–4.

Tilly, L. and Tilly, C. (eds) (1981) *Class Conflict and Collective Action.* London: Sage.

Tolliday, S. (1985) 'Government, employers and shopfloor organisation in the British motor industry.' In S. Tolliday and J. Zeitlin (eds) *Shopfloor Bargaining and the State.* Cambridge: Cambridge University Press.

Tolliday, S. (1987) 'The failure of mass production unionism in the motor industry, 1914–1939.' In C. Wrigley (ed) *A History of British Industrial Relations. Volume II: 1914–1939.* London: Edward Arnold.

Tolliday, S. and Zeitlin, J. (1986) *The Automobile Industry and Its Workers: Between Fordism and Flexibility.* Cambridge: Polity Press.

Towers, B. (1989) 'Running the gauntlet: British trade unions under Thatcher, 1979–88.' *Industrial and Labor Relations Review 42*, 163–188.

Trades Union Congress (TUC) (1988) *Meeting the Challenge.* First Report of the Special Review Body. London: TUC.

Trades Union Congress (TUC) (1994) *HRM: A Trade Union Response.* London: TUC.

Trades Union Congress (TUC) (1995) *A Trade Union's Guide to European Works Councils.* London: TUC.

Trevor, M. (1988) *Toshiba's New British Company.* London: Policy Studies Institute.

Turner, L. (1991) *Democracy at Work: Changing World Markets and the Future of Labor Unions.* Ithaca: Cornell University Press.

USDAW (1994) Written Evidence to the House of Commons Select Committee on The Future of the Unions. London: HMSO.

Visser, J. (1991) 'Trends in union membership.' *Employment Outlook 1991.* Paris: Organisation for Economic Cooperation and Development.

Visser, J. (1992) 'The strength of union movements in advanced capitalist countries: Social and democratic variations.' In M. Regini (ed) *The Future of Labour Movements.* London: Sage.

Visser, J. (1994) 'European trade unions: The transition years.' In R. Hyman and A. Ferner (eds) *New Frontiers in European Industrial Relations.* Oxford: Blackwell.

Waddington, J. (1988) 'Trade union mergers: A study of trade union structural dynamics.' *British Journal of Industrial Relations 28*, 409–430.

Waddington, J. (1992) 'Trade union membership in Britain, 1980–87: Unemployment and restructuring.' *British Journal of Industrial Relations 30*, 287–324.

Waddington, J. (1995) *The Politics of Bargaining: The Merger Process and British Trade Union Structural Developments, 1892–1987.* London: Mansell Publishing.

Wallerstein, M. (1989) 'Union organisation in advanced industrial democracies.' *American Political Science Review 83*, 481–492.

Walsh, J. (1993) 'Internalization versus decentralisation: An analysis of recent developments in pay bargaining.' *British Journal of Industrial Relations 31*, 409–432.

Walsh, K. (1983) *Strikes in Europe and the United States: Measurement and Incidence.* London: Frances Pinter.

Warde, A. (1985) 'Spatial change, politics and the division of labour.' In D. Gregory and J. Urry (eds) *Social Relations and Spatial Structures.* London: Macmillan.

Warde, A. (1987) 'Industrial discipline: Factory regime and politics in Lancaster.' *Work, Employment and Society 3,* 49–63.

Watson, G. (1994) 'The flexible workforce and patterns of working hours in the UK.' *Employment Gazette,* June, 239–247.

Webb, S. and Webb, B. (1894) *The History of Trade Unionism.* London: Longmans.

Weber, A. (1929) *Theory of the Location of Industries.* Chicago: University of Chicago Press.

Western, B. (1994) 'Unionization and labor market institutions in advanced capitalism, 1950–85.' *American Journal of Sociology 99,* 1314–1341

Western, B. (1995) 'A comparative study of working-class disorganization: Union decline in eighteen advanced capitalist countries.' *American Sociological Review 60,* 179–201.

Whitston, C. and Waddington, J. (1994) 'Why join a union?' *New Statesman and Society,* November 18.

Wilkinson, B., Morris, J. and Munday, M. (1993) 'Japan in Wales: A new IR.' *Industrial Relations Journal 24,* 273–283.

Williams, C., Williams, J. and Thomas, D. (1983) *Why are the British Bad at Manufacturing?* London: Routledge and Kegan Paul.

Williams, R. (1989) *Resources of Hope.* London: Verso.

Wills, J. (1995) *Geographies of Trade Union Tradition.* Unpublished PhD Thesis, Open University.

Wills, J. (1996a) 'Uneven reserves: Geographies of banking trade unionism.' *Regional Studies* (forthcoming).

Wills, J. (1996b) 'Geographies of trade unionism: Translating traditions across time and space.' *Antipode 2* (forthcoming).

Wood, S. (1994) *North-South Trade, Employment and Inequality: Changing Fortunes in a Skill Driven World.* Oxford: Clarendon.

Zeitlin, J. (1991) 'The internal politics of employer organisation: The EEF 1896–1939.' In S. Tolliday and J. Zeitlin (eds) *The Power to Manage? Employers and Industrial Relations in Comparative and Historical Perspective.* London: Routledge.

Subject Index

accumulation 26, 28–9
  flexible 84
  reflexive 197
  social structure of 26
agricultural workers 127
America *see* United States
armaments 46
associational unionism 203
associations *see* collective
  organizations; institutions
associative action, logics of 33
Australia 3
Austria 3, 163
'avoidance strategy' 163

ballots 131
banking 90, 141
bargaining *see* collective
  bargaining
'bargaining power' hypothesis
  162
Belgium 3
binding 'final offer' arbitration
  107
Birmingham
  early unions 42
Britain *see* United Kingdom
'British disease' 101, 125
brownfield regions 114
business units autonomy
  increases 160

Canada 3–4, 203
capital
  geographical scale of
    operation 38
capital and labour relationships
  employment relation 25–6
  exchange relations 26
  geographical complication
    16
  production relations 26
  see also industrial relations;
    labour

carpenters 41
CCT (compulsory competitive
  tendering) 38, 102, 161
Central Scotland
  early development of union
    movement 42
  post-war employment
    growth 48
  union membership
    concentration 44
centralized collective
  bargaining 163–4
check-off system 101
chemicals industry 87
Cheshire 133
class 6, 26, 148
closed shop 101
Clydeside 93
co-operative flexibility 27
coal industry 43
coal miners
  early development of union
    movement 41
  propensity to strike 127
coal mining
  early development of union
    movement 42
  geography of industrial
    action 152
  job loss 87
  South Wales communities'
    collective labourist
    identity 35
  strike rates 141
coal mining unions
  formation, early decline and
    recovery 43
collective action *see* industrial
  action; strike activity
collective bargaining 19
  'avoidance strategy' 163
  background 156
  centralized 163–4
  convergence of pay and
    employment conditions
    across
different regions 17
  coverage
    decline 159
    selected countries 8
  decentralization *see*
    decentralization
  decline 8

decollectivization 8–9
  geographical picture of
    changes 157
  geography of 167–71
  local arrangements 165, 173
  local variation 17
  marketization of public
    services, weakening 161
  multi-employer, decline 159
  national, decline 159
  non-manual workers 160
  plant-level 160
  privatization of public
    services, weakening 161
  public sector, weakening 161
  regional scope and structure
    1978 *168*
    1985 *168*
    manual workers, 1984 and
      1990 *169*
    non-manual workers, 1984
      and 1990 *170*
  restructuring 159
  structure 159
collective identities 33, 48
collective interests
  identification 33
collective organizations 33, 35
  see also institutions
collective regulation 8
collectivism 33
Combination Laws repeal 43
community
  importance to workers'
    industrial action 148
  integrated communities
    148–9
  'sense of' 150
  single-industry towns and
    villages 148
  strike propensity as function
    of 147
  traditions as basis of
    workers' collective action
    147
  working-class, cohesiveness
    148
community unionism 203, 206
competition 1
competitive world economy 10
compulsory competitive
  tendering (CCT) 38, 102,
  161

Names Index